LEARN TO READ
NEW TESTAMENT
GREEK

THIRD EDITION

DAVID ALAN BLACK

NASHVILLE, TENNESSEE

Published by B&H Publishing Group
Nashville, Tennessee

ISBN: 978-0-8054-4493-3

Dewey Decimal Classification: 225.48
Subject Heading: GREEK LANGUAGE,
BIBLICAL\BIBLE.N.T.GREEK

Printed in the United States of America
19 20 21 22 23 • 24 23 22 21 20
SB

To my Greek students—

past,
present,
and future

CONTENTS

ABOUT THIS BOOK

The Greek language has always had a peculiar attraction for both readers and expositors of the New Testament. More than a hundred introductory grammars of New Testament Greek have been produced in English alone, many of them by scholars of the first rank. It would be unusual, therefore, if the present grammar did not contain a great deal that has appeared elsewhere, and I am sure that the call for this book did not arise from the deficiencies of its predecessors. I find, nevertheless, some satisfaction in the knowledge that any subject is promoted, in however small a degree, by the independent treatment of the same material in the light of the most recent research. Accordingly, the aim of the present volume, which was written at the kind invitation of the publishers, has been to meet the need for up-to-date subject matter, a linguistically informed methodology, and an emphasis on contemporary models of language learning. The simplified explanations, basic vocabularies, and abundant exercises are designed to prepare the student for subsequent "practical" courses in exegesis, while the linguistic emphasis lays the groundwork for later courses in grammar. It is my hope that this book will prove to be not altogether unworthy of its predecessors, and that the nature of the lessons will establish it as a useful introduction to Greek linguistics, a field that is uniquely suited to provide new light on the words of Scripture.

The text is divided into 26 lessons, most of which are arranged according to the following pattern: a presentation of the grammatical concepts and forms to be learned, divided into manageable units; a list of essential vocabulary words to be mastered; and exercises based on the material covered in the lesson. The book is suitable for study or review, for individual or group work, as part of a refresher course, or as a handy reference guide. In most classroom settings it can be used for a full year of study by taking up a lesson a week, with ample time for supplementary testing and review.

Several characteristics of the lessons as a whole deserve a few words of explanation:

(1) In presenting the grammar proper, every attempt has been made not just to state rules but to give the student an understanding of the nature of

the language, especially in such fundamental topics as the significance of verbal aspect and the function of the article.

(2) Since many students are unfamiliar with grammar and particularly with grammatical nomenclature, each topic is introduced by a simple preliminary explanation of terminology with illustrations from the English language.

(3) Throughout the text I have adopted the simplest language possible to explain the subject matter, and have included only those linguistic concepts and terms that in my judgment have the clearest application to the teaching of beginning Greek.

(4) Since the most inspiring approach to ancient Greek is through original Greek sentences, the lessons contain numerous examples derived from the New Testament itself and, as far as possible, containing only grammatical forms already introduced.

(5) Rote memorization of paradigms has been kept to an absolute minimum, and the student is instead taught how to recognize basic patterns in words and how to interpret these through morphological analysis.

(6) As an aid to understanding, various visual devices have been adopted, including the use of bold type, underlining, tables, and graphs.

(7) Finally, in presenting the chief features of the language, primary principles have been set forth in large type, while matters of detail have been presented in reduced type (without implying that the topics so presented are of minor importance or can be skipped).

The various inflected and uninflected forms presented here are normal for a beginning grammar. In view of the fact that many students have had no prior exposure to verb inflection, special care has been given to the gradual description of the Greek tenses. The tenses of the active indicative are presented as follows: present and future (Lesson 3), imperfect and aorist (Lesson 7), and perfect and pluperfect (Lesson 10). Subsequent lessons treat the middle and passive voices of the indicative mood, contract and liquid verbs, participles, infinitives, the subjunctive mood, the imperative and optative moods, and finally verbs of the -μι conjugation. Considerable effort has been made to place paradigms of more or less similar forms side by side for ease of comprehension (as with the present and future active indicative), as well as to have new forms follow related ones in natural sequence (as with contract and liquid verbs). On the other hand, the introduction of the middle and passive voices has been deliberately postponed until after the entire active system has been learned, a sequence that in actual practice has achieved the goal of a clearer understanding of the significance of verbal aspect in New Testament Greek. In order that the learner may have some opportunity to become acquainted with the Greek tenses before facing the challenge of inflection, a preliminary overview of the Greek verb system is given in Lesson 2. This is supplemented by a comprehensive review of the indicative mood in Lesson 16.

The vocabularies contain words that are of great enough frequency in the Greek New Testament to justify recommending that these words be learned permanently as soon as encountered. All the words of one type have been grouped together, and an unusually full list of English cognates and derivatives has been provided in order to demonstrate the close relationship between English and Greek and to enable the student to learn the vocabulary as easily and comprehensively as possible. Wherever possible, Greek roots have been added to the word lists. This is a device for easing the burden of vocabulary acquisition, and the instructor who uses this book as a text may wish to require these forms to be learned as part of the regular vocabulary, especially by students who plan to continue their studies of Greek beyond the first year.

The Greek-to-English exercises in the text are designed to illustrate the new grammatical principles introduced in the lesson as well as those forms and grammatical usages that have been discussed previously. By going over these exercises again and again, the student will gain considerable facility in the workings of the language. For the first part of the book, these sentences have only rarely been taken from the New Testament, though I have tried not to introduce any usages that are unnatural to the New Testament idiom. Beginning with Lesson 18, however, excerpts from the Greek New Testament are used exclusively for the translation exercises. This use of genuine Greek has a twofold aim: to give students an insight into the language and thought of the New Testament writers, and to prepare them for the crowning experience of their studies—reading and understanding the original text of the New Testament. A prime consideration in the inclusion of these excerpts was that the material be interesting per se and not chosen merely because it illustrates forms and syntax.

Because the emphasis throughout this text is on reading Greek rather than on Greek composition, the treatment of Greek accents has been assigned to an appendix. Other omissions include English-to-Greek exercises, numerals, and such rare forms and constructions as the future participle and infinitive, most of the optative, and μή used as a conjunction. Thus the reader will find here little that is simply "interesting"; the subjects presented are directly relevant to the interpretation of the Greek New Testament. Hence it is all the more critical that the student learn well whatever principles are included so as to be able to move as quickly as possible from grammar to exegesis.

This volume is the third and final work in a trilogy of contributions to the study of New Testament Greek. The first volume, *Linguistics for Students of New Testament Greek: A Survey of Basic Concepts and Applications* (Baker), is designed to show the relevance of the modern science of linguistics to the interpretation of the New Testament. The second volume, *Using New Testament Greek in Ministry: A Practical Guide for Students and Pastors* (Baker), is intended to give the student a comprehensive survey of the chief features of New Testament exegesis in a practical and adaptable form. The present work completes the series by presenting in a simple-yet-comprehensive manner the elements of New Testament Greek. Since this book is primarily concerned with the rudiments of Greek for purposes of language acquisition, it will not take up detailed discussions of linguistics. The treatment of discourse analysis in Lesson 26, for example, is limited to the elements of discourse and only scratches the surface of this important field of study. Students interested in pursuing such topics should consult the bibliography provided in the Epilogue.

It now remains to acknowledge with warmest gratitude those who have helped me write this grammar and who are largely responsible for anything that may be useful in it. In the first place, my indebtedness to the authors whose works are listed in the Epilogue will be obvious to all, and I hereby record my appreciation for their helpful contributions to the study of New Testament Greek. I am also indebted to those many colleagues and friends who read and criticized the manuscript in syllabus form—Karen Jobes, Joseph Modica, Robert Smith, Stephen Veteto, John Landers, Mark Seifrid, and Chris Church should be mentioned especially—and to my own students, whose interest provided much encouragement. Special thanks goes to Dr. Ed Childs of Biola University for helping me transcribe the "Greek Alphabet Song" that appears in Appendix 2. Finally, I gratefully acknowledge the faithful support of my colleague and friend David Dockery, formerly of Broadman Press and currently dean of the School of Theology at the Southern Baptist Theological Seminary in Louisville. Although writing the grammar proved to be a far more daunting task than it appeared when I accepted his invitation, now that it is completed I am grateful to him for having given me the opportunity, as one may hope, of enlarging the readership of the Greek New Testament. At the very least, I am now more able to empathize with the ancient writer of 2 Maccabees 15:37–38:

αὐτόθι τὸν λόγον καταπαύσω. καὶ εἰ μὲν καλῶς εὐθίκτως τῇ συντάξει, τοῦτο καὶ αὐτὸς ἤθελον· εἰ δὲ εὐτελῶς καὶ μετρίως, τοῦτο ἐφικτὸν ἦν μοι.

"At this point I shall bring my work to an end. If it is found to be well written and aptly composed, that is what I myself desired; but if superficial and mediocre, it was the best I could do."

David Alan Black

FROM AUTHOR TO READER

Welcome to the study of Greek! The goal of this book is to help you learn to read and understand the Greek New Testament, even if you have never studied a foreign language before. Whether you are trying to write a solid expository sermon, prepare an accurate Sunday School lesson, express proper theology in the lyrics of a song, or translate the New Testament into a foreign language, New Testament Greek is a guide without which you are likely to stumble, or even miss the way. The focus throughout this book is on those aspects of grammar where Greek offers its greatest contributions to understanding the New Testament, contributions that are generally not attainable from an English translation.

The principles and methods used in *Learn to Read New Testament Greek* will enable you to make rapid progress in your studies. New information is introduced in small, manageable units, and points of grammar are fully explained and lavishly illustrated. After seventeen lessons you will begin reading selected passages from the Greek New Testament, and by the end of the course you will be able to read much of the New Testament without constant reference to a dictionary. You will also have an understanding of the structure of the Greek language, an ability to use commentaries and other works based on the Greek text, and a growing capacity to plumb the depths of God's revelation for yourself.

In *Learn to Read New Testament Greek*, rote memorization of grammatical forms has been kept to an absolute minimum. Instead, you will learn to recognize recurring patterns in words and how to interpret these through linguistic principles. This will equip you to read even unfamiliar passages from the New Testament with confidence. In addition, by learning the basic word lists, nearly seventy-five percent of the words of the New Testament will be familiar to you, and the rest will be within reach of an intelligent guess.

As you use this text, follow these simple instructions:

(1) When you begin a new lesson, read it through quickly. Then study it section by section, pausing at the end of each short section to assimilate its contents. Never begin a new lesson until you are thoroughly familiar with the previous one. If you are a member of a Greek class, ask questions on any point you do not understand. Your teacher will be pleased that you are sufficiently concerned to ask.

(2) When you feel you have understood the lesson, begin the exercises. To benefit most from the text, do all of the exercises. Each has been designed to give you extensive practice in using a specific Greek structure. If you are part of a Greek class, be careful not to fall behind in the exercises, since "catching up" is extremely difficult in an elementary course.

(3) Never write the English translations of words in your textbook. If you do, you will remember the English and forget the Greek. Instead, do all the exercises on a separate sheet of paper. Then read the exercises again, preferably aloud, until you are able to translate them easily and quickly.

(4) Finally, enjoy your studies and take pleasure in your progress. Don't get impatient if your pace seems slow. Learning a foreign language requires a great deal of time and effort. Claims of miracle-methods by which languages can be learned in a few days or weeks are utterly irresponsible and unfounded. On the other hand, if you make proper use of your instruction, you will be surprised how rapidly you progress. By the end of the course, you will actually be reading your New Testament in the original Greek!

Note: You will need to purchase as soon as possible an edition of the Greek New Testament. Two editions are widely used: the Nestle-Aland 27th edition (= NA[27]), and the United Bible Societies 4th (corrected) edition (= UBS[4]). UBS[4] has the same text as NA[27] but a different critical apparatus. It cites fewer variants but gives more detailed evidence for those cited. Both editions are available in a wide variety of bindings. UBS[4] is also available bound with *A Concise Greek-English Dictionary of the New Testament*. Yet another important edition of the Greek New Testament is *The New Testament in the Original Greek: Byzantine Textform*, compiled and edited by Maurice Robinson and William G. Pierpont (Chilton Book Publishing, 2005), which takes a "majority text" position.

PREFACE TO EXPANDED EDITION

In preparing this edition, I have taken into account the friendly and helpful comments of reviewers, colleagues, and students. The most obvious changes occur in the back matter, where I have added a number of helps: a key to the exercises, a summary of noun paradigms, a table of case-number suffixes, a table of person-number suffixes, a summary of prepositions, a list of words differing in accentuation or breathing, and a list of principal parts. It is hoped that these additions will enhance the usefulness of the book as a reference tool. Elsewhere, misprints have been corrected, and a few minor improvements have been made. Otherwise, the basic plan of the book remains the same, the first edition having confirmed a need for this sort of introduction to New Testament Greek.

I wish to acknowledge the helpfulness and encouragement of my students at Talbot School of Theology, Grace Bible Institute, Simon Greenleaf University, Grace Theological Seminary, Golden Gate Baptist Theological Seminary, California Graduate School of Theology, and Chong Shin Theological Seminary. I am also indebted to the following colleagues for their wise criticisms and suggestions: Peter Frick of St. Paul's College, Robert Yarbrough of Covenant Theological Seminary, Thomas Lea of Southwestern Baptist Theological Seminary, Simon Kistemaker of Reformed Theological Seminary, Thomas Friskey of Cincinnati Bible College and Seminary, Michael Martin of Golden Gate Baptist Theological Seminary, Darrell Bock of Dallas Theological Seminary, William Klein and Craig Blomberg of Denver Seminary, John Harvey of Columbia Biblical Seminary, William Warren of New Orleans Baptist Theological Seminary, Glenn Koch of Eastern Baptist Theological Seminary, Robert Sloan of Baylor University, Robert Smith of Point Loma Nazarene College, and

Carey Newman of The Southern Baptist Theological Seminary. Finally, my heartfelt thanks go to Trent Butler, John Landers, and Steve Bond of Broadman Press for their support of this project since its inception.

It is, perhaps, inevitable that some errors or omissions will still have escaped notice, and I would be grateful if users of this grammar would bring these to my attention.

David Alan Black

PREFACE TO THIRD EDITION

This revised edition of *Learn to Read New Testament Greek* was prepared at the request of the editors at B&H Academic, who felt that an updated edition of the book was needed to accompany the publication of its companion volume, *Learn to Read New Testament Greek Workbook: Supplemental Exercises for Greek Grammar Students*. In revising the book I solicited and received numerous comments from users of the grammar, both teachers and students. What was most striking to me about their remarks was how often they requested that I leave the book "as is." I thus felt that radical changes were inadvisable. Hence this third edition retains both the simplicity and conciseness of the first two editions. Changes include updated bibliographies, reworded (and hopefully improved) explanations in several places, and the addition of section numbers indicating where each word in the vocabulary first occurs in the grammar.

I wish to express my heartfelt thanks to the staff at B&H Academic, especially Ray Clendenen and David Stabnow, for their help with this revision. I sincerely hope that this new edition will prove to be as useful to seminarians, homeschoolers, and self-learners as its predecessors. No claim of infallibility is made for this update. Nevertheless, my prayer is that God may use it to equip a new generation of students to read the New Testament in its original language and to share the vast benefits of their reading with others.

David Alan Black
Rosewood Farm, Virginia

1

THE LETTERS AND
SOUNDS OF GREEK

The first step in studying New Testament Greek is learning how to read and write the Greek alphabet. Learning the order and sounds of the Greek letters will help break down the strangeness between you and Greek, enable you to find a word in a Greek-English dictionary, and reveal the relationship between Greek and English words.

1. The Language of the New Testament

You are embarking on the study of one of the most significant languages in the world. Its importance lies not so much in its wealth of forms as in the fact that God used it as an instrument to communicate his Word (just as he had earlier used Hebrew and Aramaic). History tells us that the ancient Hellenes first settled in the Greek peninsula in the thirteenth century B.C. Their language consisted of several dialects, one of which—the Attic spoken in Athens—became the most prominent. It was largely a descendent of Attic Greek that was adopted as the official language of the Greek empire after the conquests of Alexander the Great, which accounts for its use in the New Testament. This new world language has been called the "Koine," or "common," Greek since it was the common language of everyday commerce and communication. In the city of Rome itself, Greek was used as much as Latin, and when Paul wrote his letter to the Roman Christians, he wrote it in Greek. This, then, is the language of the New Testament, a language belonging to the living stream of the historical development of Greek from the ancient Hellenes to the modern Athenians, a language spoken by common and cultured people alike, a language uniquely suited to the propagation of the gospel of Christ when it began to be proclaimed among the nations of the world.

2. The Greek Alphabet

The first step in studying Greek is learning its letters and sounds. This is not as hard as you might think. All the sounds are easy to make, and Greek almost always follows the phonetic values of its letters. We should mention that the pronunciation you are learning is something of a compromise between how the sounds were probably produced in ancient times and how they are spelled. This scheme of pronunciation has the practical advantage of assigning a sound to only one letter, so that if you can remember the pronunciation of a word, you will generally be able to remember its spelling.

Below you will find the Greek letters with their closest English equivalents. When you have studied them carefully, cover the fourth and fifth columns and try to pronounce each letter.

Name	Upper-case	Lower-case	English	Pronunciation
Alpha	A	α	a	father (long) bat (short)
Beta	B	β	b	ball
Gamma	Γ	γ	g	gift
Delta	Δ	δ	d	dog
Epsilon	E	ε	e	bet
Zeta	Z	ζ	z	adze
Eta	H	η	ē	obey
Theta	Θ	θ	th	thin
Iota	I	ι	i	machine (long) pit (short)
Kappa	K	κ	k	kin
Lambda	Λ	λ	l	lamb
Mu	M	μ	m	man

2

Name	Upper-case	Lower-case	English	Pronunciation
Nu	N	ν	n	name
Xi	Ξ	ξ	x	wax
Omicron	O	ο	o	omelet
Pi	Π	π	p	pin
Rho	P	ρ	r	rat
Sigma	Σ	σ, ς	s	sing
Tau	T	τ	t	tale
Upsilon	Υ	υ	u	lute (long) put (short)
Phi	Φ	φ	ph	physics
Chi	X	χ	ch	chemist
Psi	Ψ	ψ	ps	taps
Omega	Ω	ω	ō	gold

i. Note that gamma is pronounced as a hard *g* (as in gift), never as a soft *g* (as in gem). However, before κ, χ, or another γ, γ is pronounced as an *n*. Thus ἄγγελος ("angel") is pronounced *angelos*, not *aggelos*.

ii. Did you notice that sigma has two forms? It is written ς at the end of a word, and σ in all other positions (see ἀπόστολος "apostle"). The "ς" form is called final sigma.

iii. In ancient Greek, the letter χ was probably pronounced like the *ch* in Scottish *loch* or German *Bach*. Since this sound does not occur in English, the *ch* sound in *chemist* may be used instead (i.e., approximately the same sound as for *k*).

3. Greek Phonology and Morphology

The Greek sounds represented by the letters of the alphabet are called *phonemes* (from φωνή, "sound"). Roughly speaking, phonemes are the smallest elements that contrast with each other in the phonological system of a language. In English, the words *pig* and *big* are distinguished from each other by the phonemes *p* and *b*. Likewise, κ and χ are different phonemes because they affect meaning: ἐκεῖ means "there," and ἔχει means "he has." Similarly, in Romans 5:1 one phoneme makes the difference between "*we have* [ἔχομεν] peace with God" and "*let us have* [ἔχωμεν] peace with God." Phonemes, then, are sounds that speakers of a language know to be meaningful parts of that language.

Phonemes generally combine to form what linguists call *morphemes* (from μορφή, "form"). Morphemes may be defined as the minimal units of speech that convey a specific meaning. Examples of English morphemes include -s (occurring as a plural ending in *dogs, cats, houses*), -ed (occurring as a past-tense ending in *loved, hoped, wanted*), and -ly (occurring as an adverbial ending in *badly, nicely, hardly*). Just as a knowledge of English morphemes enables us to understand the difference between *friendship, friendliness*, and *unfriendly*, so an understanding of Greek morphology will aid us in the knowledge of Greek word meanings. *You are not expected to master Greek phonology and morphology in this course.* Still, the benefits of implementing a linguistic approach, even at an introductory level, far outweigh the disadvantages of ignoring it altogether.

4. The Greek Vowels

As in English, the Greek letters may be divided into vowels and consonants. Vowels are produced by exhaling air from the lungs. Greek has seven vowels: α, ε, η, ι, ο, υ, ω. Two of these are always short (ε, ο); two are always long (η, ω); and three may be either short or long (α, ι, υ). Hence the tone value of α, ι, and υ can be learned only by observing specific Greek words.

Sometimes two different vowel sounds are combined in one syllable. This combination is called a *diphthong* (from δίφθογγος, "having two sounds"). Greek has seven common or "proper" diphthongs, four of which end in ι, and three of which end in υ:

Diphthong	Pronunciation	Example	Definition
αι	aisle	αἰών	"age" (cf. *aeon*)
ει	eight	εἰρήνη	"peace" (cf. *Irene*)
οι	oil	οἶκος	"house" (cf. *economy*)
υι	suite	υἱός	"son"
αυ	Faust	αὐτός	"self" (cf. *automobile*)
ευ	feud	εὐλογητός	"blessed" (cf. *eulogy*)
ου	soup	οὐρανός	"heaven" (cf. *Uranus*)

In some instances, the long vowels α, η, ω are combined with an ι. In this case the ι is written *beneath* the vowel (ᾳ, ῃ, ῳ) and is called an *iota subscript*. Since the ι is not pronounced, these combinations are often referred to as "improper diphthongs." Several words containing an iota subscript are found in the opening verses of the Gospel of John, which are used in the exercises to this lesson (see §11): ἀρχῇ, αὐτῷ, τῇ, σκοτίᾳ.

5. The Greek Consonants

Consonants are produced by interfering with the flow of air from the lungs. The Greek consonants can be classified according to (1) *how* one interferes with the flow (called the *manner of articulation*), (2) *where* one interferes with the flow (called the *place of articulation*), and (3) whether the vocal cords vibrate in producing the sound.

Manner of articulation involves either the *complete* interruption of the flow of air or the *incomplete* restriction of the flow. This distinction provides the basis for classifying consonants into *stops* (sometimes called *mutes*, as in β and δ) and *continuants* (sometimes called *fricatives*, as in φ and θ).

Place of articulation involves three basic possibilities: at the lips (producing *bilabials*, as in μ and π), at the teeth or just behind them (producing *dentals* or *alveolars*, as in δ and τ), or at the velum or palate (producing *velars* or *palatals*, as in γ and κ).

Finally, the vibration or lack of vibration of the vocal cords distinguishes *voiced* consonants from *unvoiced* consonants (note the difference between β and π).

Greek also contains four *sibilants*, or "s" sounds (ζ, ξ, σ, and ψ). Three of these are *double letters*, or combinations of a consonant with an "s" sound (ζ [dz], ξ [ks], and ψ [ps]). In addition, Greek has three *aspirates*, or letters combined with an "h" (θ [th], φ [ph], and χ [ch]), and four *nasals*, so called because the breath passes through the nose (λ, μ, ν, and ρ). Acquaintance with these terms will simplify the introduction of certain concepts later in this text.

6. The Use and Formation of the Greek Letters

The Greek uppercase letters are the oldest forms of the Greek letters. They are found in ancient inscriptions and are used in modern printed books to begin proper nouns, paragraphs, and direct speech (where English would use quotation marks). Greek sentences do not, however, begin

with capital letters. The lowercase letters are therefore of greater importance than the capitals and should be mastered first.

The following diagram shows you how to form the Greek lowercase
letters. The arrows indicate the easiest place to begin when writing. No-

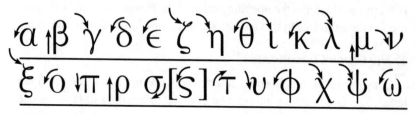

tice that many of the letters can be made without lifting pen from paper
(e.g., β and ρ are formed with a single stroke, beginning at the bottom).
Be very careful to distinguish the following pairs of letters: φ and ψ, ν and
υ, ν and γ, and o and σ.

7. Breathing Marks

Every Greek word beginning with a vowel or a diphthong has a symbol
over it called a *breathing mark*. The *rough breathing mark* (') indicates
that the word is to be pronounced with an initial "h" sound. The *smooth
breathing mark* (') indicates that the word lacks this initial "h" sound.
Thus ἕν ("one") is pronounced *hen*, and ἐν ("in") is pronounced *en*. The
breathing mark is always placed over the *second* vowel of a diphthong
(e.g., εὐλογητός, "blessed"). Initial ρ and υ always have the rough breathing mark, as in ῥῆμα ("word") and ὑποκριτής ("hypocrite"). When used
with ρ, however, the rough breathing is generally not pronounced (cf.
"rhetoric," "rhododendron"). When the initial vowel is a capital letter, the
breathing mark is placed to the left of it, as in Ἀβραάμ ("Abraham") and
Ἑβραῖος ("Hebrew").

8. Greek Punctuation

Although punctuation marks were not used in ancient Greek, they are
found today in all printed editions of the Greek New Testament. Greek
has four marks of punctuation. The *comma* (,) and the *period* (.) correspond in both form and function to the English comma and period. The

6

colon (·) and the *question mark* (;) correspond in function to the English colon and question mark but differ in form.

Since there is no punctuation in the earliest manuscripts of the New Testament, the punctuation of modern printed editions is often a matter of interpretation (e.g., John 1:3b–4). Moreover, because Greek has no quotation marks, in several New Testament passages it remains uncertain where direct speech begins and ends (e.g., Jesus' discourse with Nicodemus in John 3). These and other problems of punctuation are best treated when encountered in the New Testament.

9. Greek Diacritical Marks

Modern printed editions of the Greek New Testament employ three different diacritical marks. The *apostrophe* (') indicates the omission of a final short vowel before a word that begins with a vowel or diphthong, as in δι' αὐτοῦ ("through him") for διὰ αὐτοῦ (John 1:3). This process is called *elision* (from Lat. *elido*, "I leave out"). The *diaeresis* (¨) occurs where two vowels that normally combine to form a diphthong are to be pronounced separately, as in 'Ησαΐας (the Greek form of "Isaiah"; John 1:23). Notice that this word consists of four syllables ('H-σα-ι-ας), not three ('H-σαι-ας). Finally, the *coronis* (') indicates the combination of two words with the loss of an intermediate letter or letters. This process of merging two words is known as *crasis* (from κρᾶσις, "a mingling") and is found in such English forms as "I'm," "you're," and "don't." In the New Testament, crasis occurs in a number of specific combinations, the most common of which include κἀγώ (for καὶ ἐγώ, "and I"; John 1:31) and κἀκεῖνος (for καὶ ἐκεῖνος, "and he"; John 6:57).

10. The Greek Accents

Printed editions of the Greek New Testament use three accent marks: the *acute* (´), the *grave* (`), and the *circumflex* (^). The importance of accents for the study of Greek is twofold: (1) accents occasionally distinguish between words that are otherwise identical (e.g., εἰ means "if," but εἶ means "you are"); and (2) accents serve to indicate which syllable in a Greek word is to be stressed in pronunciation. Otherwise, it is possible to read New Testament Greek without knowing any more about accents. In subsequent lessons, accents will be treated where relevant. For those with a special interest in learning the rules of Greek accentuation, Appendix 1 provides a detailed summary.

The Greek accents were invented about 200 B.C. as an aid to the correct pronunciation of Greek among foreigners. The accents originally indicated pitch rather than stress. The acute marked a rise in the voice, and the circumflex marked a rise followed by a fall. The grave accent was not usually used. Accents were not regularly employed in texts until after the fifth century A.D.

11. Exercises

a. Study the pronunciation of the Greek letters and diphthongs, and practice saying each sound aloud. It is exceedingly important to be able to read the characters accurately and quickly before proceeding further. An incorrect pronunciation will hamper the learning process and easily mislead you into a confusion about words and forms. For the Greek alphabet set to a traditional tune, see Appendix 2: "The Greek Alphabet Song."

b. Pronounce the following Greek words. Notice their similarity to English words.

ἀπόστολος	apostle
σῶμα	body (cf. *soma*tic)
φωνή	sound (cf. *phone*)
καρδία	heart (cf. *cardi*ac)
φόβος	fear (cf. *phob*ia)
γένος	race (cf. *gen*us)
Φίλιππος	Philip
ἔξοδος	departure (cf. *Exod*us)
ζωή	life (cf. *zo*ology)
Πέτρος	Peter
θεός	God (cf. *theo*logy)
γυνή	woman (cf. *gyne*cology)
πατήρ	father (cf. *pater*nal)
ψυχή	soul (cf. *psycho*logy)
πόλις	city (cf. *poli*tical)
Χριστός	Christ

c. Practice writing the Greek lowercase letters in proper order, aiming at simplicity and ease of recognition. It is helpful to pronounce the *name* of each letter while writing, since the name contains the sound of the letter.

d. The following passage from John 1:1–5 contains all but three letters of the Greek alphabet (only μ, ξ, and ψ are absent). Read these verses aloud with proper accentuation, striving for fluency in pronunciation. Remember that there are no silent letters in Greek except for the iota subscript.

'Εν ἀρχῇ ἦν ὁ λόγος, καὶ ὁ λόγος ἦν πρὸς τὸν θεόν, καὶ θεὸς ἦν ὁ λόγος. οὗτος ἦν ἐν ἀρχῇ πρὸς τὸν θεόν. πάντα δι' αὐτοῦ ἐγένετο, καὶ χωρὶς αὐτοῦ ἐγένετο οὐδὲ ἕν. ὃ γέγονεν ἐν αὐτῷ ζωὴ ἦν, καὶ ἡ ζωὴ ἦν τὸ φῶς τῶν ἀνθρώπων. καὶ τὸ φῶς ἐν τῇ σκοτίᾳ φαίνει, καὶ ἡ σκοτία αὐτὸ οὐ κατέλαβεν.

e. It is important to know something of the history and development of the Greek language. Try to read the article "Language of the New Testament" in a reference book or Bible encyclopedia. For some suggestions, see the bibliography given in the Epilogue (§181).

2

THE GREEK VERB SYSTEM
A BIRD'S EYE VIEW

As in English, the great majority of Greek sentences contain verbs as essential elements. The primary goal of this lesson is understanding the concept of inflection in the Greek verb, The word inflection comes from the Latin *inflecto*, "I bend." Inflected words are "bent" or altered from the simplest form either by changes to the stem of the word or by changes caused by the addition of morphemes to the stem. It is essential to grasp the concept of inflection as well as the broad perspective of the Greek verb system before studying the changes themselves.

12. Inflection

Greek, unlike English, is a highly *inflected* language. Inflection refers to the changes words undergo in accordance with their grammatical function in a sentence. Although Greek contains numerous uninflected words, most Greek words undergo inflection. These words—verbs, nouns, pronouns, adjectives, participles, and the article "the"—have different forms to indicate such matters as gender (masculine, feminine, neuter), number (singular or plural), and case (nominative, accusative, etc.).

This lesson introduces inflection in the Greek verb system. A verb is a word that makes a statement about a subject (e.g., "I *am* an apostle") or transfers an action from the subject to an object (e.g., "I *see* an apostle"). Each of the above examples is a *clause*—a group of words forming a sense unit and containing one finite verb. A finite verb is one that functions as the basic verbal element of a clause. We can say "Christ died" because "died" is a finite form of the verb "die." We cannot say "Christ dying" (as a complete sentence) because "dying" is a non-finite form.

Finite verbs in Greek consist of two basic parts: a stem, which contains the lexical or dictionary meaning of the word, and one or more *affixes*, which indicate the function of the word in the particular sentence where it occurs. An affix added to the beginning of a word is called a *prefix*, one that is added within a word is called an *infix*, and one that is added to the end of a word is called a *suffix*. English verbs such as "break" are illustrative: "break-" is the present stem, and to it the suffix of the third person singular is added, giving "breaks." "Brok-" is the past stem, giving us "broken" for the past participle. In Greek, affixes are used to convey similar types of grammatical information.

The beginning student of Greek is sometimes bewildered by the complexity of Greek verbs in comparison with English verbs. Notice, for example, the forms for the English verb "have":

	Singular	Plural
First Person	I have	we have
Second Person	you have	you have
Third Person	he *has*	they have

Here English makes use of independent pronouns to indicate person and number ("I," "you," "we," etc.), except in the third person singular (where "have" becomes "has"). *But what English can do in only one of its six forms, other languages can do in each of the six forms by means of inflection.* For example, the Spanish forms for *tener*, "to have," are as follows:

(yo)	tengo	(nosotros)	tenemos
(tú)	tienes	(vosotros)	tenéis
(él)	tiene	(ellos)	tienen

Here the pronouns in parentheses are optional elements, so that "I have" is simply *tengo*, "we have" is *tenemos*, and so forth. French uses a combination of personal endings and personal pronouns to get the message across, as in *avoir*, "to have":

j'	ai	nous	avons
tu	as	vous	avez
il	a	ils	ont

German does much the same thing, as in *haben*, "to have":

ich	habe	wir	haben
du	hast	ihr	habt
er	hat	sie	haben

Notice that in both French and German the personal pronouns "I," "you," "we," and the like are *not* optional, just like in English. Greek, however, is more like Spanish in that a different form of the verb is used to indicate both person and number. This is accomplished by the affixing of *person-number suffixes* to the verb stem. This stem is called the *lexical morpheme* since it conveys the lexical meaning of the word (i.e., the meaning found in the dictionary). Thus the Greek word for "I have," ἔχω, consists of the lexical morpheme ἐχ- (meaning "have") plus the person-number suffix ω (meaning "I"). If the various suffixes of the present tense are now added to this stem, we get the following forms:

ἔχω	*I have*	ἔχομεν	*we have*
ἔχεις	*you have*	ἔχετε	*you have*
ἔχει	*he has*	ἔχουσι	*they have*

These suffixes are also used in many other verbs. When the same pattern of suffixes is used by several words, that pattern is called a *paradigm* (from παράδειγμα, "pattern").

13. Mood

Notice that each form of ἔχω given above makes an affirmation. In Greek an affirmation is said to be in the *indicative mood*. The term "mood" comes from the Latin *modus*, meaning "measure" or "manner." Mood refers to the manner in which the speaker relates the verbal idea to reality. The indicative mood indicates that the speaker affirms the factuality of the statement (as in "*I have* mercy"). Greek has other moods as well: a verb can express a command (the *imperative mood*: "Lord, *have* mercy"); it can express contingency (the *subjunctive mood*: "though *he have* mercy"); and it can express a verbal idea without limiting it by specifying person and number (the *infinitive mood*: "*to have* mercy is better than to offer sacrifices"). These four moods—indicative, imperative, subjunctive, and infinitive—are the ones most frequently encountered in

12

the New Testament. The *optative mood*, which generally expresses a polite request (*"may he have* mercy"), is not widely used.

Because the indicative mood affirms the factuality of an action, it is called the *mood of reality*. It is also the customary or "unmarked" mood in Greek. The other moods are variations of the indicative, and are called *potential moods* because they represent action that is possible but not actual. It should be emphasized that the speaker's choice of mood does not necessarily correspond to objective reality. The speaker may be deliberately masking the real mood or even be lying. When, for example, Peter was asked whether he was a disciple of Jesus, he replied "I am not" (John 18:17). Here the indicative mood refers only to *purported* reality, since Peter was, of course, a disciple.

14. Voice

In addition to mood, Greek verbs are also said to express *voice*. Whereas mood refers to the way in which the speaker chooses to affirm the reality or unreality of an action, voice refers to the way in which the speaker chooses to relate the grammatical subject of a verb to the action of that verb. A verb is said to be in the *active* voice when the subject is presented as performing the action, as in "I hear a man" (ἀκούω ἄνθρωπον). Here ἀκούω ("I hear") is an *active* verb since the subject of the verb is doing the hearing rather than being heard. There are two other voices in Greek: the *passive* and the *middle*. In the passive voice the subject is pictured as being acted upon (e.g., "I am being heard"). In the middle voice the subject is pictured as acting in its own interest. Something of the force of the middle voice can be seen by comparing the following New Testament verses:

(a) Active: "They *put on* him his own clothes" (Matt 27:31).
(b) Middle: "Do not *put on* two tunics" (Mark 6:9).

Both by frequency and emphasis the active is the normal or "unmarked" voice in Greek. It highlights the *action* of the verb, whereas the middle and passive highlight the grammatical *subject*.

15. Tense (Aspect)

In addition to mood and voice, a Greek verb is also said to have *tense*. The tenses in Greek are the *present*, the *future*, the *imperfect*, the *aorist* (pronounced " air-rist"), the *perfect*, the *pluperfect*, and the *future perfect*.

The present, future, perfect, and future perfect are sometimes called *primary* (or *principal*) tenses, while the imperfect, aorist, and pluperfect are sometimes called *secondary* (or *historical*) tenses. In the indicative mood, the usual English equivalents of these tenses are as follows:

Tense	Active Voice	Passive Voice
Present	*I love*	*I am being loved*
Future	*I will love*	*I will be loved*
Imperfect	*I was loving*	*I was being loved*
Aorist	*I loved*	*I was loved*
Perfect	*I have loved*	*I have been loved*
Pluperfect	*I had loved*	*I had been loved*
Future perfect	*I will have loved*	*I will have been loved*

Notice how many tenses in English are formed with the present or past tense of the verb in question together with some part of "will," "have," or "be." When so used, the latter are called *auxiliary verbs*, and the resulting combinations (e.g., "I will have been loved") are called *composite tenses*. Other auxiliary verbs in English are "should" and "would." Koine Greek has a much smaller number of composite tenses and only one auxiliary verb.

Besides tense, linguists also speak of *aspect* in describing the Greek verb system. The term "aspect" refers to the view of the action that the speaker chooses to present to the hearer. There are three categories of aspect in Greek: imperfective, perfective, and aoristic. *Imperfective* aspect focuses on the process or duration of the action. *Perfective* aspect focuses on the state or condition resulting from a completed action. *Aoristic* aspect focuses on the verbal idea in its entirety, without commenting upon either the process or the abiding results of the action. The aorist does not deny that these aspects may be present; in keeping with its name—ἀ-όριστος "un-defined"—it simply chooses not to comment. The aoristic is the normal or "unmarked" aspect in Greek. A deviation from the aoristic to another aspect is generally exegetically significant.

Each of these categories of aspect intersects with the Greek tenses (with some overlapping). Imperfective aspect intersects with the present, imperfect, and future tenses; aoristic aspect intersects with the aorist, present, and future tenses; and perfective aspect intersects with the perfect, pluperfect, and future perfect tenses. This may be illustrated by the following diagram:

	Time of Action		
Kind of Action	Past	Present	Future
Imperfective	Imperfect *I was loving*	Present *I am loving*	Future *I will be loving*
Aoristic	Aorist *I loved*	Present *I love*	Future *I will love*
Perfective	Pluperfect *I had loved*	Perfect *I have loved*	Future Perfect *I will have loved*

Notice that the imperfect tense is always imperfective; the aorist tense is always aoristic; and the pluperfect, perfect, and future perfect tenses are always perfective. The present is basically imperfective ("I am loving"), though it may also be aoristic ("I love"). Likewise, the future tense is sometimes imperfective ("I will be loving") and sometimes aoristic ("I will love"), the context alone conveying this information. Since the future tense is primarily concerned with future time, its aspectual significance is less marked than the other tenses.

16. The Significance of Tense (Aspect) for Reading Greek

Even in the early stages of learning, it is important to become aware of both the importance and the function of aspect in the Greek verb system. Unlike English, the most significant feature of tense in Greek is *kind of action*. A secondary consideration of tense, and one that applies only in the indicative mood, is *time of action*. But the essential signification of the Greek tense system is the kind of action—whether it is represented as ongoing, finished, or simply as an occurrence. Hence there are really only three tenses in Greek (as in English): past, present, and future. The other "tenses" are, in fact, merely alternative uses of these three tenses in conjunction with the three aspects (imperfective, perfective, and aoristic).

In summary, then, tense in Greek is determined by the writer's portrayal of the action with regard to aspect and (in the indicative mood) to time. This accounts for the fact that two different authors may portray the action of the same event differently. For instance, Matthew writes that Jesus "gave" (ἔδωκεν, aorist indicative) the loaves to the disciples (Matt 14:19), while Mark writes that Jesus "kept giving" (ἐδίδου, imperfect indicative) them out (Mark 6:41). Here Matthew focuses on the bare idea of the action, while Mark emphasizes its continuance, implying that the miracle took place in the very hands of Jesus. Even the same writer may portray the same action differently in different contexts. Paul, for example, uses the aorist participle in reference to the resurrection of Christ when viewing it as a simple event (Rom 8:11) and the perfect participle when emphasizing the state of Christ's risenness (2 Tim 2:8). *Hence the basic issue with regard to tense is always the question of how much—or how little—the writer wishes to say about the kind of action involved.*

17. Exercises

The chief aim of this lesson is to provide you with an awareness, in a general way, of the Greek verb system, enabling you to see the work ahead of you in its totality and to get an idea of its scope. *You are not expected to memorize anything in this lesson.* Instead, read the lesson carefully, concentrating particularly on those areas of the Greek verb that are newest to you. If you do this, you will have a much better feel for the overall functioning of the Greek language as you progress through this grammar.

3

PRESENT AND FUTURE ACTIVE INDICATIVE

> Related patterns of verbs are known as conjugations (from Lat. *coniugo*, "I join together"). The entire Greek verb system may be divided into two basic conjugations: the -ω conjugation, and the -μι conjugation. These terms refer to the ending of the first person singular suffix in the present active indicative. The older but much smaller of the two systems is the -μι conjugation. The most common -μι verb is εἰμί ("I am"), used about 2,500 times in the Greek New Testament. However, the great majority of New Testament verbs belong to the -ω conjugation. Mastering this conjugation is, therefore, essential before attempting to read the Greek New Testament. This lesson introduces the conjugations of λύω ("I loose") in the present and future active indicative and the conjugation of εἰμί ("I am") in the present indicative.

18. The Primary Active Suffixes

You will recall that the Greek primary tenses are the present, the future, the perfect, and the future perfect (see §15). In the indicative mood, the primary tenses deal with present or future time, whereas the secondary tenses are oriented to the past. Greek has separate sets of person-number suffixes for the primary tenses and for the secondary tenses. Only the primary suffixes concern us in this lesson. In the active indicative, these suffixes are:

	Singular	Plural
1.	-ω	-μεν
2.	-εις	-τε
3.	-ει	-ουσι(ν)

These suffixes have the following meanings:

	Singular	Plural
1.	I	we
2.	you	you
3.	he (she, it)	they

In addition, Greek adds a vowel before the suffixes -μεν and -τε. This vowel, known as a *connecting vowel*, functions as a phonological cushion between the verb stem and the suffix. The connecting vowel is o before μ and ν, and ε before all other letters. The connecting vowel is sometimes called a *neutral morpheme* since it is added solely for the sake of pronunciation and does not affect meaning.

19. The Present and Future Active Indicative of λύω

The primary suffixes and connecting vowels discussed above are used in forming the present and future active indicative tenses. Note the forms of the model verb λύω ("I loose"):

		Present		Future	
Sg.	1.	λύω	I loose	λύσω	I will loose
	2.	λύεις	you loose	λύσεις	you will loose
	3.	λύει	he looses	λύσει	he will loose
Pl.	1.	λύομεν	we loose	λύσομεν	we will loose
	2.	λύετε	you loose	λύσετε	you will loose
	3.	λύουσι(ν)	they loose	λύσουσι(ν)	they will loose

The main feature distinguishing these two paradigms is the stem. By removing the -ω from λύω, we obtain the present stem λυ-. The conjugation of the present active indicative of any -ω verb can be obtained by (a) substituting the present stem of that verb for λυ-, and then (b) adding the primary active suffixes along with the appropriate connecting vowels. Thus, for example, the present active indicative of γράφω ("I write") is: γράφω, γράφεις, γράφει, γράφομεν, γράφετε, γράφουσι(ν).

By removing the -ω from λύσω, we obtain the future stem λυσ-. Notice that Greek indicates future time by adding a σ to the present stem. This σ is called the *future time morpheme* and is equivalent in meaning to the English auxiliary verb "will." Thus the analysis of λύσομεν ("we will loose") is λυ- (lexical morpheme), -σ- (future time morpheme), -ο- (neutral morpheme), and -μεν (person-number suffix). This may also be shown graphically as follows (the symbol # refers to "zero" significance):

λυ	+	σ	+	ο	+	μεν	=	λύσομεν
"loose"	+	"will"	+	#	+	"we"	=	"we will loose"

Observe that the only difference between the forms of the present tense and the future tense is that the future tense forms contain the future time morpheme σ. The first person singular form λύω is called the *present active principal part*, while the first person singular form λύσω is called the *future active principal part*. A verb that is regular has six principal parts, each of which has the first person singular ending. Present and future principal parts are presented together in the vocabulary to this lesson (§26).

20. Amalgamation in the Future Tense

Numerous Greek verbs form the future tense by adding a σ to the present stem. However, when the stem of a verb ends in a consonant, a phonological change will occur when the future time morpheme σ is attached. These changes may be summarized as follows:

(a) π, β, φ + σ form the double consonant ψ. Thus the future of πέμπω ("I send") is πέμψω (from πεμπ + σω).

(b) κ, γ, χ + σ form the double consonant ξ. Thus the future of ἄγω ("I lead") is ἄξω (from ἀγ + σω).

19

(c) τ, δ, θ drop out before σ. Thus the future of πείθω ("I trust in") is πείσω.

Note, however, that if the *verb* stem is different from the *present* stem (as is sometimes the case), the future time morpheme σ is added to the verb stem instead of the present stem. For example, the verb stem of κηρύσσω ("I preach") is not κηρυσσ-, but κηρυκ-. From κηρυκ- is formed the future κηρύξω by the rules given above (κηρυκ + σω = κηρύξω). Similarly, the verb stem of βαπτίζω ("I baptize") is not βαπτιζ- but βαπτιδ-. From βαπτιδ- is formed the future βαπτίσω from the same rules (βαπτιδ + σω = βαπτίσω). In all these cases, *amalgamation* is said to have occurred.

21. More on the Person-Number Suffixes

The person-number suffixes -ω, -εις, -ει, -μεν, -τε, -ουσι(ν) probably had their origin in the attachment of independent personal pronouns to the stem of the verb. This means that each Greek verb has a built-in *internal subject*. When an *external subject* for a verb is given, the internal subject is not translated. Thus λύει is "he looses," but Ἰησοῦς λύει is "Jesus looses," not "Jesus he looses." Since pronoun suffixes do not indicate gender, λύει may also be translated "she looses" or "it looses," depending on the context.

Notice also that Greek distinguishes between second person singular and second person plural, a distinction not made by English (see John 4:20–22). Greek does not, however, have familiar and polite forms of the second person as in French, German, and other languages. A slave and a master would have addressed each other in the second person singular.

Finally, the phoneme ν is sometimes added to the third person plural suffix -ουσι, especially before a word beginning with a vowel or at the end of a clause or sentence, as in λύουσιν ἀνθρώπους, "they loose men." This usage is called the *movable ν*. As with "a" and "an" in English (e.g., "*an* apple"), this type of phonetic modification does not affect the meaning of the individual word or morpheme. Slightly different forms of a morpheme (e.g., -ουσι and -ουσιν) are called *allomorphs* (from ἄλλος, "another [kind]").

22. Uses of the Present and Future

As we have seen, the aspect denoted by the present indicative may be aoristic, though it is usually imperfective (see §15). Hence λύω may be rendered either "I loose" or "I am loosing," depending on the context. These uses are called the *simple present* and the *progressive present*, respectively. The progressive present is frequently found in narrative material, as in Matthew 8:25: "Lord, save us! *We are drowning.*" One other use of the present tense deserves brief mention here. The *historical present* is used when a past event is viewed with the vividness of a present occurrence, as in Mark 1:40: "And a leper *comes* to him." This usage is characteristic of lively narrative in general and is a special feature of Mark's Gospel (151 times), where it frequently introduces new scenes or participants. Note that even when an action occurred in the past, an author may choose to *depict* that action in present time. Hence one must always carefully distinguish between reality (how the action happened) and depiction (how the author presents the action).

The future tense, as its name implies, is usually *predictive* in force, as in John 14:26: "He *will teach* you all things." However, the future may also be used *imperatively* to express a command, as in Luke 1:31: "*you will call* [i.e., you are to call] his name Jesus." This usage reflects Hebrew influence. Finally, the statement of a generally accepted fact is occasionally expressed by the future tense, as in Ephesians 5:31: "A man *will leave* father and mother." This latter example is neither predictive nor imperatival; it simply asserts a performance that may rightfully be expected under normal conditions. This usage is sometimes called the *gnomic* future (from γνώμη, "maxim"). It will be recalled that the kind of action in the future tense may be either aoristic ("I will loose") or imperfective ("I will be loosing"). Its usual aspect in the New Testament is aoristic, with greater emphasis on the time element than the present. "I *will prepare* a place for you" (John 14:3) is aoristic, while "the one who began a good work in you *will bring* it to completion" (Phil 1:6) is imperfective.

i. The names "progressive," "predictive," "gnomic," and so forth, are at best conventional designations. As labels they are quite unimportant. What *is* important are the *meanings* associated with the names. It is the context and *not* the tense that determines these meanings. This fact should be borne in mind here and in subsequent lessons wherever such labels are used.

ii. You will recall that the Greek question mark is ; (see §8). Hence λύομεν means "we loose" or "we are loosing," but λύομεν; means "do we loose?" or "are we loosing?"

23. The Present Indicative of εἰμί

As already observed, the most frequently occurring verb of the -μι conjugation is εἰμί ("I am"). Grammarians label εἰμί a *copulative* verb (from Lat. *copulo*, "I link together") because it links subject and predicate, as in 1 John 1:5: ὁ θεὸς φῶς ἐστιν, "God [subject] is light [predicate]." Since εἰμί expresses a state of being rather than an action, it has neither active, middle, nor passive voice. Note the movable ν in the third person singular and plural.

	Singular		Plural	
1.	εἰμί	I am	ἐσμέν	we are
2.	εἶ	you are	ἐστέ	you are
3.	ἐστί(ν)	he is	εἰσί(ν)	they are

Except for εἶ, the present tense of εἰμί is said to be *enclitic*, throwing its accent back on the last syllable of the preceding word, as in ὁ δὲ ἀγρός ἐστιν ὁ κόσμος, "Now the field is the world" (Matt 13:38). For further discussion of enclitics and of Greek accents in general, see Appendix 1.

24. Negatives

The negative *not* is expressed in Greek by the adverb οὐ. This word is used as the negative with verbs in the *indicative* mood. A different word, μή, is used with all other moods. Both negatives precede the word to which they refer. Thus οὐ λύω means "I do not loose," οὐ λύομεν means "we do not loose," etc. Before a word beginning with a vowel, οὐκ is used (e.g., οὐκ ἀκούω, "I do not hear"), and before a rough breathing, οὐχ is used (e.g., οὐχ ἑτοιμάζω, "I do not prepare"). In linguistics, all of these forms—οὐ, μή, οὐκ, and οὐχ—are considered allomorphs of the same Greek negative adverb.

25. Parsing

Finite verbs in Greek convey tense, voice, mood, person, and number. To *parse* a verb is to identify these five elements along with the source (lexical or vocabulary form) of the verb. For example, to parse λύομεν, we say that it is present tense, active voice, indicative mood, first person, plural number, from the verb λύω. For practical usage, we can say, "Present active indicative, first plural, from λύω."

26. Vocabulary

a. Present and future active indicative principal parts of -ω verbs.

ἄγω, ἄξω	*I lead, I will lead* (*ag*ent)
ἀκούω, ἀκούσω	*I hear, I will hear* (*acous*tics)
βαπτίζω, βαπτίσω	*I baptize, I will baptize* (√ βαπτιδ, *bapti*sm)
βλέπω, βλέψω	*I see, I will see*
γράφω, γράψω	*I write, I will write* (*graph*ics)
διδάσκω, διδάξω	*I teach, I will teach* (√ διδακ, *didac*tic)
δοξάζω, δοξάσω	*I glorify, I will glorify* (√ δοξαδ, *dox*ology)
ἑτοιμάζω, ἑτοιμάσω	*I prepare, I will prepare* (√ ἑτοιμαδ)
ἔχω, ἕξω	*I have, I will have* (√ ἐχ, *hec*tic [from ἑκτικός, "habitual"])
θεραπεύω, θεραπεύσω	*I heal, I will heal* (*therapeu*tic)
κηρύσσω, κηρύξω	*I preach, I will preach* (√ κηρυκ, *keryg*ma)
λύω, λύσω	*I loose, I will loose* (*analysis*)
πείθω, πείσω	*I trust in, I will trust in* (√ πιθ [Lat. *fid*], *fid*elity)
πέμπω, πέμψω	*I send, I will send* (*pomp*)
πιστεύω, πιστεύσω	*I believe, I will believe*
σώζω, σώσω	*I save, I will save* (√ σωδ, *soz*in [an animal protein])

b. -μι verb.

εἰμί	*I am* (√ ἐσ, *is*)

c. Adverbs

μή	*not* (with non-indicative moods)
οὐ	*not* (with indicative mood)

27. Exercises

a. Read the lesson carefully, attempting to become familiar with the new material and to gain an initial understanding of Greek verbs. Learn by heart: (1) the paradigm of λύω in the present active indicative, and

23

(2) the paradigm of εἰμί in the present indicative. It is not necessary to memorize the future paradigm of λύω since it is identical to the present except for the future time morpheme. In memorizing all paradigms, be sure to say them aloud, for this provides the help of two senses, both sight and sound.

b. Beginning with this lesson, you will find a list of the most frequently used words in the New Testament. (This first vocabulary contains words that occur a total of 6,487 times in the Greek New Testament!) The English words in parentheses are related to the Greek words and are given to aid memorization, while the symbol √ indicates the basic stem of the word in question. For example, the verb stem of διδάσκω ("I teach") is not διδασκ, but διδακ, as seen in *didac*tic ("intended to teach"). It is often helpful to learn the stem of a word along with the word itself.

It is important to remember that Greek words (like English ones) have a meaning that is context-determined to a significant degree. For instance, the Greek of John 1:1a ("In the beginning was the Word") could, in an appropriate context, be translated, "The treasurer was in the midst of a body of troops"! Keep in mind, therefore, that *the semantic field (area of meaning) of a Greek word is much wider than can be summarized in the vocabulary of a beginning grammar, and that the definitions given in this text represent only the most common meanings of the words as they are used in the New Testament.*

Study the vocabulary to this lesson with the following suggestions in mind: (1) read each Greek word aloud several times, noting its meaning; (2) cover the English column and see if you can remember the meaning of the Greek word; and (3) cover the Greek column and write the Greek word corresponding to the English word. Follow these same instructions in subsequent lessons. As you enlarge your vocabulary, you may find it helpful to make your own system of flash cards for review.

c. Translate the following sentences.

1. βλέπεις. γράφεις. οὐ πέμπεις.

2. ἄγει. βαπτίζει. οὐ λύει.

3. ἀκούομεν. ἑτοιμάζομεν. οὐ πιστεύομεν.

4. γράφετε. πείθετε. οὐ σώζετε.

5. βλέπουσιν. διδάσκουσιν. οὐ λύουσιν.

6. βαπτίζει. διδάσκομεν. οὐκ ἀκούουσιν.

7. σώζω; θεραπεύει; πέμπουσιν;

8. εἶ. ἐσμέν. ἐστέ.

9. ἀκούσει. βαπτίσει. ἕξει.

10. γράψομεν. διδάξομεν. κηρύξομεν.

11. οὐ λύσετε. οὐ δοξάσεις. οὐ πείσομεν.

4

NOUNS OF THE
SECOND DECLENSION

The primary goal of this lesson is understanding the concept of inflection (word change) in the Greek noun. The inflection of a noun is called a declension. Nouns of the second declension are studied first because of their greater regularity and because this declension contains the largest number of New Testament nouns.

28. Introducing the Greek Cases

In any type of expression where it occurs, a noun (or pronoun) stands in a certain relationship to the other words around it, and this relationship is determined by the meaning we want to convey. "Men see apostles" and "Apostles see men" contain exactly the same words but have opposite meanings, which are indicated by the relationship in each sentence of the nouns "men" and "apostles" to the verb "see." As is normal in English, this relationship is indicated by word order: the subject precedes the verb, and the object follows it, without any change in form. In Greek, where word order has a different function, grammatical relationships are indicated by particular suffixes applied to the nouns. If a noun is the subject of a verb (i.e., if it precedes the verb in a simple English sentence), it must, in Greek, be put into the *nominative case* with the appropriate suffix. If it is the object of a verb (i.e., if it follows the verb in English), Greek puts it into the *accusative case*. Thus "Men see apostles" would be ἄνθρωποι βλέπουσιν ἀποστόλους, where the suffixes -οι (nominative plural) and -ους (accusative plural) indicate subject and object, respectively. Case in Greek means that it is *not* the order of words, as in English, that decides the meaning of a sentence. The subject will not always be found before the verb, nor will the object always be found after the verb. In Greek it is the *case form* that decides which word is the subject or the object.

Greek has four basic cases:

(1) The *nominative*, representing the *subject* ("*Men* see apostles").

(2) The *genitive*, representing the *possessor* ("The wisdom *of men*").

(3) The *dative*, representing the *indirect object* ("He gave gifts *to men*").

(4) The *accusative*, representing the *object* ("Apostles see *men*").

The *vocative*, which represents the person or thing *addressed* ("Forward, men!"), is not widely used. In English, the only surviving case ending in nouns is that of the genitive (e.g., *men's*, *boy's*). Elsewhere the function of a noun is shown by its position (as with "*Men* see apostles" and "Apostles see *men*"), or by a preposition: "The wisdom *of men*" (for the genitive case) or "He gave gifts *to men*" (for the dative case). In the latter two instances, notice that in English we can also say with the same meaning, "*Men's* wisdom" and "He gave *men* gifts," respectively.

29. Gender

In addition to case, Greek nouns are also said to have gender. In English we observe natural gender: "man" is masculine, "girl" is feminine, and "car" is neuter. When referring to these, we would say "he, "she," and "it," respectively. Greek observes natural gender with living beings (generally), but other nouns, which may describe things, qualities, and so on, are not necessarily neuter. For example, ἀνήρ ("man") is masculine and γυνή ("woman") is feminine, but θάνατος ("death") is masculine, ἁμαρτία ("sin") is feminine, and τέκνον ("child") is neuter. Generally, we cannot see why a particular noun is a particular gender, but the gender of individual nouns is not difficult to learn since in most instances it is shown by its ending.

30. Second Declension Nouns

Because Greek indicates case function by means of different forms, Greek nouns can be grouped together according to the manner in which their endings change. These changes indicate both *case* and *number*. Case, as we have seen, involves the function of the noun in its relation to the verb or other parts of the sentence. Number indicates whether the noun is *singular* or *plural*. Both case and number are indicated by different forms called *case-number suffixes*. Nouns with the same pattern of endings are called *declensions* (from Lat. *declino*, "I fall away [i.e., from the nominative case]"). There are three basic declensions in Greek. The second declension is introduced here because it is the easiest of the three to learn and because it contains a larger number of words than the others.

The second declension may be divided into two main groups: (1) nouns whose nominative singular ends in -ος, which, with a few exceptions, are masculine; and (2) nouns whose nominative singular ends in -ον, which are all neuters. Both groups have identical endings except for the nominative, vocative, and accusative. Compare the declension of ὁ ἄνθρωπος ("man"), a masculine noun, with the declension of τὸ δῶρον ("gift"), a neuter noun:

Singular			
Masculine		**Neuter**	
N.	ἄνθρωπος	a man	δῶρον	a gift
G.	ἀνθρώπου	of a man	δώρου	of a gift
D.	ἀνθρώπῳ	to a man	δώρῳ	to a gift
A.	ἄνθρωπον	a man	δῶρον	a gift
V.	ἄνθρωπε	man	δῶρον	gift

Plural			
Masculine		**Neuter**	
N.V.	ἄνθρωποι	men	δῶρα	gifts
G.	ἀνθρώπων	of men	δώρων	of gifts
D.	ἀνθρώποις	to men	δώροις	to gifts
A.	ἀνθρώπους	men	δῶρα	gifts

By removing the -ος from ἄνθρωπος, we obtain the stem ἄνθρωπ-. This stem remains constant when the various endings (i.e., the case-number suffixes) are added to it. These endings may be used with any *masculine* noun given in the vocabulary to this lesson.

The stem of δῶρον is δῶρ-. Notice that the nominative, vocative, and accusative of neuter nouns are identical in both the singular and the plural (these forms are underlined). δῶρον is the paradigm word for all the *neuter* nouns given in the vocabulary to this lesson. It should be noted that neuter *plural* nouns regularly take *singular* verbs.

Omitting names and compound forms, there are 595 second declension nouns in the New Testament, 347 of which are masculine and follow the declension ἄνθρωπος, and 196 of which are neuter and follow the declension of δῶρον. There are also several *feminine* nouns of the second declension. These nouns follow the declension of ἄνθρωπος but use the feminine definite article (e.g., ἡ ὁδός, "the way"; see John 14:6). Some second declension nouns are irregular in their formation. For example, the name "Jesus" is declined as follows: N. Ἰησοῦς; G.D.V. Ἰησοῦ; A. Ἰησοῦν.

31. Additional Uses of the Cases

Although the genitive case usually expresses possession, it has many other important uses. One of these is the *ablatival genitive*, which indicates source: ἄγω δοῦλον οἴκου, "I lead a servant *from* a house." The dative also has many other important uses, including the *locative dative* (ἀγρῷ, "*in* a field"), the *instrumental dative* (λόγῳ, "*by* a word"), and the *dative of personal advantage* (ἀνθρώπῳ, "*for* a man"). These and other uses of the cases must be learned by observation.

32. Complements

As a copulative verb (see §23), εἰμί equates what follows with what precedes. It therefore requires a *complement* in the *nominative* case (to "complete" the idea) instead of an *object* in the *accusative* case. If it is remembered that εἰμί is virtually equivalent to an equal sign (=), its use will be easily understood:

βλέπω **ἄνθρωπον.**	"I see **a man**."
εἰμὶ **ἄνθρωπος.**	"I am **a man** (i.e., 'I' = 'man')."

33. The Use of the Definite Article

Greek has no *indefinite* article (Eng. "a" or "an"). Thus ἄνθρωπος means "man" or "a man." When Greek wants to indicate that a noun is definite, it places the *definite article* in front of it. Thus ὁ ἄνθρωπος means "the man." In general, the presence of the article emphasizes *particular identity*, while the absence of the article emphasizes *quality* or *characteristics*. In Luke 18:13, for example, the tax collector, by using the article, identifies himself as "the sinner," a point largely missed in English translations. On the other hand, Paul's claim in Galatians 1:1 to be "an apostle" emphasizes the dignity and authority of his apostleship without excluding others from that office.

Where no article appears in Greek, the indefinite article "a" or "an" may be used in English when the context suggests this translation. Sometimes an English definite article has to be supplied where Greek lacks the article (as in John 1:1: "in *the* beginning"). Conversely, Greek frequently uses the article with abstract nouns where English usage omits the article (as in 1 Corinthians 13:13: "the greatest of these is [the] love"). The importance of the article for understanding the New Testament is treated in greater detail in Lesson 26.

A noun that has an article is called an *arthrous* noun (from ἄρθρον, "article"). A noun that has no article is called an *anarthrous* (i.e., "not-arthrous") noun.

34. Conjunctions

A conjunction (from Lat. *coniugo*, "I join together") is a word whose function is to join together words, phrases, clauses, and sentences: "the apostle *and* the slave"; "the law *or* the gift"; "he goes *but* they come"; etc. Conjunctions are classified either as *coordinate* (from Lat. *cum*, "with," plus *ordinatus*, "placed in order") or as *subordinate* (from Lat. *sub*, "under"). Coordinate conjunctions connect parallel words or clauses. They may show such relationships as connection ("and"), contrast ("but"), or consequence ("therefore"). Subordinate conjunctions introduce clauses that are dependent on some other clause. Subordinate clauses may be conditional ("if"), concessive ("although"), temporal ("when"), causal ("because"), final ("in order that"), or consecutive ("that").

This lesson contains three common New Testament coordinating conjunctions: καί ("and"), occurring 8,947 times; δέ ("now," "but"), occurring 2,771 times; and ἀλλά ("but"), occurring 635 times. καί is the basic or "unmarked" means of conjoining sentences and implies continuity with the preceding context. δέ marks the introduction of a new and significant development in the story or argument. ἀλλά marks a contrast between sentences and bears more semantic weight than either δέ or καί.

i. δέ is *postpositive* in Greek, i.e., it cannot stand first in its clause or sentence. It is, however, almost always translated first in English.

ii. The final vowel of ἀλλά is elided before a word beginning with a vowel or diphthong, as in βλέπεις, ἀλλ᾿ ἀκούω, "You see, but I hear."

iii. Greek does not have a conjunction meaning "both." Instead, καί is used, as in εἰμὶ καὶ υἱὸς καὶ δοῦλος, "I am *both* a son *and* a servant." καί may also be used adverbially, in which case it is translated "also" or "even." Compare Matt 10:30: "But *even* [καί] the hairs of your head are all numbered."

35. Greek Word Order

As we have seen, word order in Greek is far more flexible than in English. New Testament writers typically placed the subject after the verb (e.g., βλέπει ἄνθρωπος ἀπόστολον, "A man sees an apostle"). This tendency to place the verb at the beginning of its clause is probably due to Semitic influence, the normal word order in biblical Hebrew being verb, subject, object. Elements of the sentence that are "fronted" (moved forward) often receive special emphasis: ἀπόστολον βλέπει ἄνθρωπος would imply "It is *an apostle* that a man sees." Similarly, the normal position for genitives is after their noun: εἰμὶ δοῦλος θεοῦ, "I am a servant of God." Here emphasis would be achieved by pre-positioning the genitive: εἰμὶ θεοῦ δοῦλος, "I am *God's* servant." The significance of Greek word order is discussed more fully in Lesson 26.

36. Vocabulary

a. Masculine nouns of the second declension.

ἄγγελος, ὁ	angel, messenger (*angel*ic)
ἀγρός, ὁ	field (*agr*arian)
ἀδελφός, ὁ	brother, fellow believer (Phil*adelph*ia)
ἀμαρτωλός, ὁ	sinner (*hamart*iology [the study of sin])
ἄνθρωπος, ὁ	man, person (*anthrop*ology)
ἀπόστολος, ὁ	apostle, messenger (*apostol*ic)
διάκονος, ὁ	minister (*deacon*)
δοῦλος, ὁ	servant, slave
θάνατος, ὁ	death (*thanat*ology [the study of death and dying])
θεός, ὁ	God, god (*the*ology)
Ἰησοῦς, ὁ	Jesus

31

κόσμος, ὁ	*world* (*cosm*ic)
κύριος, ὁ	*Lord, master* (*kyrie* eleison, "Lord, have mercy")
λίθος, ὁ	*stone* (*lith*ography)
λόγος, ὁ	*word, message* (*log*ical)
νόμος, ὁ	*law* (antі*nom*ian)
οἶκος, ὁ	*house, household* (*econom*y)
ὄχλος, ὁ	*crowd* (*ochl*ocracy [mob rule])
υἱός, ὁ	*son*
Χριστός, ὁ	*Christ*

b. Neuter nouns of the second declension.

δῶρον, τό	*gift* (√ δο, *do*nate)
ἔργον, τό	*work* (*erg* [a unit of work], cf. en*erg*y)
εὐαγγέλιον, τό	*gospel* (*evangeli*cal)
ἱερόν, τό	*temple* (*hier*archy)
τέκνον, τό	*child*

c. Feminine nouns of the second declension.

ἔρημος, ἡ	*wilderness, desert* (*herm*it)
ὁδός, ἡ	*road, way* (*od*ometer)

d. Additional -ω verbs.

γινώσκω	*I know* (√ γνο, *Gno*stic)
λαμβάνω	*I take, I receive* (√ λαβ, *lab*yrinth)
λέγω	*I say, I speak* (*leg*end)
φέρω	*I bring, I bear* (Christo*pher* ["bearer of Christ"])

e. Conjunctions.

ἀλλά	*but*
δέ	*now, but*
καί	*and, also, even*
καὶ . . . καί	*both . . . and*

37. Exercises

a. Read the lesson carefully. Make use of the lesson material to gain an understanding of declension. This will consolidate your overall understanding of Greek nouns. Learn by heart the paradigms of ἄνθρωπος and δῶρον, carefully noting where they differ.

b. Memorize the vocabulary to this lesson. Remember to study the vocabularies in accordance with the instructions given in Lesson 3.

c. Translate the sentences given below. Since these sentences are more difficult than those in Lesson 3, it is necessary to approach them in a logical and systematic way. The following steps are suggested:

(1) Mark all finite verbs. This will indicate the number of clauses in the sentence.

(2) Taking each clause separately, determine how each word relates to the finite verb in its clause (e.g., look for a subject in the nominative case, an object in the accusative case).

(3) Finally, observe how the clauses are related to each other, and work out the overall meaning of the sentence. For example, in sentence (1) below, γράφει is the only finite verb, and therefore we have only one clause ("he writes"). The noun δοῦλος is nominative and therefore must be the subject of γράφει ("a servant writes"). The noun νόμον is accusative and therefore is the object of γράφει ("writes a law"). Putting all this together, we arrive at the meaning of the sentence: "A servant writes a law."

1. γράφει δοῦλος νόμον.

2. γινώσκετε θάνατον.

3. λύουσιν ἀδελφοὶ δούλους.

4. φέρουσιν υἱοὶ δῶρα.

5. γράφεις λόγους ἀποστόλοις.

6. βλέπει υἱὸς ἱερὰ καὶ οἴκους.

7. οὐ λέγει ἀδελφὸς λόγον ἀνθρώπῳ.

8. φέρει δοῦλος δῶρον ἀποστόλῳ.

9. γινώσκομεν ὁδὸν ἱερῷ.

10. οὐκ ἀκούομεν λόγους θανάτου.

11. λέγεις δούλοις, ἀλλὰ λέγω ἀδελφοῖς.

12. λύουσιν υἱοὶ δούλους ἀποστόλων.

13. καὶ ἀποστόλοις καὶ ἀνθρώποις λέγομεν λόγους θανάτου.

14. οὐ γράφετε λόγους υἱοῖς.

15. ἀκούει τέκνα λόγους οἴκῳ, ἀλλ᾽ ἀκούουσιν ὄχλοι λόγους ἐρήμῳ.

16. γινώσκει ἀποστόλους καὶ φέρει δῶρα τέκνοις.

17. δούλους βλέψεις, ἀνθρώπους δὲ βλέψομεν.

18. σῴζουσιν ἀπόστολοι ἀδελφούς.

19. εἰμὶ ἀπόστολος, ἀλλ᾽ υἱοί ἐστε.

20. δοῦλοί ἐσμεν, ἀλλὰ δούλους διδάξομεν.

21. ἐστὲ ἄγγελοι καὶ φέρετε δῶρα ἀνθρώποις.

22. σώσουσιν ἀπόστολοι ἀνθρώπους θανάτου.

5

NOUNS OF THE FIRST DECLENSION

As we have seen, there are three major declensions, or patterns of inflection, of Greek nouns. The second declension (Lesson 4) is the most common and the most regular. The next most regular is the first declension. The primary goal of this lesson is mastering the five paradigms of the Greek first declension.

38. First Declension Nouns

There are five paradigms in the first declension. Differences between these paradigms are due to certain phonetic changes and are confined to the singular. There are no neuter nouns of the first declension. The five paradigms of the first declension are given below:

	Singular				
	Feminine Nouns			**Masculine Nouns**	
	"day"	"glory"	"voice"	"disciple"	"young man"
N.	ἡμέρα	δόξα	φωνή	μαθητής	νεανίας
G.	ἡμέρας	δόξης	φωνῆς	μαθητοῦ	νεανίου
D.	ἡμέρᾳ	δόξῃ	φωνῇ	μαθητῇ	νεανίᾳ
A.	ἡμέραν	δόξαν	φωνήν	μαθητήν	νεανίαν
V.	ἡμέρα	δόξα	φωνή	μαθητά	νεανία

35

	Plural				
	Feminine Nouns			**Masculine Nouns**	
N. V.	ἡμέραι	δόξαι	φωναί	μαθηταί	νεανίαι
G.	ἡμερῶν	δοξῶν	φωνῶν	μαθητῶν	νεανιῶν
D.	ἡμέραις	δόξαις	φωναῖς	μαθηταῖς	νεανίαις
A.	ἡμέρας	δόξας	φωνάς	μαθητάς	νεανίας

Notice that if the stem of a word ends in the phonemes ε, ι, or ρ, then the α of the nominative singular is retained throughout the declension (as in ἡμέρα). If the stem of a word ends in a sibilant phoneme (ζ, σ, or a double letter containing σ, i.e., ξ, or ψ), then the α of the nominative singular lengthens to -ης and -η in the genitive and dative singular (as in δόξα). If the stem of a word ends in a phoneme other than ε, ι, ρ, or a sibilant, then the η in the nominative singular is retained throughout the singular (as in φωνή).

The three classes of nouns discussed above comprise the largest group of first declension nouns in the New Testament. Excluding names, there are 310 New Testament nouns that follow the paradigm of ἡμέρα, 22 nouns that follow the paradigm of δόξα, and 191 nouns that follow the paradigm of φωνή. These words are all feminine in gender.

There are, however, 112 *masculine* nouns of the first declension in the New Testament. The genitive singular (-ου) ending of the masculine nouns was borrowed from the second declension. The genitive suffix -ου became necessary in order to distinguish the genitive from the nominative (otherwise the patterns would have been -ης, -ης and -ας, -ας).

For ease of comprehension, the case-number suffixes of the first declension paradigms may be presented in chart form (omitting the vocative, which is rarely found in the New Testament):

1	2	3	4	5	Plural
-α	-α	-η	-ης	-ας	-αι
-ας	-ης	-ης	-ου	-ου	-ων
-ᾳ	-η	-η	-η	-ᾳ	-αις
-αν	-αν	-ην	-ην	-αν	-ας

39. The Paradigm of the Definite Article

The paradigm of the Greek definite article ("the") may now be set out in full (see also §33). The feminine article follows the paradigm of φων-ή (see above), while the masculine and neuter inflections of the article follow the masculine and neuter paradigms of the second declension introduced in Lesson 4 (ἄνθρωπος and δῶρον), with the exception of the nominative singular. The root of the definite article is the rough breathing in the nominative masculine and feminine (singular and plural) and τ elsewhere. Since the article provides the basic declension patterns for nouns, its mastery will assure rapid control of much of the Greek noun system.

	Singular			Plural		
	M	F.	N.	M.	F.	N.
N.	ὁ	ἡ	τό	οἱ	αἱ	τά
G.	τοῦ	τῆς	τοῦ	τῶν	τῶν	τῶν
D.	τῷ	τῇ	τῷ	τοῖς	ταῖς	τοῖς
A.	τόν	τήν	τό	τούς	τάς	τά

40. Prepositions with One Case

A *preposition* is a word used with a noun (or pronoun) in order to clarify the relationship of the noun to some other word in a sentence, as in "I go *into* the church." Prepositions are always located before the noun (hence the name "pre-position"). In English, the noun (or pronoun) is always in the accusative case, though it is only with pronouns that there is any difference in form (we say "about *her*," not "about *she*"). In Greek, numerous prepositions take a single case, but others take two or even three cases (see Lesson 8). In addition, most prepositions have both a core meaning (which is the general meaning) and a number of extended meanings.

This lesson introduces four Greek prepositions that are used with a single case:

(1) ἀπό (645 occurrences) always takes the genitive case. It is most frequently rendered "from" (its core meaning), "away from," or "of." Example: "I received the book *from the brother* [ἀπὸ τοῦ ἀδελφοῦ]." ἀπό

37

contains the allomorphs ἀπ’ before a vowel (as in ἀπ’ ἐμοῦ, "from me") and ἀφ’ before a rough breathing (as in ἀφ’ ἡμῶν, "from us").

(2) εἰς (1,753 occurrences) always takes the accusative case. It is most frequently rendered "into" (its core meaning), "to," "for," or "in." Example: "I walked *into the house* [εἰς τὸν οἶκον]."

(3) ἐκ (915 occurrences) always takes the genitive case. It is most frequently rendered "out of" (its core meaning), "from," or "by." Example: "I went *out of the temple* [ἐκ τοῦ ἱεροῦ]." ἐκ contains the allomorph ἐξ before a vowel, as in ἐξ οἴκου, "out of a house."

(4) ἐν (2,713 occurrences) always takes the dative case. It is most frequently rendered "in" (its core meaning), "within," "by," "with," or "among." Example: "I got lost *in the crowd* [ἐν τῷ ὄχλῳ]." ἐν is sometimes used to express impersonal agency (see §84).

It should be emphasized that a preposition is always to be read in conjunction with what it governs in a sentence. This combination is called a *prepositional phrase* and is a single unit of meaning. Hence ἐν τῷ ὄχλῳ is not to be read as ἐν ("in") plus τῷ ὄχλῳ ("to the crowd") but rather as a single unit of thought ("in the crowd").

41. Vocabulary

a. Feminine nouns of the ἡμέρα type.

ἀλήθεια, ἡ	*truth*
ἁμαρτία, ἡ	*sin (hamarti*ology [the study of sin])
βασιλεία, ἡ	*kingdom, reign (basi*lica)
διακονία, ἡ	*ministry, service (diacon*ate)
ἐκκλησία, ἡ	*church (ecclesi*astical [related to the church])
ἐξουσία, ἡ	*authority, right*
ἐπιθυμία, ἡ	*desire, lust*
ἡμέρα, ἡ	*day (ephemera*l)
καρδία, ἡ	*heart (cardi*ac)
μαρτυρία, ἡ	*testimony (martyr)*
οἰκία, ἡ	*house* (cf. οἶκος)
παρρησία, ἡ	*boldness, confidence*
σοφία, ἡ	*wisdom (sophis*ticated)
σωτηρία, ἡ	*salvation (soteri*ology)

χαρά, ἡ	*joy* (*Chari*ssa)
ὥρα, ἡ	*hour* (*hor*oscope)

b. Feminine nouns of the δόξα type.

γλῶσσα, ἡ	*tongue, language* (*gloss*alalia)
δόξα, ἡ	*glory* (*dox*ology)
θάλασσα, ἡ	*sea* (*thallas*ic [pertaining to the sea])

c. Feminine nouns of the φωνή type.

ἀγάπη, ἡ	*love* (the *Agape* [the love feast])
ἀρχή, ἡ	*beginning* (*arch*aic)
γῆ, ἡ	*earth, land* (*ge*ology)
γραφή, ἡ	*Scripture, writing* (*graph*ics)
διαθήκη, ἡ	*covenant*
διδαχή, ἡ	*teaching* (the *Didache* [an early Christian writing])
δικαιοσύνη, ἡ	*righteousness*
εἰρήνη, ἡ	*peace* (*Irene*)
ἐντολή, ἡ	*commandment*
ἐπιστολή, ἡ	*letter* (*epistle*)
ζωή, ἡ	*life* (*zo*ology)
κεφαλή, ἡ	*head* (en*cepha*litis [inflammation of the brain])
ὀργή, ἡ	*anger, wrath*
παραβολή, ἡ	*parable* (*parabol*ic)
περιτομή, ἡ	*circumcision*
προσευχή, ἡ	*prayer*
συναγωγή, ἡ	*synagogue*
ὑπομονή, ἡ	*endurance, steadfastness*
φωνή, ἡ	*voice, sound* (*phon*ology)
ψυχή, ἡ	*soul, life* (*psych*ology)

d. Masculine nouns of the μαθητής type.

μαθητής, ὁ	*disciple* (√ μαθ, *math*ematics)
προφήτης, ὁ	*prophet* (*prophet*ic)
στρατιώτης, ὁ	*soldier* (*strat*egic)
τελώνης, ὁ	*tax collector*
ὑποκριτής, ὁ	*hypocrite* (*hypocrit*ical)

e. Masculine nouns of the νεανίας type.

Μεσσίας, ὁ	*Messiah* (*messi*anic)
νεανίας, ὁ	*young man* (from νέος ["new"], *neo*-orthodox)

f. The definite article.

ὁ, ἡ, τό	*the*

g. Prepositions with one case.

ἀπό	*from; away from, of* (with gen.) (*apo*stasy)
εἰς	*into; to, for, in* (with acc.) (*esoteric*)
ἐκ	*out of; from, by* (with gen.) (*eccentric*)
ἐν	*in; within, by, with, among* (with dat.) (*en*ergy)

42. Exercises

a. Read the lesson carefully, studying the chart of first declension endings and comparing them with the feminine article. You will need to be thoroughly familiar with these endings. Learn by heart the paradigm of the Greek definite article. When you have mastered Lessons 3, 4, and 5, you will have made great progress toward your goal of reading the New Testament in Greek.

b. Memorize the vocabulary to this lesson. The core meanings of the prepositions have been set off by a semicolon. Let it be emphasized again that for maximum value you should say all the Greek words *aloud*, and that you should have studied each lesson carefully through the vocabulary before doing the translation exercises.

c. Translate the following sentences.

1. λύω τὸν δοῦλον ἐν τῇ ἐκκλησίᾳ.

2. βλέπομεν τοὺς οἴκους τῶν νεανιῶν.

3. λέγει ὁ ἄγγελος λόγους θανάτου τοῖς στρατιώταις.

4. οἱ ἀδελφοὶ τῶν μαθητῶν ἀκούσουσι τοὺς λόγους τοῦ θεοῦ.

5. γράψει ὁ ἀπόστολος παραβολὴν τοῖς ὄχλοις.

6. ἀγάπην καὶ σοφίαν καὶ χαρὰν ἔχουσιν οἱ υἱοὶ τῶν ἀποστόλων.

7. γινώσκουσιν οἱ μαθηταὶ τὴν διδαχὴν τοῦ ἀποστόλου.

8. γράφει τοὺς λόγους γραφῆς ὁ προφήτης τοῦ θεοῦ.

9. ἡ ὁδὸς τοῦ κυρίου ἐστὶν ἡ ὁδὸς χαρᾶς καὶ παρρησίας.

10. οἱ ὑποκριταὶ οὐ γινώσκουσι τὴν ὁδὸν ζωῆς καὶ ἀληθείας.

11. δῶρα ἀπὸ τῶν συναγωγῶν λαμβάνει ὁ ἀπόστολος τοῦ Μεσσίου.

12. γινώσκει τὴν καρδίαν ἀνθρώπου ὁ θεός.

13. εἰμὶ ἡ ὁδὸς καὶ ἡ ἀλήθεια καὶ ἡ ζωή.

14. τοὺς μαθητὰς τοῦ κυρίου καὶ τοὺς προφήτας τοῦ θεοῦ καὶ τοὺς υἱοὺς τῶν ἀποστόλων ἄξομεν ἐκ τῶν οἴκων ἁμαρτίας.

15. οἱ ἄγγελοι γινώσκουσι τὸ εὐαγγέλιον ἀληθείας, ἀλλὰ τελῶναι οὐ γινώσκουσι τὴν ὁδὸν εἰς τὴν βασιλείαν δικαιοσύνης.

16. λαμβάνουσι στρατιῶται τὰ δῶρα ἀπὸ τῶν υἱῶν τῶν ἀποστόλων.

17. εἰμὶ νεανίας, ἀλλ' εἶ ἄνθρωπος τοῦ θεοῦ.

18. τὴν ἡμέραν καὶ τὴν ὥραν σωτηρίας οὐ γινώσκομεν.

6

ADJECTIVES OF THE
FIRST AND SECOND
DECLENSIONS

Adjectives constitute one of the most prominent classes of words in the New Testament and provide a prolific area for discriminative study. This lesson introduces the paradigms of first and second declension adjectives as well as the more characteristic features of the Greek use of the adjective.

43. The Inflection of Adjectives

An adjective is a word that describes a noun, as in "the *good* apostle," "*evil* servants," "the gift is *beautiful*," and so forth. A Greek adjective agrees with the noun that it modifies in gender, number, and case. Most adjectives will therefore have 24 forms (like the article). These adjectives are called *three-termination adjectives* since they have inflections for masculine, feminine, and neuter genders. A smaller number of *two-termination adjectives* have no separate forms for the feminine, but instead use the masculine forms for both masculine and feminine. This category frequently includes *compound* adjectives, that is, adjectives that are composed of two or more constituent parts (e.g., ἀδύνατος, "impossible").

The great majority of New Testament adjectives (546, or 85%) are three-termination adjectives of the first and second declensions. In this pattern, the feminine forms of the adjective follow the first declension (see §38) and the masculine and neuter forms follow the second declension (see §30). When the stem of the adjective ends in ε, ι, or ρ, the feminine singular will use α (as in ἡμέρα); otherwise it will use η (as in φωνή).

a. The declension of ἀγαθός ("good"), a consonant-stem adjective, is given below:

	Singular			Plural		
	Masculine	Feminine	Neuter	Masculine	Feminine	Neuter
N.	ἀγαθός	ἀγαθή	ἀγαθόν	ἀγαθοί	ἀγαθαί	ἀγαθά
G.	ἀγαθοῦ	ἀγαθῆς	ἀγαθοῦ	ἀγαθῶν	ἀγαθῶν	ἀγαθῶν
D.	ἀγαθῷ	ἀγαθῇ	ἀγαθῷ	ἀγαθοῖς	ἀγαθαῖς	ἀγαθοῖς
A.	ἀγαθόν	ἀγαθήν	ἀγαθόν	ἀγαθούς	ἀγαθάς	ἀγαθά
V.	ἀγαθέ	ἀγαθή	ἀγαθόν	ἀγαθοί	ἀγαθαί	ἀγαθά

b. The declension of μικρός ("small"), an ε-, ι-, ρ-stem adjective, is given below:

	Singular			Plural		
	Masculine	Feminine	Neuter	Masculine	Feminine	Neuter
N.	μικρός	μικρά	μικρόν	μικροί	μικραί	μικρά
G.	μικροῦ	μικρᾶς	μικροῦ	μικρῶν	μικρῶν	μικρῶν
D.	μικρῷ	μικρᾷ	μικρῷ	μικροῖς	μικραῖς	μικροῖς
A.	μικρόν	μικράν	μικρόν	μικρούς	μικράς	μικρά
V.	μικρέ	μικρά	μικρόν	μικροί	μικραί	μικρά

c. The declension of ἀδύνατος ("impossible"), a two-termination adjective, is given below:

	Singular		Plural	
	Masc./Fem.	Neuter	Masc./Fem.	Neuter
N.	ἀδύνατος	ἀδύνατον	ἀδύνατοι	ἀδύνατα
G.	ἀδυνάτου	ἀδυνάτου	ἀδυνάτων	ἀδυνάτων
D.	ἀδυνάτῳ	ἀδυνάτῳ	ἀδυνάτοις	ἀδυνάτοις
A.	ἀδύνατον	ἀδύνατον	ἀδυνάτους	ἀδύνατα
V.	ἀδύνατε	ἀδύνατον	ἀδύνατοι	ἀδύνατα

44. Uses of the Adjective

Greek adjectives are used in three distinct ways: (1) attributively, (2) predicatively, and (3) substantivally.

(1) The *attributive adjective* attributes a quality to the noun it modifies, as in ὁ ἀγαθὸς ἄνθρωπος, "the good man." Notice that the adjective in this example stands between the definite article and the noun. This position is called the *ascriptive attributive position*. A Greek adjective may also follow the noun, though in this case the adjective as well as the noun must have the article: ὁ ἄνθρωπος ὁ ἀγαθός, "the good man" (literally, "the man, the good one"). This latter position is called the *restrictive attributive position* and is somewhat more emphatic than the ascriptive attributive position, the implication being that there are other men who are not good. Attributive adjectives in English occasionally occur in postposition, as in "He preached about life *everlasting*," or "God *almighty* will save you." In John 10:11 the restrictive attributive adjective is used of Jesus: ὁ ποιμὴν ὁ καλός, "the good shepherd." Observe that the adjective in the attributive position *immediately follows* the article: either ὁ **ἀγαθὸς** ἄνθρωπος, or ὁ ἄνθρωπος ὁ **ἀγαθός**.

(2) In contrast to the attributive adjective, an adjective may also be used as the complement of the verb "to be," even when the verb is only implied. Here it is said to be the *predicate adjective* because it tells us what is predicated of, or asserted about, a person or thing (e.g., "The man is good"). In this use, the adjective in Greek is placed either *before* or *after* the article and its noun but never *between* the article and its noun. This position is called the *predicate position*, and the adjective used in this way is called a *predicate adjective*. Thus, "the man is good" may be expressed as either ὁ ἄνθρωπος **ἀγαθός,** or **ἀγαθὸς** ὁ ἄνθρωπος. Notice that whereas in the attributive position the article immediately precedes the adjective, in the predicate position there is no immediately preceding article. This means that it is possible for Greek to drop the verb "to be" without any confusion in meaning; see Romans 7:12: ὁ νόμος ἅγιος, καὶ ἡ ἐντολὴ ἁγία, "the law is holy, and the commandment is holy." Although the New Testament writers generally used the verb "to be" with predicate adjectives, in cases where there is no verb you must be able to distinguish between the attributive and predicate position.

(3) Finally, as in English, the Greek adjective may serve as a noun (i.e., as a substantive): "only *the good* die young," "a word to *the wise* is sufficient," etc. This use is called the *substantival adjective*. In Greek, this

function of the adjective is considerably more common than in English, and Greek can use its endings to make distinctions that are impossible with English adjectives. Hence the masculine οἱ ἀγαθοί means "the good men" or "the good people," but the feminine αἱ ἀγαθαί, and the neuter τὰ ἀγαθά, mean "the good women" and "the good things," respectively. Likewise, an adjective may be used substantivally in the singular, as in ὁ ἀγαθός, "the good man," or ἡ ἀγαθή, "the good woman." Some words, among them ἁμαρτωλός ("sinner"), were originally adjectives but were used so frequently as nouns that they are normally regarded as both. A New Testament example of a substantival adjective is found in Matthew 13:19: "the evil one [ὁ πονηρός] comes and snatches away what has been sown."

It should be noted that agreement of adjectives does not necessarily mean that an adjective will have the same suffixes as its noun, although this frequently happens. *Grammatical* agreement may take place even when there is lack of *phonetic* agreement. An example is οἱ ἀγαθοὶ μαθηταί, "the good disciples." Here the endings -οι and -αι are in agreement, even though they differ in both spelling and pronunciation. Later we will study a large group of adjectives that belong to the third declension (Lesson 18). When these adjectives are used with nouns from other declensions, they naturally retain the forms of their own declension.

Sometimes an adjective is found in an *indefinite* construction where the English "a" or "an" is used. Since Greek has no indefinite article, neither the noun nor the adjective will have an article. In such instances only the context can determine whether the adjective is being used attributively or predicatively. For example, if we find ἀγαθὸς ἄνθρωπος standing alone as a complete sentence, the adjective will be a predicate adjective ("A man is good"). However, in a sentence such as ἀγαθὸς ἄνθρωπος βλέπει τὸν ἀπόστολον, the adjective is obviously an attributive adjective ("A good man sees the apostle"). In the New Testament, an attributive adjective generally has the article, but not always (see Phil 1:6: ἔργον ἀγαθόν, "a good work").

45. Summary of the Uses of the Adjective

The uses of the adjective in Greek may now be summarized:

1. *The Attributive Adjective.*	ὁ ἀγαθὸς ἄνθρωπος
	or = "the good man"
	ὁ ἄνθρωπος ὁ ἀγαθός
2. *The Predicate Adjective.*	ὁ ἄνθρωπος ἀγαθός
	or = "the man is good"
	ἀγαθὸς ὁ ἄνθρωπος

3. *The Substantival Adjective.*

ὁ ἀγαθός	= "the good man"
οἱ ἀγαθοί	= "the good men"
ἡ ἀγαθή	= "the good woman"
αἱ ἀγαθαί	= "the good women"
τὸ ἀγαθόν	= "the good thing"
τὰ ἀγαθά	= "the good things"

46. Vocabulary

a. Consonant-stem adjectives.

ἀγαθός, -ή, -όν	*good* (*Agatha*)
ἀγαπητός, -ή, -όν	*beloved* (the *Agape* [the love feast])
ἄλλος, -η, -ο	*other* (neuter nom./acc. is irregular)
δυνατός, -ή, -όν	*powerful, possible* (*dyna*mic)
ἕκαστος, -η, -ον	*each, every*
ἔσχατος, -η, -ον	*last* (*escha*tology [the study of last things])
καινός, -ή, -όν	*new*
κακός, -ή, -όν	*bad* (*ca*cophony [a bad sound])
καλός, -ή, -όν	*good, beautiful* (*call*igraphy [beautiful writing])
μόνος, -η, -ον	*only* (*mono*theism)
πιστός, -ή, -όν	*faithful* (√ πιθ [see πείθω, §26])
πρῶτος, -η, -ον	*first* (*proto*type)
σοφός, -ή, -όν	*wise* (*soph*isticated)
τρίτος, -η, -ον	*third*

b. ε-, ι-, ρ-stem adjectives.

ἅγιος, -α, -ον	*holy, saint* (*hagi*ography [a writing about a saint])
ἄξιος, -α, ον	*worthy* (*axi*om [a worthy statement])
δεύτερος, -α, -ον	*second* (*Deuter*onomy [the second statement of the law])
δίκαιος, -α, -ον	*righteous, just* (√ δικ ["to point out"], *dic*tate)
ἕτερος, -α, -ον	*other, different* (*hetero*sexual)
ἰσχυρός, -ά, -όν	*strong*

μακάριος, -α, -ον	*blessed* (*macari*sm [a word of blessing])
μικρός, -ά, -όν	*small, little* (*micro*scope)
νεκρός, -ά, -όν	*dead* (*necro*mancy [conversation with the dead])
νεός, -ά, -όν	*new* (*neo*natal)
πονηρός, -ά, -όν	*evil*

c. Two-termination adjectives.

ἀδύνατος, -ον	*impossible* (*dyn*amic)
αἰώνιος, -ον	*eternal* (*aeon*)
ἀκάθαρτος, -ον	*unclean* (*cathar*sis)
ἄπιστος, -ον	*unbelieving, faithless* (cf. πιστεύω)

47. Exercises

a. There are no new paradigms to be learned in this lesson, since you have already encountered all of the suffixes involved. Instead, read the lesson carefully, aiming especially at an understanding of the various uses of the Greek adjective. You will often come across adjectives in your reading of Greek, so be sure you understand their uses now.

b. Memorize the vocabulary to this lesson.

c. Translate the following sentences.

1. ὁ ἀγαπητὸς ἀπόστολος διδάσκει τὸν δοῦλον.

2. ἡ ἐκκλησία ἀγαθή.

3. βλέπουσιν οἱ μαθηταὶ τοὺς νεκρούς.

4. ὁ ἕτερος ἄνθρωπος ἀκούει τὸν λόγον τοῦ θεοῦ ἐν τῇ ἐκκλησίᾳ.

5. λέγουσιν οἱ πονηροὶ κακοὺς λόγους ἐν ταῖς ἐσχάταις ἡμέραις.

6. καινὰς παραβολὰς λέγουσιν οἱ ἀγαθοὶ προφῆται καὶ τοῖς πιστοῖς καὶ ταῖς πισταῖς.

7. λέγομεν ἀγαθοὺς λόγους τοῖς ἀγαθοῖς ἀποστόλοις.

8. τοὺς πιστοὺς καὶ τὰς πιστὰς σῴζει ὁ Μεσσίας τῆς βασιλείας.

9. ἡ ἀγαθὴ βλέψει τὰς ἀγαθὰς ἡμέρας τῆς βασιλείας ἀγάπης.

10. οἱ ἀδελφοὶ πρῶτοι καὶ οἱ δοῦλοι ἔσχατοι.

11. αἱ σοφαὶ ἀγαθὰ λέγουσιν.

12. εἰς τὴν συναγωγὴν ἄξουσιν οἱ δίκαιοι τοὺς ἀκαθάρτους.

13. λέγει ὁ ἀπόστολος τοῦ κυρίου ἀγαθὴν παραβολὴν τοῖς ἀγαπητοῖς μαθηταῖς.

14. αἱ ὁδοὶ ἀγαθαί, ἀλλ᾽ οἱ ἄνθρωποι πονηροί.

15. τὰς ἀγαθὰς ἡμέρας τοῦ κυρίου ζωῆς βλέψεις.

16. βλέπει ὁ υἱὸς τοῦ ἀπίστου ἀδελφοῦ τοὺς ἀξίους.

17. ἀγαθὴ ἡ ἀλήθεια καὶ κακὴ ἡ ὥρα.

18. τοὺς ἀγαθοὺς λόγους λέγετε ταῖς πονηραῖς ἐκκλησίαις καὶ τοὺς κακοὺς λόγους τοῖς ἀδελφοῖς.

19. δοξάσουσιν αἱ ἄπιστοι τὸν θεόν.

7

IMPERFECT AND AORIST ACTIVE INDICATIVE

We have seen that kind of action (i.e., verbal aspect) is more important than time of action in the Greek verb system. Nevertheless, Greek is fully capable of expressing action in past, present, and future time. The paradigms of the present and future active indicative were given in Lesson 3. This lesson introduces the most frequently encountered past tenses of the active indicative.

48. The Secondary Active Suffixes

As explained in Lesson 2 (see §15), Greek verbs have three sets of forms for indicating action in past time. Some forms express imperfective aspect; these forms comprise the *imperfect indicative*. Other forms express aoristic aspect; these forms make up the *aorist indicative*. Still other forms represent perfective aspect; these forms comprise the *pluperfect indicative*. In all of these forms, past time is indicated by the prefixing of the *past time morpheme* (also called an *augment* and usually appearing as ἐ) to the beginning of the verb. The augment is present only in the *secondary* (i.e., historical) tenses of the indicative mood. The tenses thus affected are the imperfect, the aorist, and the pluperfect.

The secondary tenses all use the Greek *secondary suffixes*. In the active voice of the indicative mood, these suffixes appear as follows:

	Singular	Plural
1.	-ν	-μεν
2.	-ς	-τε
3.	none (or movable ν)	-ν or -σαν

49. The Imperfect and Aorist Active Indicative of λύω

The imperfect and aorist active indicative of λύω are given below:

		Imperfect		Aorist	
Sg.	1.	ἔλυον	I was loosing	ἔλυσα	I loosed
	2.	ἔλυες	you were loosing	ἔλυσας	you loosed
	3.	ἔλυε(ν)	he was loosing	ἔλυσε(ν)	he loosed
Pl.	1.	ἐλύομεν	we were loosing	ἐλύσαμεν	we loosed
	2.	ἐλύετε	you were loosing	ἐλύσατε	you loosed
	3.	ἔλυον	they were loosing	ἔλυσαν	they loosed

Notice that the forms of the imperfect tense are obtained by (a) augmenting the present stem, (b) attaching the connecting vowels o/ε to the verb stem, and then (c) adding the secondary active suffixes -ν, -ς, none, -μεν, -τε, -ν.

The forms of the aorist active indicative are obtained by (a) augmenting the present stem, (b) adding the *aoristic aspect morpheme* σα to the stem, and then (c) adding the secondary active suffixes. Because the first person singular does not use ν or any other consonant in its suffix, the third person singular modifies the σα to σε (without a person-number suffix), thereby differentiating the first and third person singular forms. The aorist active indicative, first person singular form (ἔλυσα) is called the *aorist active principal part*.

Observe that the major difference between the two paradigms given above is the addition of the aoristic aspect morpheme σα to the stem of the present tense forms. In the imperfect paradigm, no such morpheme is added to indicate aspect. Instead, where the aoristic aspect morpheme would be used, the *neutral morpheme* (i.e., connecting vowel) is used (see §18). Compare the following examples:

(a) ἐλύετε = ἐ (past time morpheme), λυ (lexical morpheme), ε (neutral morpheme), τε (person-number suffix): "you were loosing."

(b) ἐλύσατε = ἐ (past time morpheme), λυ (lexical morpheme), σα (aoristic aspect morpheme), τε (person-number suffix): "you loosed."

The ability to identify such recurring patterns in words and to interpret them through morphological analysis is the key to translating verbs of increasing complexity.

50. Amalgamation in the Aorist Tense

When the aoristic aspect morpheme σα is attached to the present stem to form the aorist stem, the same kinds of modifications are made in the final consonants of the stem as are made when the future time morpheme σ is added to form the future stem (see §20):

$$κ, γ, χ + σ = ξ$$
$$π, β, φ + σ = ψ$$
$$τ, δ, θ + σ = σ$$

Note these examples:

Present Act. Ind.		Future Act. Ind.		Aorist Act. Ind.	
κηρύσσω (κηρυκ)	(I preach)	κηρύξω	(I will preach)	ἐκήρυξα	(I preached)
βλέπω	(I see)	βλέψω	(I will see)	ἔβλεψα	(I saw)
πείθω	(I trust in)	πείσω	(I will trust in)	ἔπεισα	(I trusted in)

51. More on the Augment

The augment has several important allomorphs:

(1) As already observed, if the verb stem begins with a consonant, it has an *additive morpheme* in the form of a prefixed ἐ, which is called the *syllabic augment* because it adds a syllable to the word (as in λύω, imperfect ἔλυον).

(2) If the verb stem begins with a short vowel, the augment consists of a *process morpheme* called the *temporal augment*, which lengthens the short vowel to the corresponding long vowel (as in ἀκούω, imperfect ἤκουον).

(3) Finally, a verb commencing with a long vowel or long diphthong has a *zero morpheme augment*—"zero" because there is no visible phonetic change (as in εἰρηνεύω ["I make peace"], imperfect εἰρήνευον).

51

Some Greek verbs take a *double augment*—both an additive and a process morpheme. Thus ἄγω reduplicates (doubles) its first syllable to form ἀγαγ- and then takes the temporal augment, producing ἤγαγον in the aorist indicative. In other verbs, the augment is irregular (e.g., the imperfect of ἔχω is εἶχον, εἶχες).

52. First and Second Aorists

Greek contains not one but two basic patterns for forming the aorist tense. The difference between these patterns is one of form only (cf. the past forms of Eng. *bake/baked, make/made, take/took, wake/awoke*). Verbs that have aorist forms containing the aoristic aspect morpheme σα are called *first aorists*, and the forms are called *first aorist forms*. Most Greek verbs have first aorist forms, and the majority of these form their first aorists as set forth above. However, a number of Greek verbs have *second aorist forms*, which are identical to the forms of the *imperfect tense* except for their stems. This can be seen by comparing the forms for the *imperfect* and *second aorist* active indicative of λείπω ("I leave"):

		Imperfect		Second Aorist	
Sg.	1.	ἔλειπον	*I was leaving*	ἔλιπον	*I left*
	2.	ἔλειπες	*you were leaving*	ἔλιπες	*you left*
	3.	ἔλειπε(ν)	*he was leaving*	ἔλιπε(ν)	*he left*
Pl.	1.	ἐλείπομεν	*we were leaving*	ἐλίπομεν	*we left*
	2.	ἐλείπετε	*you were leaving*	ἐλίπετε	*you left*
	3.	ἔλειπον	*they were leaving*	ἔλιπον	*they left*

Notice that the second aorist differs from the imperfect, not by adding σα or any other aspect morpheme to the stem of the verb, but by differences *within* the stem itself: the stem of the imperfect form ἔλειπον is λειπ, but the stem of the second aorist form ἔλιπον is λιπ. *Thus the only difference between the imperfect and the second aorist indicative is that the imperfect is formed on the present stem, while the second aorist is formed on the aorist stem.* This type of internal vowel change is called *vowel gradation* (cf. Eng. *sing, sang, sung*).

i. Occasionally, a Greek verb will have both a first and a second aorist (cf. Eng. *dived* and *dove* as past tense forms of *dive*). For instance, the aorist indicative of ἁμαρτάνω ("I sin") may be given as ἡμάρτησα (first aorist) or as ἥμαρτον (second aorist). There is, however, no difference in meaning between these two forms (both may be translated "I sinned").

ii. Some verbs form their second aorists by substituting entirely different forms. These forms, known as *suppletives*, must simply be memorized. For example, λέγω means "I speak," but εἶπον means "I spoke." The reason for the existence of such forms is that the aorist tense of one verb and the present tense of another verb of similar meaning both fell into disuse. The remaining present and aorist tense forms came to be associated with each other as if they were related morphologically. An English example of suppletion is *went*, which is the past tense form of *go,* though originally the past tense form of *wend.*

53. Second Aorist Stems

The original stem of a Greek verb is often preserved in the second aorist stem. For example, the second aorist indicative of μανθάνω ("I learn") is ἔμαθον, the stem of which (μαθ) forms the basis of both μαθητεύω ("I make a disciple") and μαθητής ("disciple," "learner"). Compare also the following forms:

Present	Aorist	Verb Stem	English Derivative
ἁμαρτάνω (I sin)	ἥμαρτον (I sinned)	ἁμαρτ	hamartiology
εὑρίσκω (I find)	εὗρον (I found)	εὑρ	heuristic
λαμβάνω (I take)	ἔλαβον (I took)	λαβ	labyrinth
πάσχω (I suffer)	ἔπαθον (I suffered)	παθ	pathetic
φεύγω (I flee)	ἔφυγον (I fled)	φυγ	fugitive

i. Note that the stem of γινώσκω is γνο (cf. *Gno*stic), which is usually lengthened to γνω. Its second aorist is ἔγνων, ἔγνως, ἔγνω, ἔγνωμεν, ἔγνωτε, ἔγνωσαν.

ii. εἶδον ("I saw") is the second aorist of ὁράω ("I see"), which is a *contract* verb. Contract verbs will be studied in Lesson 19, but familiarity with εἶδον cannot be postponed. In the New Testament εἶδον frequently has *first* aorist endings, but in this text it is treated as a second aorist throughout. The stem of εἶδον is Ϝιδ (the Ϝ, or digamma, is an obsolete Greek letter that was pronounced as "w" or "v"). This stem means "see," as in *video.*

54. Uses of the Imperfect and Aorist

The imperfect and aorist tenses are used in a wide variety of ways. The imperfect has four main uses:

(1) The *progressive imperfect* expresses continuous action in the past ("I kept loosing").

(2) The *customary imperfect* expresses habitual action in the past ("I used to loose").

(3) The *conative imperfect* expresses attempted action in the past ("I tried to loose").

(4) The *inceptive imperfect* expresses the initiation of an action in the past ("I began to loose").

It is the context, and not the tense itself, that shows which meaning we should choose. For example, the use of the imperfect in Luke 23:34 ("Jesus *kept saying*" instead of "Jesus *said*") suggests that Jesus pled, over and over, "Father, forgive them, for they do not know what they are doing." Similarly, the use of the imperfect in Matthew 27:30 ("*they kept beating* him on the head") implies that the Roman soldiers beat Jesus "again and again."

In keeping with its name, the aorist refrains from commenting on the kind of action involved in the verb. However, when one examines how the aorist interacts with other features such as context and lexical meaning, the following uses of the aorist indicative emerge:

(1) The *constative aorist* views an action in its totality, as in John 2:20: "This temple *was built* in forty-six years."

(2) The *ingressive aorist* emphasizes the beginning of an action, as in Romans 14:9: "Christ died and *lived* [i.e., returned to life]."

(3) The *effective aorist* views an action from the vantage point of its conclusion, as in Philippians 4:11: "*I have learned* to be content in whatever circumstance I am."

Because the aorist is of much higher frequency in the New Testament than the imperfect, it is always proper to ask why an imperfect was chosen rather than an aorist. A striking example of the careful selection of tenses is Galatians 1:13–14: "For *you have heard* [effective aorist] of my former manner of life in Judaism, how *I used to persecute* [customary imperfect] the church of God beyond measure and *tried to destroy* [conative imperfect] it; and *I kept advancing* [progressive imperfect] in Judaism beyond many of my contemporaries." These are but a few shades of meaning that are important to grasp, if only because they usually defy translation.

It should be emphasized that the aorist tense does not necessarily refer to "once-for-all" action. The aorist *may* be used to describe a "once-only" occurrence, but this is due to the nature of the event described and *not* to the presence of the aorist tense (see Acts 5:5: "Ananias . . . *breathed his last*"). Hence the "once-for-all" nature of the aorist, so often celebrated in sermon and commentary, is little more than nonsense if one is arguing that it is the aorist tense per se that proves the nature of the action behind it. It should also be noted that even in the indicative mood the aorist does not always refer to past time. Note Mark 1:11: "In you *I am well pleased* [εὐδόκησα]" and 1 Pet 1:24: "the grass *withers* [ἐξηράνθη]." In both instances, aorist *indicative* verbs are used. What gives the aorist—or any tense—its particular significance is the relation of the verb to its specific context.

55. The Imperfect Indicative of εἰμί

The imperfect indicative of εἰμί ("I am") is given below. Its person-number suffixes are those of the secondary active tenses with the exception of the first person singular, which takes a middle/passive suffix (see §94), and the third person singular, which adds a ν.

	Singular		Plural	
1.	ἤμην	I was	ἦμεν	we were
2.	ἦς	you were	ἦτε	you were
3.	ἦν	he was	ἦσαν	they were

56. Vocabulary

a. Additional -ω verbs.

ἁμαρτάνω	I sin (√ ἁμαρτ, *hamarti*ology [the study of sin])
βάλλω	I throw (√ βαλ, *ball*istic)
ἐσθίω	I eat
εὑρίσκω	I find (√ εὑρ, *heuri*stic)
λείπω	I leave (√ λιπ, *lip*oid ["fatty"], from λίπος ["fat"])
μανθάνω	I learn (√ μαθ, *math*ematics)
πάσχω	I suffer (√ παθ, *path*etic)
φεύγω	I flee (√ φυγ, *fugi*tive)

b. First aorist active indicative principal parts.

ἤκουσα	I heard
ἡμάρτησα	I sinned (cf. ἥμαρτον below)
ἐβάπτισα	I baptized

ἔβλεψα	*I saw*
ἔγραψα	*I wrote*
ἐδίδαξα	*I taught*
ἐδόξασα	*I glorified*
ἡτοίμασα	*I prepared*
ἐθεράπευσα	*I healed*
ἐκήρυξα	*I preached*
ἔλυσα	*I loosed*
ἔπεισα	*I trusted in*
ἔπεμψα	*I sent*
ἐπίστευσα	*I believed*
ἔσωσα	*I saved*
ἤνεγκα	*I bore, I brought* (cf. ἤνεγκον below)

c. Second aorist active principal parts.

ἤγαγον	*I led*
ἥμαρτον	*I sinned* (cf. ἡμάρτησα above)
ἔβαλον	*I threw*
ἔγνων	*I knew*
ἔφαγον	*I ate* (√ φαγ, eso*phag*ous)
εὗρον	*I found*
ἔσχον	*I had* (imperfect εἶχον)
ἔλαβον	*I took, I received*
εἶπον	*I said, I spoke*
ἔλιπον	*I left*
ἔμαθον	*I learned*
εἶδον	*I saw* (from ὁράω; see §127)
ἔπαθον	*I suffered*
ἔφυγον	*I fled*
ἤνεγκον	*I bore, I brought* (cf. ἤνεγκα above)

57. Exercises

a. Read the lesson carefully. Compare the paradigms of λύω in the imperfect and first aorist active indicative. Be sure that you understand the verb patterns of these tenses, including their characteristic morphemes. Learn by heart: (1) the Greek secondary active suffixes (§48), and (2) the paradigm of εἰμί in the imperfect indicative. This is also a good time to review the Greek tense system (§15).

56

b. Memorize the vocabulary to this lesson.

c. Translate the following sentences.

1. ἔλυσαν οἱ ἀπόστολοι τοὺς δούλους.

2. εἴδομεν τοὺς μακαρίους υἱούς.

3. ἐκήρυξαν οἱ μαθηταὶ ἁμαρτωλοῖς.

4. τοὺς πονηροὺς ἔσῳζεν ὁ κύριος ζωῆς.

5. ἔλιπον οἱ πονηροί, ἀλλ᾽ οἱ ἀγαθοὶ ἐπίστευσαν τὸ εὐαγγέλιον.

6. ἐφύγετε ἐκ τῶν πονηρῶν οἴκων καὶ εἰς τὴν ἐκκλησίαν τοῦ θεοῦ.

7. ἐν ἀρχῇ ἦν ὁ λόγος, καὶ θεὸς ἦν ὁ λόγος.

8. ἔπαθεν ὁ Ἰησοῦς, οἱ δὲ μαθηταὶ ἔλαβον ζωὴν καὶ σωτηρίαν ἀπὸ τοῦ θεοῦ.

9. ἐδίδαξεν ὁ ἀπόστολος τοὺς μαθητὰς καὶ ἦγε τοὺς ἀγαθοὺς ἀνθρώπους εἰς τὴν βασιλείαν ἀγάπης.

10. ἔβλεψεν ὁ κύριος τοὺς πονηρούς, ἀλλὰ βλέπομεν τοὺς ἀγαθούς.

11. ἐπιστεύσατε τὴν ἀλήθειαν καὶ ἐκηρύσσετε τὸ εὐαγγέλιον.

12. ἤκουσα καὶ ἔβλεψα τοὺς μαθητάς, ἀλλ᾽ ἤκουσας καὶ ἔβλεψας τὸν κύριον.

13. ἦμεν ἐν τῇ ἐκκλησίᾳ, ἦτε δὲ ἐν τοῖς οἴκοις ἁμαρτίας.

14. ἐβαπτίζετε τοὺς ἀνθρώπους τοὺς πιστούς, ἐδιδάσκομεν δὲ τοὺς μαθητὰς καὶ ἐδοξάζομεν τὸν θεόν.

15. ἔσωσεν ὁ κύριος τὰς πονηρὰς ἀφ᾽ ἁμαρτίας.

16. οὐκ ἐλέγετε λόγους ἀληθείας, ἐπίστευον δὲ πονηροὶ τὸ εὐαγγέλιον.

17. εἶχεν ὁ κύριος χαρὰν καὶ εἰρήνην ἐν τῷ κόσμῳ.

18. ἐν τῷ κόσμῳ ἦν, ὁ δὲ κόσμος οὐκ ἔλαβε τὴν ἀλήθειαν.

19. ἐδίδαξεν ὁ Μεσσίας καὶ ἐν τῷ ἱερῷ καὶ ἐν τῇ συναγωγῇ.

8

ADDITIONAL PREPOSITIONS

Because prepositions are involved in exegesis at numerous points, an understanding of their nature and function is essential. Some mention has already been made of the Greek prepositions. This lesson introduces several additional prepositions that occur frequently in the Greek New Testament.

58. Prepositions with Two or Three Cases

Lesson 5 introduced four of the most common Greek prepositions: ἀπό, εἰς, ἐκ, and ἐν. These prepositions are used with a single case: ἀπό and ἐκ with the genitive, ἐν with the dative, and εἰς with the accusative.

Several prepositions in New Testament Greek can be used with two or even with three cases. The major prepositions of this type are set forth below, together with brief phrases to assist in remembering their core meanings. Additional prepositions taking only one case are given in the vocabulary to this lesson.

Prepositions with Two Cases

(1) διά (666 occurrences)

Gen. *through*	διὰ τῆς γῆς	*through the earth*
Acc. *because of*	διὰ τὸν κύριον	*because of the Lord*

διά with the genitive is frequently used with a passive verb to express *intermediate agency* ("by"; see §84).

(2) κατά (471 occurrences)

Gen. *against*	κατὰ τοῦ νόμου	*against the law*
Acc. *according to*	ΚΑΤΑ ΜΑΡΚΟΝ	*(the Gospel) according to Mark*

A common New Testament idiom is καθ' ἡμέραν, "daily."

(3) μετά (467 occurrences)

Gen. *with*	μετὰ τοῦ κυρίου	*with the Lord*
Acc. *after*	μετὰ θάνατον	*after death*

(4) περί (331 occurrences)

Gen. *about*	περὶ τοῦ εὐαγγελίου	*about the gospel*
Acc. *around*	περὶ τὴν θάλασσαν	*around the sea*

(5) ὑπέρ (149 occurrences)

Gen. *for*	ὑπὲρ ἁμαρτιῶν	*for sins*
Acc. *above*	ὑπὲρ τὴν γήν	*above the earth*

(6) ὑπό (217 occurrences)

Gen. *by*	ὑπὸ τοῦ κυρίου	*by the Lord*
Acc. *under*	ὑπὸ τὴν γήν	*under the earth*

ὑπό with the genitive is commonly used with a passive verb to express *direct agency* (see §84).

Prepositions with Three Cases

(1) ἐπί (878 occurrences)

Gen. *upon*	ἐπὶ γῆς	*upon earth*
Dat. *upon*	ἐπὶ γῇ	*upon earth*
Acc. *upon*	ἐπὶ γήν	*upon earth*

In the New Testament, the distinction between the uses of ἐπί with the various cases has become blurred.

(2) παρά (191 occurrences)

Gen. *from*	παρὰ τοῦ θεοῦ	*from God*
Dat. *with*	παρὰ τῷ κυρίῳ	*with the Lord*
Acc. *beside*	παρὰ τὴν θάλασσαν	*beside the sea*

59. Directional Functions of Prepositions

Numerous Greek prepositions are used with a directional or local function. It is helpful to be able to visualize these uses diagrammatically:

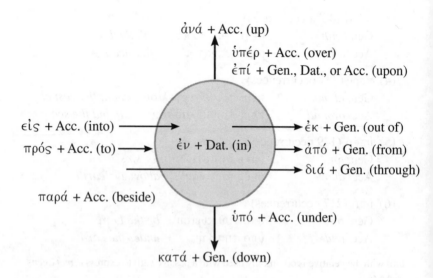

60. Elision of Final Vowels of Prepositions

Prepositions (other than περί and πρό) that end in a vowel drop the final vowel when the next word begins with a vowel. This process of eliminating a vowel is called *elision* (see §9). Note that the final vowel is replaced by an apostrophe except when the preposition is combined with a verb to form a *compound verb*:

ἀπ’ ἀδελφοῦ	(= ἀπό + ἀδελφοῦ)	*from a brother*
ἀπάγω	(= ἀπό + ἄγω)	*I lead away*

Preposition	Before Smooth Breathing	Before Rough Breathing
ἀνά	ἀν'	ἀν'
ἀντί	ἀντ'	ἀνθ'
ἀπό	ἀπ'	ἀφ'
διά	δι'	δι'
ἐπί	ἐπ'	ἐφ'
κατά	κατ'	καθ'
μετά	μετ'	μεθ'
παρά	παρ'	παρ'
ὑπό	ὑπ'	ὑφ'

But	περί	περί	περί
	πρό	πρό	πρό

There are only a few exceptions to these rules. For example, ὑπὸ ἐξουσίαν ("under authority") is the form always found in the New Testament (e.g., Matt 8:9).

61. Compound Verbs

Several New Testament verbs are *compound verbs*, that is, verbs composed of a *simplex* verb and a preposition that has been affixed to it. This preposition is called a *prepositional prefix morpheme*. Sometimes the meaning of a compound verb can be determined from the meanings of its component parts. An example is ἐκβάλλω, which means "I throw out" (from ἐκ, "out," and βάλλω, "I throw"). At other times, the meaning of the verb is modified by the preposition in a way that makes it difficult, if not impossible, to explain its meaning (e.g., ἀναγινώσκω means "I read," not "I know up"). When a compound verb is augmented, the augment is placed *between* the preposition and the simplex verb. Hence the imperfect of ἐκβάλλω is ἐξέβαλλον. If the preposition ends in a vowel, the vowel is usually dropped (elided) before a verb that begins with a vowel and before an augment (as in ἀποθνῄσκω, imperfect ἀπέθνῃσκον). In the New Testament, the preposition used in a prefix is often repeated with a noun or pronoun in the appropriate case, without any additional significance (e.g., ἐκβάλλω τὸν πονηρὸν ἐκ τοῦ οἴκου, "I throw the evil man *out of* the house").

62. Vocabulary

a. Prepositions with two cases.

διά	*through; by* (with gen.) (*dia*meter)
	because of; on account of (with acc.) (*dia*critical)
κατά	*against; down* (with gen.) (*cata*pult)
	according to (with acc.) (*cata*log)
μετά	*with* (with gen.) (*meta*bolic)
	after (with acc.) (*meta*morphosis)
περί	*about; concerning, for* (with gen.)
	around (with acc.) (*peri*meter)
ὑπέρ	*for* (with gen.)
	above; over (with acc.) (*hyper*tension)
ὑπό	*by* (with gen.)
	under (with acc.) (*hypo*thermia)

b. Prepositions with three cases.

ἐπί	*upon; on, at, about* (with gen., dat., and acc.) (*epi*dermis)
παρά	*from* (with gen.)
	with (with dat.)
	beside; by (with acc.) (*para*llel)

c. Additional prepositions with one case.

ἀνά	*up* (with acc.) (*ana*lysis)
ἀντί	*instead of; in place of, for* (with gen.) (*Anti*christ)
πρό	*before* (with gen.) (*pro*logue)
πρός	*to; toward, with* (with acc.) (*pros*thesis)
σύν	*with* (with dat.) (*syn*thesis)

d. Compound verbs.

ἀναγινώσκω	*I read*
ἀνοίγω	*I open* (√ οιγ; 1 aor. ἀνέῳξα)
ἀποθνήσκω	*I die* (√ θαν; 2 aor. ἀπέθανον)
ἐκβάλλω	*I throw out, I cast out*

63. Exercises

a. Read the lesson carefully, noting the various prepositions used in Greek, the cases they take, and the differences in their meaning.

b. Memorize the vocabulary to this lesson. As in Lesson 5, the core meanings of the prepositions have been set off by a semicolon.

c. Translate the following sentences.

1. ἀναγινώσκει ὁ μαθητὴς παραβολὴν περὶ τῆς βασιλείας.

2. ἐκβάλλομεν τὰ πονηρὰ ἐκ τοῦ οἴκου.

3. ἔλαβον αἱ ἀγαθαὶ ἀγαθὰ ἀπὸ τοῦ πιστοῦ ἀδελφοῦ.

4. εἶπον οἱ υἱοὶ τῶν προφητῶν λόγους κατὰ τὴν ἀλήθειαν.

5. διὰ τὴν δόξαν τοῦ κυρίου ἠκούομεν παραβολὴν ἀγάπης καὶ εἰρήνης.

6. διὰ τῶν γραφῶν γινώσκομεν τὸν νόμον τοῦ θεοῦ.

7. ἔπεμψεν ὁ θεὸς ἀγγέλους εἰς τὸν κόσμον.

8. μετὰ τῶν ἀποστόλων τῶν ἀγαθῶν ἦμεν ἐν τῇ ἐκκλησίᾳ.

9. εἰς τὸ ἱερὸν φέρουσι τοὺς στρατιώτας τοὺς πονηρούς.

10. ἤγαγον οἱ νεανίαι τοὺς ἀγαθοὺς δούλους καὶ τοὺς υἱοὺς τῶν προφητῶν πρὸς τοὺς οἴκους τῶν μαθητῶν.

11. εἰσὶν οἱ υἱοὶ ἀνθρώπων ἐν τῷ ἱερῷ.

12. λέγεις κατὰ τοῦ νόμου, ἀλλὰ λέγω λόγους ἀληθείας.

13. ἔπαθεν ὁ Ἰησοῦς ὑπὲρ τῶν ἁμαρτιῶν τοῦ κόσμου.

14. ὑπὸ τὴν γήν εἰσιν οἱ νεκροί.

15. ἔλεγεν ὁ ἀπόστολος περὶ τῶν ἁμαρτιῶν τῶν τέκνων.

16. ἔπεμψεν ὁ θεὸς τοὺς προφήτας πρὸ τῶν ἀποστόλων.

17. ἦμεν σὺν τοῖς μαθηταῖς ἐν τῇ ἐρήμῳ.

18. ἀντὶ τοῦ Μεσσίου ἐκήρυξεν ὁ ἀπόστολος ὁ πιστός.

19. ἦγεν ὁ κύριος τοὺς μαθητὰς περὶ τὴν θάλασσαν καὶ εἰς τὴν ἔρημον.

20. καθ᾽ ἡμέραν ἐδίδασκον οἱ ἀπόστολοι ἐν τῷ ἱερῷ.

21. Χριστὸς ἀπέθανεν ὑπὲρ τῶν ἁμαρτιῶν ἀνθρώπων κατὰ τὰς γραφάς.

9

PERSONAL PRONOUNS

The word "pronoun" is derived from the Latin *pro* and *nomen*, meaning "for a noun." The name is appropriate, since pronouns are employed to avoid the repetition of the noun. There are nine classes of pronouns in the New Testament, one of which, the personal pronoun, is introduced in this lesson.

64. The Greek Personal Pronouns

A pronoun is a word that takes the place of a noun or another substantive. *Personal pronouns* are those which stand in the place of persons. Those pronouns that refer to or include the person(s) speaking are said to be in the *first person* (e.g., "I," "me," "us," "our"). Those relating to the person(s) being spoken to are said to be in the *second person* (e.g., "you," "your"). Finally, those referring to a person or thing being spoken about are said to be in the *third person* (e.g., "he," "her," "its," "their"). Pronouns are useful words since they enable the speaker to avoid constant repetition of nouns. For example, "I see the disciple and teach him" means the same thing as "I see the disciple and teach the disciple," but the first sentence avoids the redundancy of the second.

a. The declension of the personal pronoun of the first person is given below:

	Singular		Plural	
N.	ἐγώ	*I*	ἡμεῖς	*we*
G.	ἐμοῦ or μου	*of me, my*	ἡμῶν	*of us, our*
D.	ἐμοί or μοι	*to me*	ἡμῖν	*to us*
A.	ἐμέ or με	*me*	ἡμᾶς	*us*

Note the following:

(1) There are no vocatives in the first person pronouns.

(2) The forms ἐμοῦ, ἐμοί, ἐμέ are used when emphasis is desired. The forms μου, μοι, με are enclitics, throwing their accent on the preceding word (enclitics are discussed in Appendix 1). The enclitic forms are used when there is no particular emphasis on the pronoun.

b. The declension of the personal pronoun of the second person is given below:

	Singular		Plural	
N.V.	σύ	*you*	ὑμεῖς	*you*
G.	σοῦ or σου	*of you, your*	ὑμῶν	*of you, your*
D.	σοί or σοι	*to you*	ὑμῖν	*to you*
A.	σέ or σε	*you*	ὑμᾶς	*you*

Note the following:

(1) The vocative is the same as the nominative.

(2) The forms σοῦ, σοί, σέ are enclitic, that is, they lose their accent *except when they are emphatic* (see Appendix 1).

(3) The formal similarity between ἡμεῖς ("we") and ὑμεῖς ("you") is very close. The tendency to confuse the meanings of these pronouns may be overcome by recalling that the *last* letter of the English word is the *first* letter of the Greek equivalent: w*e* = ἡμεῖς; yo*u* = ὑμεῖς.

c. The declension of the personal pronoun of the third person is given below:

	Singular					
	Masculine		Feminine		Neuter	
N.	αὐτός	*he*	αὐτή	*she*	αὐτό	*it*
G.	αὐτοῦ	*of him, his*	αὐτῆς	*of her, her*	αὐτοῦ	*of it, its*
D.	αὐτῷ	*to him*	αὐτῇ	*to her*	αὐτῷ	*to it*
A.	αὐτόν	*him*	αὐτήν	*her*	αὐτό	*it*

			Plural			
	Masculine		**Feminine**		**Neuter**	
N.	αὐτοί	*they*	αὐταί	*they*	αὐτά	*they*
G.	αὐτῶν	*of them, their*	αὐτῶν	*of them, their*	αὐτῶν	*of them, their*
D.	αὐτοῖς	*to them*	αὐταῖς	*to them*	αὐτοῖς	*to them*
A.	αὐτούς	*them*	αὐτάς	*them*	αὐτά	*them*

Note the following:

(1) The declension of αὐτός, αὐτή, αὐτό is identical to that of ἀγαθός (see §43), except for the neuter nominative/accusative singular form αὐτό (cf. the neuter article τό).

(2) There are no vocatives.

65. Characteristics of Personal Pronouns

The major characteristics of the Greek personal pronouns may be described as follows:

(1) As already observed, personal pronouns are used in place of nouns and other substantives in order to avoid monotony. For example, ὁ ἄνθρωπος γινώσκει τὸν ἀπόστολον καὶ ἀκούει τὸν ἀπόστολον ("The man knows the apostle and hears the apostle") is less redundantly expressed by the use of the pronoun αὐτόν ("him") in place of the second occurrence of τὸν ἀπόστολον.

(2) The noun for which a pronoun stands is called an *antecedent*. A Greek pronoun agrees with its antecedent in gender and number, but its case depends on its *use* in the sentence in which it occurs. For example, in the sentence βλέπω τὸν κύριον καὶ γινώσκω αὐτόν ("I see the Lord and know him"), the antecedent of αὐτόν is τὸν κύριον. Since τὸν κύριον is masculine singular, the personal pronoun αὐτόν is also masculine singular. In this particular sentence, αὐτόν is also the *direct object* of the verb γινώσκω and thus is in the *accusative* case. However, in the sentence βλέπω τὸν κύριον καὶ πιστεύω ἐν αὐτῷ ("I see the Lord and believe in him"), the context of the pronoun requires the *dative* case, though its gender and number remain masculine singular as in the first sentence.

(3) Since the subject of a Greek verb is already expressed in its person-number suffix (cf. Span. *tengo*, "I have"), personal pronouns are used in

67

the nominative case only when emphasis is intended. For example, λέγω means "I say," the suffix -ω sufficiently indicating the subject. If ἐγώ is added to the construction, special emphasis is being placed on the subject, as in Matthew 5:22: ἐγὼ δὲ λέγω ὑμῖν, "But *I* say to you." Here "I" is contrasted with "those in former times" (v 21).

(4) Personal pronouns in the genitive case are frequently used to express possession. The enclitic (unemphatic) forms are used throughout. Note the following examples:

ὁ λόγος μου	= "my word"	(lit., "the word of me")
ὁ οἶκος σου	= "your house"	(lit., "the house of you")
ὁ δοῦλος ἡμῶν	= "our slave"	(lit., "the slave of us")
ὁ δοῦλος αὐτοῦ	= "his slave"	(lit., "the slave of him")
ὁ δοῦλος αὐτῆς	= "her slave"	(lit., "the slave of her")
ὁ δοῦλος αὐτῶν	= "their slave"	(lit., "the slave of them")

(5) The emphatic forms of the personal pronouns are normally used after prepositions:

	ἀπ᾽ ἐμοῦ	(*instead of* ἀπό μου)	= "from me"
	ἐκ σοῦ	(*instead of* ἐκ σου)	= "out of you"
	ἐν ἐμοί	(*instead of* ἔν μοι)	= "in me"
but	πρός με	(*instead of* πρὸς ἐμέ)	= "to me"

Note that an apostrophe (᾽) marks the place where elision has occurred (see §9).

66. Special Uses of αὐτός

Αὐτός has two special uses:

(1) When used with the article, that is, in the *attributive* position, it corresponds to the English adjective *same*. This use is called "adjectival αὐτός."

(2) When used without the article, that is, in the *predicate* position, it corresponds to the English pronoun *self* (e.g., "himself," "herself," "themselves"). This use is called "intensive αὐτός."

Compare adjectival αὐτός with the adjective ἀγαθός when used in the attributive position:

(1) ὁ ἀγαθὸς ἀπόστολος   "the good apostle"
     ὁ αὐτὸς ἀπόστολος   "the same apostle"

(2) ὁ ἀπόστολος ὁ ἀγαθός   "the good apostle"
     ὁ ἀπόστολος ὁ αὐτός   "the same apostle"

(3) βλέπω τὸν ἀγαθὸν ἀπόστολον.   "I see the good apostle."
     βλέπω τὸν αὐτὸν ἀπόστολον.   "I see the same apostle."

Now *contrast* intensive αὐτός and the adjective ἀγαθός when used in the predicate position:

(1) ὁ ἀπόστολος ἀγαθός   "the apostle is good"
     ὁ ἀπόστολος αὐτός   "the apostle himself"

(2) ἀγαθὸς ὁ ἀπόστολος   "the apostle is good"
     αὐτὸς ὁ ἀπόστολος   "the apostle himself"

Intensive αὐτός may also be used with other pronouns or with the unexpressed subject of the verb:

(1) αὐτὸς ἐγὼ λέγω   "I myself say"
     or
     αὐτὸς λέγω

(2) αὐτὸς σὺ λέγεις   "you yourself say"
     or
     αὐτὸς λέγεις

(3) αὐτὸς λέγει   "he himself says"

(4) αὐτὴ λέγει   "she herself says"

(5) αὐτοὶ ἡμεῖς λέγομεν   "we ourselves say"
     or
     αὐτοὶ λέγομεν

67. Examples of Personal Pronouns

The principal uses of the Greek personal pronouns may be reviewed by studying the following New Testament examples:

(1) John 6:35: **ἐγώ** εἰμι ὁ ἄρτος τῆς ζωῆς.
"**I** am the bread of life."

(2) Luke 4:41: **σὺ** εἶ ὁ υἱὸς τοῦ θεοῦ.
"**You** are the Son of God."

(3) John 19:7: **ἡμεῖς** νόμον ἔχομεν.
"**We** have a law."

(4) Matt 1:21: **αὐτὸς** σώσει τὸν λαὸν **αὐτοῦ**.
"He **himself** will save **his** people."

(5) John 15:3: **ὑμεῖς** καθαροί ἐστε.
"**You** are clean."

(6) John 17:4: **ἐγώ σε** ἐδόξασα.
"**I** glorified **you**."

(7) John 4:29: εἶπέν **μοι** πάντα.
"He told **me** all things."

(8) 1 Cor 15:51: μυστήριον **ὑμῖν** λέγω.
"I tell **you** a secret."

(9) Acts 10:26: **ἐγὼ αὐτὸς** ἄνθρωπός εἰμι.
"**I myself** am a man."

(10) Rev 21:3: **αὐτὸς** ὁ θεὸς μετ' **αὐτῶν** ἔσται.
"God **himself** will be with **them**."

(11) John 14:11: διὰ τὰ ἔργα **αὐτὰ** πιστεύετε.
"Because of the works **themselves** you believe."

(12) John 1:42: ὁ Ἰησοῦς εἶπεν, **Σὺ** εἶ Σίμων ὁ υἱὸς Ἰωάννου.
"Jesus said, '**You** are Simon, the son of John.'"

(13) John 1:25 τί βαπτίζεις εἰ **σὺ** οὐκ εἶ ὁ Χριστός;
"Why do you baptize if **you** are not the Christ?"

(14) 1 Cor 12:6 ὁ δὲ **αὐτὸς** θεὸς ὁ ἐνεργῶν τὰ πάντα ἐν πᾶσιν.

"Now the **same** God is the one who works all things in all people."

(15) John 11:25: εἶπεν **αὐτῇ** ὁ Ἰησοῦς, Ἐγώ εἰμι ἡ ἀ-νάστασις καὶ ἡ ζωή.

"Jesus said **to her**, 'I am the resurrection and the life.'"

68. Vocabulary

Personal pronouns.

αὐτός, -ή, -ό	*he, same, self* (*auto*mobile)
ἐγώ	*I* (*ego*centric)
σύ	*you*

69. Exercises

a. Read the lesson carefully. Learn by heart the paradigms of the first and second person pronouns.

b. Memorize the vocabulary to this lesson.

c. Translate the following sentences.

1. γινώσκουσιν οἱ μαθηταί σου τὸν ἀπόστολον καὶ ἄγουσιν αὐτὸν εἰς τὸν οἶκον αὐτῶν.

2. διδάσκω τοὺς υἱούς μου καὶ λέγω αὐτοῖς τὸν λόγον τοῦ θεοῦ.

3. ἐγώ εἰμι δοῦλος, σὺ δὲ εἶ ὁ κύριος.

4. οἱ ἀδελφοὶ ἡμῶν εἶδον ἡμᾶς καὶ εἴδομεν αὐτούς.

5. ἄξει με ὁ κύριος αὐτὸς εἰς τὴν βασιλείαν αὐτοῦ.

6. σὺ βλέψεις θάνατον, ἐγὼ δὲ βλέψω ζωήν.

7. ὁ ἀπόστολος πιστός, οἱ δὲ δοῦλοι αὐτοῦ κακοί.

8. σὲ εἴδομεν καὶ εἴπομέν σοι παραβολὴν ἀγάπης.

9. ἐφύγετε ἀφ' ἡμῶν, ἀλλ' ἡμεῖς ἐδιδάσκομεν ἐν τῇ ἐκκλησίᾳ.

10. ἐν ταῖς ἡμέραις ταῖς ἐσχάταις ὁ Ἰησοῦς ἄξει τοὺς μαθητὰς αὐτοῦ εἰς τὴν βασιλείαν.

11. εὗρον οἱ ἄνθρωποι τὰ τέκνα αὐτῶν καὶ ἤγαγον αὐτὰ εἰς τοὺς οἴκους αὐτῶν.

12. ὑμεῖς ἐλάβετε τὸν κύριον εἰς τὰς καρδίας ὑμῶν, ἀλλ᾽ ἡμεῖς ἐφύγομεν ἀπὸ τῆς ἐκκλησίας.

13. ἐγὼ ἔπαθον, σὺ ἡμάρτησας, ἀλλ᾽ αὐτὸς ἔσωσεν ἡμᾶς.

14. μετὰ τῶν ἀδελφῶν ἡμῶν ἐβλέψαμεν τοὺς μαθητὰς τοῦ κυρίου ἡμῶν.

15. διὰ σοῦ ἄξει ὁ θεὸς τὰ τέκνα αὐτοῦ εἰς τὴν βασιλείαν ἀγάπης.

16. ἀφ᾽ ὑμῶν ἔλαβεν ὁ ἀδελφός μου δῶρα καλά.

17. μετὰ τὰς ἡμέρας τὰς πονηρὰς αὐτοὶ βλέψομεν τὰς ἡμέρας τὰς ἀγαθάς.

18. μεθ᾽ ὑμῶν ἐσμεν ἐν τοῖς οἴκοις ὑμῶν.

19. αὐτοὶ γινώσκομεν τὴν ὁδόν, καὶ δι᾽ αὐτῆς ἄξομέν σε εἰς τὴν ἐκκλησίαν τὴν αὐτήν.

20. δι᾽ ἐμὲ βλέψεις τὸν κύριον.

10

PERFECT AND PLUPER-FECT ACTIVE INDICATIVE

Often called the most exegetically significant of the Greek tenses, the perfect appears in three forms: the perfect, the pluperfect (i.e., the perfect of past time), and the future perfect. By far the most common form is the perfect. Because the New Testament often draws a sharp distinction between the perfect and the other tenses, mastery of the Greek perfect is essential for accurate exegesis.

70. The Perfect Active Indicative of λύω

In our study of the Greek verb, we have thus far considered three of its principal parts: the present active, the future active, and the aorist active. This lesson introduces the fourth principal part, that is, the *perfect active*. From this principal part are obtained the forms of the perfect, pluperfect, and future perfect tenses of the verb.

The perfect active indicative of λύω is given below:

	Singular		Plural	
1.	λέλυκα	*I have loosed*	λελύκαμεν	*we have loosed*
2.	λέλυκας	*you have loosed*	λελύκατε	*you have loosed*
3.	λέλυκε(ν)	*he has loosed*	λελύκασι(ν)	*they have loosed*

Notice that the perfect tense is obtained by (a) affixing the *perfective aspect morpheme* κα to the stem of the verb, (b) attaching the secondary active suffixes (see §48), and (c) prefixing a *reduplicated syllable* to the beginning of the verb. Perfective reduplication consists of the initial consonant of the verb stem plus the vowel ∈. Thus λυ- becomes λελυ-, γραφ- becomes γεγραφ-, etc. Exceptions to this general rule derive from the phonetic characteristics of the initial phoneme of the verb:

(1) If the verb stem begins with an aspirated consonant (φ, θ, or χ), then the corresponding unaspirated consonant is used to form the redupli-cated syllable, as in θεραπεύω ("I heal"), perfect τεθεράπευκα ("I have healed"). This phonological process is called *deaspiration*.

(2) If the verb stem begins with a double consonant (ψ, ζ, or ξ) or with two consonants other than a consonant plus λ or ρ, then the reduplicating syllable is simply ἐ-, as in γινώσκω ("I know," √ γνο), perfect ἔγνωκα ("I have known").

(3) If the verb stem begins with a vowel, then the reduplication takes the form of the temporal augment, as in ἑτοιμάζω ("I prepare"), perfect ἡτοίμακα ("I have prepared"). Other changes are best learned by obser-vation in vocabulary study.

Notice that the first person singular of the perfect active indicative does not have the ν. In the third person singular the ∈ alone appears, thereby distinguishing the first and third persons in the singular. It should also be noted that the phonemes τ, δ, or θ are dropped before the κ of the perfect, as in ἐλπίζω ("I hope," root ἐλπιδ), perfect ἤλπικα.

71. Second Perfects

Some verbs do not contain the κ of the perfective aspect morpheme κα in their perfect, pluperfect, or future perfect forms. These verbs are known as second perfects. They are conjugated exactly like first perfects except for the absence of the κ. As with first and second aorists, the dis-tinction is one of form only and not of function (see §52). An example of a second perfect verb is γράφω ("I write"):

	Singular		Plural	
1.	γέγραφα	*I have written*	γεγράφαμεν	*we have written*
2.	γέγραφας	*you have written*	γεγράφατε	*you have written*
3.	γέγραφε(ν)	*he has written*	γεγράφασι(ν)	*they have written*

The New Testament contains 21 verbs containing second perfect forms. The most common of these include:

Present		Second Perfect	
ἀκούω	(I hear)	ἀκήκοα	(I have heard)
πείθω	(I trust in)	πέποιθα	(I have trusted in)
πέμπω	(I send)	πέπομφα	(I have sent)
πάσχω	(I suffer)	πέπονθα	(I have suffered)

72. The Significance of the Perfect Tense

The Greek perfect refers to a state resulting from a completed action. As such, the temporal focus is often more on the present than the past, though the perfect depicts action that is already completed. Note the difference between Acts 2:2 and Acts 5:28.

"A sound *filled* [aorist indicative] the whole house."

"You *have filled* [perfect indicative] Jerusalem with your teaching."

Here the aorist emphasizes the action of the verb "fill" without reference to its effect, while the perfect emphasizes a present state that has resulted from the action. Similarly, when the Greek philosopher Archimedes discovered the law of buoyancy while taking a bath, he is reported to have scampered (without his clothes) through the streets of Athens shouting, εὕρηκα, εὕρηκα, "I have found it, I have found it!" What Archimedes apparently meant by the use of εὕρηκα (the perfect of εὑρίσκω) was that his discovery had become a part of his intellectual awareness. If, on the other hand, he had found a drachma on the street and then lost it before he got home, he probably would have used the aorist εὗρον, "I found it," which says nothing about the existing state of affairs.

In the New Testament, the genius of the Greek perfect is clearly seen in 1 Corinthians 15:4, where Paul uses the perfect tense ("Christ . . . was raised") to emphasize that the risen Christ remains in a state of risenness, in contrast to his death and subsequent burial and appearances (aorists are used to describe these actions). Other New Testament examples of the perfect include:

John 1:41:   "*We have found* the Messiah [and the finding is still vivid]."

John 7:22:	"Moses *has given* you circumcision [as a continuing rite]."
John 19:22:	"What *I have written I have written* [and it cannot be changed]."
2 Cor 12:9:	"*He has said* to me, 'My grace is sufficient for you' [and the answer is still valid]."
2 Tim 4:7:	"*I have kept* the faith [from beginning to end]."
Heb 1:4:	"*He has inherited* [and still possesses] a more excellent name than they."

It is to be remembered that the choice between the perfect and some other tense is not necessarily determined by the objective facts, but by the writer's point of view of the action (see §§15–16). As always, the significance of each occurrence of the perfect tense must be determined by the context.

73. The Pluperfect Active Indicative of λύω

The Greek pluperfect represents the past tense of the perfect. It too is formed on the stem of the fourth (i.e., the perfect active) principal part. Since the pluperfect is a past tense, it has an augment in addition to the reduplication. To the perfect stem are affixed the secondary active suffixes, using -ει- as the connecting vowel(s). Because the pluperfect forms are adequately identified by reduplication and by their distinctive endings, the augment is often omitted.

The pluperfect active indicative of λύω is given below:

	Singular		Plural	
1.	ἐλελύκειν	*I had loosed*	ἐλελύκειμεν	*we had loosed*
2.	ἐλελύκεις	*you had loosed*	ἐλελύκειτε	*you had loosed*
3.	ἐλελύκει	*he had loosed*	ἐλελύκεισαν	*they had loosed*

An example of the pluperfect tense is found in John 9:22: "the Jews *had agreed* that anyone who acknowledged him [i.e., Jesus] as Messiah should be banned from the synagogue." Here the pluperfect emphasizes that the previous arrangement of the Jewish leaders was still in effect.

The pluperfect is seldom used in the New Testament, and the future perfect tense is even rarer. The future perfect expresses perfective aspect in future time. Its few occurrences are best interpreted as they are encountered in exegesis.

74. The Verb οἶδα

Because of its frequency in the Greek New Testament (321 occurrences), the verb οἶδα ("I know"), a synonym of γινώσκω, deserves special attention. This verb has only perfect and pluperfect *forms*, but these are used with present and past *meanings*. For purposes of parsing, οἶδα is regarded as a *present* tense verb, and ᾔδειν as an *imperfect* tense verb ("I was knowing" or "I knew").

		Present Active Indicative		Imperfect Active Indicative	
Sg.	1.	οἶδα	I know	ᾔδειν	I was knowing
	2.	οἶδας	etc.	ᾔδεις	etc.
	3.	οἶδε(ν)		ᾔδει	
Pl.	1.	οἴδαμεν		ᾔδειμεν	
	2.	οἴδατε		ᾔδειτε	
	3.	οἴδασι(ν)		ᾔδεισαν	

75. Vocabulary

a. Additional -ω verb.

οἶδα   *I know*

b. Perfect active indicative principal parts.

ἡμάρτηκα   *I have sinned*
βέβληκα   *I have thrown*
ἔγνωκα   *I have known*
ἡτοίμακα   *I have prepared*
εὕρηκα   *I have found*
ἔσχηκα   *I have had*
τεθεράπευκα   *I have healed*
εἴρηκα   *I have said, I have spoken*

λέλυκα	*I have loosed*
μεμάθηκα	*I have learned*
ἑώρακα	*I have seen* (from ὁράω; see §127)
πεπίστευκα	*I have believed*
σέσωκα	*I have saved*

c. Second perfect active indicative principal parts.

ἀκήκοα	*I have heard*
γέγραφα	*I have written*
πέπονθα	*I have suffered*
πέποιθα	*I have trusted in*
πέπομφα	*I have sent*
πέφευγα	*I have fled*

d. Additional conjunction.

ὅτι	*that, because*

76. Exercises

a. Read the lesson carefully. Learn by heart the paradigm of λύω in the perfect active indicative.

b. Memorize the vocabulary to this lesson.

c. Translate the following sentences.

1. ἀκηκόαμεν τὴν ἀλήθειαν.

2. ἐγνώκαμεν ὅτι ὁ θεὸς ἀγάπη ἐστίν.

3. πεπιστεύκαμεν ὅτι σὺ εἶ ὁ ἅγιος τοῦ θεοῦ.

4. λελύκατε τὸν δοῦλον καὶ πεπόμφατε αὐτὸν εἰς τὴν ἐκκλησίαν.

5. γεγράφαμεν λόγους ἀληθείας διὰ τὴν ἀγάπην ἡμῶν ὑπὲρ τοῦ ἀποστόλου.

6. πέπονθεν ὁ Μεσσίας καὶ ἔγνωκε θάνατον.

7. τοὺς δούλους τῶν πιστῶν ἀνθρώπων ἐλελύκεις ὅτι σὺ ἦς ἀγαθός.

8. οἴδατε ὅτι ὑμᾶς σέσωκεν ὁ υἱὸς τοῦ θεοῦ.

9. γινώσκομεν ὅτι ἐγνώκαμεν αὐτόν, ὅτι πεπιστεύκαμεν ἐν αὐτῷ.

10. ἐγὼ εἴρηκα τὴν ἀλήθειαν, ἀλλ᾽ οὐκ ἐπιστεύσατέ με.

11. ὑπὲρ ἡμῶν ἡτοίμακεν ὁ θεὸς βασιλείαν.

12. ἀκηκόατε ὅτι ἡμάρτηκα κατὰ τοῦ κυρίου.

13. ἐγὼ ἔσχηκα χαρὰν καὶ εἰρήνην, ἀλλὰ σὺ πέπονθας ὅτι οὐ πέποιθας τὸν κύριον.

11

DEMONSTRATIVE
PRONOUNS

When it is desired to call attention to a designated object, a demonstrative construction is used (from Lat. *demonstro*, "I point out"). This construction normally consists of a demonstrative pronoun. The near demonstrative, οὗτος ("this"), points out something near at hand, while the remote demonstrative, ἐκεῖνος ("that"), points out something further removed.

77. Paradigms of the Demonstrative Pronouns

The following paradigms of the demonstrative pronouns should be compared with those of αὐτός (§64) and the definite article (§39). In particular, the forms αὕτη and αὗται (demonstrative pronouns) should be distinguished from αὐτή and αὐταί (personal pronouns).

a. The declension of οὗτος, αὕτη, τοῦτο ("this") is given below:

	Singular			Plural		
	Masculine	Feminine	Neuter	Masculine	Feminine	Neuter
N	οὗτος	αὕτη	τοῦτο	οὗτοι	αὗται	ταῦτα
G.	τούτου	ταύτης	τούτου	τούτων	τούτων	τούτων
D.	τούτῳ	ταύτῃ	τούτῳ	τούτοις	ταύταις	τούτοις
A.	τοῦτον	ταύτην	τοῦτο	τούτους	ταύτας	ταῦτα

Notice that the rough breathing occurs in the nominative masculine and feminine in both the singular and plural; all other forms begin with τ (cf. the paradigm of the definite article [§39]). It should also be observed that the diphthong of the stem of the near demonstrative, ου or αυ, varies in accordance with the vowel of the ending, ο (ω) or α (η).

b. The declension of ἐκεῖνος, ἐκείνη, ἐκεῖνο ("that") is given below:

	Singular			Plural		
	Masculine	**Feminine**	**Neuter**	**Masculine**	**Feminine**	**Neuter**
N.	ἐκεῖνος	ἐκείνη	ἐκεῖνο	ἐκεῖνοι	ἐκεῖναι	ἐκεῖνα
G.	ἐκείνου	ἐκείνης	ἐκείνου	ἐκείνων	ἐκείνων	ἐκείνων
D.	ἐκείνῳ	ἐκείνῃ	ἐκείνῳ	ἐκείνοις	ἐκείναις	ἐκείνοις
A.	ἐκεῖνον	ἐκείνην	ἐκεῖνο	ἐκείνους	ἐκείνας	ἐκεῖνα

The declension of ἐκεῖνος is identical to that of αὐτός (§64).

78. Uses of the Demonstratives

There are three main uses of the Greek demonstratives:

(1) They are most frequently used to modify nouns, in which case they agree with the noun in gender, number, and case (cf. αὐτός and adjectives like ἀγαθός). In this use the noun always has the definite article, and the demonstrative pronoun stands in the *predicate* position; that is, the pronoun is *never* immediately preceded by the definite article. Hence "this man" would be either οὗτος ὁ ἄνθρωπος or ὁ ἄνθρωπος οὗτος. The same position may be used in any case function, as in:

βλέπω τοῦτον τὸν ἄνθρωπον.   "I see this man."

βλέπω ἐκεῖνον τὸν ἄνθρωπον.   "I see that man."

λέγω τούτοις τοῖς ἀνθρώποις.   "I speak to these men."

Note the following New Testament examples:

Heb 7:1:   **οὗτος** ὁ Μελχισεδὲκ μένει ἱερεύς.
            "**This** Melchizedek remains a priest."

Rev 22:6:   **Οὗτοι** οἱ λόγοι πιστοὶ καὶ ἀληθινοί.
            "**These** words are faithful and true."

Luke 13:6: ἔλεγεν **ταύτην** τὴν παραβολήν.
"He was speaking **this** parable."

Matt 24:14: κηρυχθήσεται **τοῦτο** τὸ εὐαγγέλιον.
"**This** gospel will be preached."

1 Cor 11:25: **τοῦτο** τὸ ποτήριον ἡ καινὴ διαθήκη ἐστίν.
"**This** cup is the new covenant."

Matt 13:44: ἀγοράζει τὸν ἀγρὸν **ἐκεῖνον**.
"He buys **that** field."

Luke 12:46: ἥξει ὁ κύριος τοῦ δούλου **ἐκείνου**.
"The master of **that** slave will come."

To repeat, Greek demonstrative pronouns always modify *arthrous* nouns, and they always occur in the *predicate* position.

(2) Both οὗτος and ἐκεῖνος may also be used by themselves with the force of a substantive. In this usage οὗτος could mean "this one," "this man," "this person," and ἐκεῖνος could mean "that one," "that man," "that person." New Testament examples include:

Matt 9:3: **οὗτος** βλασφημεῖ.
"**This man** is blaspheming."

Matt 3:17: **οὗτός** ἐστιν ὁ υἱός.
"**This one** is the son."

Acts 9:36: **αὕτη** ἦν πλήρης ἔργων ἀγαθῶν.
"**This woman** was full of good works."

It is to be carefully observed that when the demonstrative pronouns occur with *anarthrous* nouns, they are not modifiers of these nouns, but pronouns:

John 10:1: **ἐκεῖνος** κλέπτης ἐστὶν καὶ λῃστής.
"**That man** is a thief and a robber."

Contrast: **ἐκεῖνος** ὁ κλέπτης ἐστὶν καὶ λῃστής.
"**That** thief is also a robber."

(3) Finally, the demonstrative pronouns may be used to refer to persons mentioned in the immediately preceding context. In such cases, they are best translated simply *he, she,* or *they:*

John 1:2: **οὗτος** ἦν ἐν ἀρχῇ πρὸς τὸν θεόν.
"**He** [i.e., the Word] was in the beginning with God."

John 1:8: οὐκ ἦν **ἐκεῖνος** τὸ φῶς.
"**He** [i.e., John the Baptist] was not the light."

79. Vocabulary

a. Demonstrative pronouns.

ἐκεῖνος, -η, -ο	*that*
οὗτος, αὕτη, τοῦτο	*this*

b. Additional masculine nouns of the second declension.

ἀμνός, ὁ	*lamb*
ἄρτος, ὁ	*bread*
διάβολος, ὁ	*slanderer, devil (diabolic)*
ἐχθρός, ὁ	*enemy*
ἥλιος, ὁ	*sun (Heliopolis [city of the sun])*
θρόνος, ὁ	*throne*
καιρός, ὁ	*time, occasion*
καρπός, ὁ	*fruit*
λαός, ὁ	*people (laity)*
ναός, ὁ	*temple, sanctuary*
οὐρανός, ὁ	*heaven (Uranus)*
ὀφθαλμός, ὁ	*eye (ophthalmology)*
Πέτρος, ὁ	*Peter*
σταυρός, ὁ	*cross*
τόπος, ὁ	*place (topography)*
τυφλός, ὁ	*blind man*
φίλος, ὁ	*friend (philanthropic)*
φόβος, ὁ	*fear (phobic)*
χρόνος, ὁ	*time (chronology)*

c. Additional neuter nouns of the second declension.

βιβλίον, τό	*book (bibliography)*
δαιμόνιον, τό	*demon (daimonic)*
ἱμάτιον, τό	*cloak, garment*

μυστήριον, τό   *secret* (*mystery*)
παιδίον, τό   *child* (*pediatrics*)
πλοῖον, τό   *boat*
σάββατον, τό   *Sabbath*
σημεῖον, τό   *sign* (*semantics*)

80. Exercises

a. Read the lesson carefully. Study the paradigms of οὗτος and ἐκεῖνος.

b. Memorize the vocabulary to this lesson. A reminder: the vocabulary words in this textbook are found with great frequency in the New Testament and should be mastered.

c. Translate the following sentences.

1. οὗτος ὁ ἀπόστολος γινώσκει ἐκεῖνον τὸν ἀπόστολον.

2. οὗτοι οἱ ἄνθρωποι ἀκούουσιν ἐκεῖνα τὰ παιδία.

3. οὗτος βλέπει ἐκεῖνον ἐν τῷ ναῷ.

4. αὕτη ἔχει εἰρήνην ἐν τῇ καρδίᾳ αὐτῆς.

5. ἀκούσομεν ταύτην τὴν παραβολὴν περὶ τῶν πονηρῶν δαιμονίων.

6. οὗτοι ἔχουσι χαράν, ἐκεῖνοι δὲ ἔχουσιν ἁμαρτίαν ἐν ταῖς καρδίαις αὐτῶν.

7. οὗτός ἐστιν ὁ λόγος τοῦ κυρίου.

8. γινώσκομεν τοῦτον καὶ ἄγομεν αὐτὸν μετὰ τοῦ ἱματίου αὐτοῦ εἰς τοὺς οἴκους ἡμῶν.

9. φέρομεν ταῦτα τὰ δῶρα ἀπὸ τοῦ ἀποστόλου εἰς τὴν ἐκκλησίαν ἡμῶν.

10. οὗτός ἐστιν ἄνθρωπος τοῦ κόσμου καὶ ἐχθρὸς τοῦ θεοῦ, ἐκεῖνος δέ ἐστιν φίλος τοῦ θεοῦ.

11. ἐκεῖνοι οἱ ἀπόστολοί εἰσι μαθηταὶ τούτου τοῦ κυρίου.

12. μετὰ τὰς ἡμέρας ἐκείνας ἄξομεν τούτους τοὺς μαθητὰς εἰς τὸ πλοῖον.

13. οἱ ἀπόστολοι τοῦ κυρίου ἔφαγον ἄρτον καὶ καρπὸν ἐν τῇ ἐρήμῳ.

14. αὐτὸς εἶδεν ἐκεῖνα τὰ σημεῖα ἐν οὐρανῷ.

15. μετὰ τούτων τῶν πιστῶν ἤκουσαν οἱ μαθηταὶ παραβολὰς ἀγαθάς, ὁ δὲ λαὸς ἀκούσει λόγους θανάτου.

16. αὕτη ἔγνωκε τὴν ἀλήθειαν αὐτήν.

17. εἰς τὴν αὐτὴν ἐκκλησίαν ἤγαγεν ὁ Πέτρος τούτους τοὺς τυφλοὺς τοὺς ἀγαθούς.

18. ἐν ἐκείναις ταῖς ἡμέραις ἦμεν ἐν τῷ ἀγρῷ καὶ ἐδιδάσκομεν ἐκεῖνα τὰ παιδία.

19. αὕτη ἐστὶν ἡ ὁδὸς θανάτου καὶ ἁμαρτίας, καὶ πονηροὶ ἄγουσι τὰ τέκνα αὐτῶν εἰς αὐτήν.

20. τοῦτο τὸ βιβλίον ἐστὶν ὁ λόγος τοῦ θεοῦ.

21. οὗτοι οὐ γινώσκουσι τὸν χρόνον τῆς ἡμέρας τοῦ κυρίου.

12

PRESENT MIDDLE AND PASSIVE INDICATIVE

We have seen that voice in Greek is concerned with the relation of the action of the verb to the subject. To this point we have studied the active voice, which expresses the idea that the subject of the verb is the doer of the action. This lesson introduces the other two voices in Greek: the middle and the passive.

81. The Present Middle and Passive Indicative of λύω

In addition to the active voice, the Greek verb system has middle and passive voices (see §14). The significance of the passive voice is the same in Greek as it is in English: the subject is receiving the action of the verb. The middle voice, on the other hand, represents the subject as acting in its own interest or in such a way as to participate in the results of the action of the verb. *Just how the action is related to the subject is not indicated by the middle voice itself but by the context or the verbal idea.*

In English, passive forms are made up of the past passive participle of a verb preceded by the appropriate part of the verb "be" (e.g., "is loved," "was hidden"). The verb "be" may itself be used as an auxiliary, as in "is being loved" and "had been hidden." In Greek, such composite tenses are not used. Instead, Greek uses single-word forms (e.g., λύομαι, "I am being loosed").

The following are the primary middle/passive suffixes:

	Singular	Plural
1.	-μαι	-μεθα
2.	-σαι	-σθε
3.	-ται	-νται

These suffixes are used in the conjugation of the present middle and passive indicative of λύω, which is given below. Notice that the connecting vowels ο/ε are clearly observable in all forms, except the second person singular. This form, λύῃ, has been shortened from λύεσαι by the dropping of the σ, the contracting (combining) of the ε and α, and the subscripting of the ι.

	Singular	Plural
1.	λύομαι	λυόμεθα
2.	λύῃ	λύεσθε
3.	λύεται	λύονται

Since the forms of the middle voice are identical with those of the passive, the context alone will indicate whether the construction is middle or passive in function. The translation of the middle voice requires special discussion (see below). With regard to the translation of the passive voice, it will be recalled that the present *active* indicative of λύω may be translated "I loose" or "I am loosing" (see §22). In English, the passive of "I loose" is "I am loosed," and the passive of "I am loosing" is "I am being loosed." However, because "I am loosed" would normally be expressed by the Greek *perfect* passive (see Lesson 13), the student is advised to adopt the alternative translation wherever possible. Thus λύομαι (as a passive) should be translated "I am being loosed," λύῃ should be translated "you are being loosed," etc. These translations clearly bring out the imperfective aspect of the present tense (see §15). A New Testament example is Romans 1:18: ἀποκαλύπτεται ὀργὴ θεοῦ ἀπ᾽ οὐρανοῦ, "The wrath of God *is being revealed* from heaven."

As with the active voice, the normal position of the negative adverb οὐ is immediately before the verb, as in οὐ λύομαι, "I am not being loosed," οὐ λύῃ, "you are not being loosed," etc.

82. Uses of the Middle Voice

In the middle voice, the subject is involved in the action of the verb, but the manner of the involvement must be inferred from the context. Hence there is no single way of translating the middle voice into English. Suggested translations for λύομαι (as a middle) include "I am loosing myself," "I am loosing for myself," "I myself am loosing." The following uses of the middle voice represent the general idea of the construction:

(1) The *reflexive middle* refers the result of the action of the verb directly to the subject, as in Matthew 27:5: "[Judas] hanged himself." Here the reflexive pronoun "himself" does not occur in the Greek; it is implied from the middle voice of the verb. Other New Testament examples of the reflexive middle include 1 Corinthians 6:11 ("you washed yourselves") and 2 Corinthians 11:14 ("Satan disguises himself"). The proportion of strictly reflexive middles in the New Testament is actually very small. It is more common to find the reflexive sense expressed by a verb in the *active* voice accompanied by a Greek reflexive pronoun, as in John 17:19: "I sanctify myself [ἐγὼ ἁγιάζω ἐμαυτόν]."

(2) The *intensive middle* emphasizes the agent as producing the action rather than participating in its results, as in Hebrews 9:12: "he himself secured eternal redemption." Here the idea is that "Jesus and no other" has accomplished redemption. Once again, the word "himself" has been supplied from the middle voice.

(3) The *reciprocal middle* is the use of a plural subject engaged in an interchange of action, as in John 9:22: "The Jews were agreeing with one another." Usually, however, this idea is expressed by an active verb plus the pronoun ἀλλήλους ("one another").

83. Deponent Verbs

A number of Greek verbs have middle or passive forms without any corresponding active forms. These verbs are called *deponent* verbs, the term "deponent" coming from the Latin *depono*, "I lay aside." It is thought that somewhere in the development of the language the active forms of these verbs were "laid aside" out of preference for the middle forms. An example of a deponent verb is ἔρχομαι, "I go," which is middle in form but active in meaning. Most verbs that are deponent in the present tense are deponent in one or more of their other tenses also.

Some deponent verbs can be explained as true middles in which the subject is being emphasized in some manner. The following categories seem to be involved:

(1) *Reciprocity*. These verbs describe situations in which two parties are involved and, if one were removed, no action would be possible. Examples include δέχομαι ("I welcome"), λυτρόομαι ("I redeem"), χαρίζομαι ("I forgive"), ἰάομαι ("I heal"), μάχομαι ("I fight"), ψεύδομαι ("I lie"), ἀσπάζομαι ("I greet"), and ἀποκρίνομαι ("I answer").

(2) *Reflexivity*. In these verbs the verbal idea turns back upon the subject. Examples include τυφόομαι ("I am conceited"), ἐπενδύομαι ("I put on"), μιμέομαι ("I imitate"), and ἐγκρατεύομαι ("I abstain").

(3) *Self-involvement*. These verbs describe processes that the subject alone can experience. Examples include ἔρχομαι ("I go"), διαλογίζομαι ("I ponder"), ἡγέομαι ("I consider"), ὀργίζομαι ("I am angry"), and βούλομαι ("I wish").

i. It should be noted that with some verbs the active form has one meaning and the middle another, as with ἄρχω, "I rule," but ἄρχομαι, "I begin."

ii. A number of deponent verbs occur with a prepositional prefix. For example, ἔρχομαι ("I go") may be compounded with several prepositions: ἀπέρχομαι, "I go away," εἰσέρχομαι, "I go into," ἐξέρχομαι, "I go out."

iii. Several New Testament verbs (deponent or otherwise) take their direct objects in a case other than the accusative. Examples include ἄρχω ("I rule"), which takes the genitive, and ἀποκρίνομαι ("I answer"), which takes the dative.

84. Agency

A verb in the passive voice will often be followed by the identification of an *agent*, that is, the person or thing producing the action. Greek expresses agency in three ways:

(1) The *direct* agent, by whom an action is performed, is expressed by ὑπό and the genitive, as in οἱ ἁμαρτωλοὶ σώζονται ὑπὸ τοῦ θεοῦ, "The sinners are being saved by God."

(2) The *intermediate* agent, through whom the original agent acts, is expressed by διά and the genitive, as in οἱ ἁμαρτωλοὶ σώζονται διὰ τοῦ ἀποστόλου, "The sinners are being saved by the apostle." Here the apostle is looked upon as the intermediate agent of salvation; God would be the original agent (as in sentence 1).

(3) *Impersonal agency* is expressed by the dative case, with or without
ἐν, as in οἱ ἁμαρτωλοὶ σώζονται τῷ λόγῳ [or ἐν τῷ λόγῳ] τοῦ κυρίου,
"The sinners are being saved by the word of the Lord."

Of course, the passive voice frequently occurs when no agent is expressed (e.g., ἁμαρτωλοὶ σώζονται, "The sinners are being saved"). The
name "divine passive" is given to the passive voice when it is used to
avoid naming God directly, as in Matthew 5:5: "they will be comforted
[by God]." This usage occurs frequently in the sayings of Jesus.

85. Vocabulary

a. Additional -ω verbs.

ἄρχω	*I rule* (takes the gen.)
ὑπάρχω	*I am, I exist*

b. Deponent verbs.

ἀποκρίνομαι	*I answer* (takes the dat.)
ἄρχομαι	*I begin* (cf. ἀρχή)
ἀσπάζομαι	*I greet*
βούλομαι	*I wish*
γίνομαι	*I become, I am* (takes a complement)
δέχομαι	*I receive*
ἐκπορεύομαι	*I come out, I go out*
ἐργάζομαι	*I work* (cf. ἔργον)
ἔρχομαι	*I come, I go* (used with numerous preps.; 2 aor. ἦλθον)
εὐαγγελίζομαι	*I preach the gospel, I bring good news* (cf. εὐαγγέλιον)
λογίζομαι	*I consider*
πορεύομαι	*I come, I go*
προσεύχομαι	*I pray* (cf. προσευχή)
ψεύδομαι	*I lie* (*pseudo*nym)

86. Exercises

a. Read the lesson carefully. Learn by heart the primary middle/passive
suffixes (§81). Note carefully how the second person singular suffix -σαι
is modified to -ῃ in the paradigm of λύω.

b. Memorize the vocabulary to this lesson.

c. Translate the following sentences.

1. λύονται οἱ δοῦλοι ὑπὸ τῶν ἀποστόλων.

2. διδάσκεται ἡ ἀλήθεια διὰ τῶν υἱῶν τῶν μαθητῶν.

3. σώζεται ὁ πιστὸς μαθητὴς ὑπὸ τοῦ κυρίου.

4. πέμπεται ὁ ἄγγελος ὑπὸ τοῦ ἀποστόλου ἐκ τοῦ οἴκου καὶ εἰς τὴν ἐκκλησίαν.

5. σώζονται οἱ ὄχλοι ἐκ τοῦ κόσμου.

6. πονηροὶ ἄνθρωποι δοξάζονται, ἀλλὰ δίκαιοι ἄνθρωποι δοξάζουσι τὸν θεόν.

7. ἐκβάλλονται ἐκ τῶν ἐκκλησιῶν οἱ πονηροὶ μαθηταί.

8. οἱ ἄνθρωποι λαμβάνονται ζωὴν ἀπὸ τοῦ κυρίου.

9. ἀναγινώσκονται αἱ γραφαὶ ὑπὸ τῶν πιστῶν μαθητῶν.

10. διδάσκονται οἱ μαθηταὶ οἱ καλοὶ τὸν λόγον ἀληθείας.

11. αἱ πισταὶ ἔρχονται καὶ βαπτίζονται ὑπὸ τῶν ἀποστόλων.

12. γινώσκεται τὰ τέκνα τὰ πιστὰ ὑπὸ τοῦ θεοῦ.

13. γίνῃ μαθητὴς ἀγαθός.

14. ἄγεται ὁ ἀπόστολος μετὰ τῶν ἀδελφῶν αὐτοῦ εἰς τὴν ἐκκλησίαν τοῦ θεοῦ.

15. πορεύεσθε ἐκ τῆς ἐρήμου καὶ εἰς τὸν οἶκον.

16. διὰ τοῦ υἱοῦ τοῦ θεοῦ σώζῃ ἀπὸ τῶν ἁμαρτιῶν σου.

17. οἱ ἁμαρτωλοὶ οὐκ ἐξέρχονται ἐκ τῶν οἴκων τῶν πονηρῶν ὅτι οὐ πιστεύονται ἐν τῷ θεῷ.

18. σώζεται ἡ πιστὴ ὑπὸ τοῦ κυρίου αὐτῆς.

19. οἱ ἁμαρτωλοὶ δέχονται Χριστὸν εἰς τὰς καρδίας αὐτῶν.

20. ἀπόστολοι καὶ προσεύχονται ὑπὲρ ἁμαρτωλῶν καὶ εὐαγγελίζονται αὐτοῖς.

13

PERFECT MIDDLE AND PASSIVE, FUTURE MIDDLE INDICATIVE

The perfect is the tense of completed action. This lesson introduces the perfect middle and passive indicative as well as the future middle indicative.

87. The Perfect Middle and Passive Indicative of λύω

As we saw in Lesson 3 (§19), the Greek verb has six principal parts. We now come to the *fifth* principal part of λύω: the perfect middle and passive (λέλυμαι). Like the present middle and passive indicative, this tense uses the *primary* middle/passive personal endings -μαι, -σαι, -ται, -μεθα, -σθε, -νται (see §81). These endings are attached directly to the reduplicated verb stem *without a connecting vowel*. The reduplication is the same as that of the perfect active (cf. §70).

	Singular	Plural
1.	λέλυμαι	λελύμεθα
2.	λέλυσαι	λέλυσθε
3.	λέλυται	λέλυνται

As with the perfect active, the perfect middle and passive denotes a present state resulting from a completed action. As a middle, λέλυμαι may be rendered "I have loosed myself," "I have loosed for myself," "I myself have loosed," etc. As a passive, λέλυμαι may be rendered "I have been loosed" or "I am loosed." These translations are, however, approximations at best. Sometimes the Greek perfect passive has to be translated by the English simple past, as in 1 Corinthians 15:3–4: "Christ *died* [aorist active] . . . and *was raised* [perfect passive]." Here, however, the perfect "was raised" (ἐγήγερται) contains the further thought: "and is still alive today!"

It should be noted that verbs whose stems end with a consonant undergo certain changes when the perfect middle and passive endings are added to them. For example, the perfect of γράφω is γέγραμμαι in the *first* person singular, but γέγραπται in the *third* person singular. It is not necessary to learn these modifications at this stage. Once the principal parts of a verb are known, the forms are usually easy to recognize.

88. The Future Middle Indicative of λύω

The future middle indicative is formed on the *future* stem, derived from the *second* principal part of the verb. (The future *passive* indicative is formed on another stem and will be learned in a later lesson.) As we have seen, the identifying mark of the future tense is the future time morpheme σ that is added to the verb stem (see §19). Thus the future stem of λύω is λυσ-. To form the future middle indicative of λύω, we simply attach the primary middle/passive personal endings, with the appropriate connecting vowel, to the future stem:

	Singular	Plural
1.	λύσομαι	λυσόμεθα
2.	λύσῃ	λύσεσθε
3.	λύσεται	λύσονται

i. The irregularity in the second person singular form is explained in §81.

ii. The same uses of the middle voice given in §82 apply here also. Thus λύσομαι may be rendered "I will loose myself," "I will loose for myself," "I myself will loose," etc.

89. The Future Indicative of εἰμί

The future indicative of εἰμί is formed on the stem ἐσ- and takes the primary middle/passive endings:

	Singular		Plural	
1.	ἔσομαι	*I will be*	ἐσόμεθα	*we will be*
2.	ἔσῃ	*you will be*	ἔσεσθε	*you will be*
3.	ἔσται	*he will be*	ἔσονται	*they will be*

The complete paradigm of εἰμί in all its tenses has now been studied (see §§23, 55).

90. Adverbs

An adverb is a word that qualifies a verb (hence its name), an adjective, or another adverb. In the sentence "*Immediately* he called him" (Mark 1:20), the adverb "immediately" qualifies the verb "called." Some adverbs are formed from adjectives by substituting ς for ν at the end of the genitive plural. For example, from καλῶν (the genitive plural of καλός) is formed καλῶς ("rightly," "well"). Other adverbs reflect various case endings, as for example σήμερον ("today" = accusative singular). Many adverbs, however, are of diverse forms that must be learned by observation.

91. μέν and δέ

The conjunctions μέν and δέ are often used to express contrast. In this case, μέν means something like "on the one hand," while δέ means something like "on the other hand." Note, for example, 1 Corinthians 1:12: ἐγὼ μέν εἰμι Παύλου, ἐγὼ δὲ Ἀπολλῶ, "I, on the one hand, am of Paul; I, on the other hand, am of Apollos." However, it is often best to leave μέν untranslated and to translate δέ by "but" (e.g., "I am of Paul, but I am of Apollos"). The μέν . . . δέ construction is unusually frequent in the epistle to the Hebrews, where contrast is an essential element in the author's argument (cf. 1:7; 3:5; 9:6; 10:11; 11:15).

μέν and δέ can also be used with the plural definite article to express "some . . . others." A New Testament example is Acts 14:4: οἱ μὲν ἦσαν σὺν τοῖς Ἰουδαίοις, οἱ δὲ σὺν τοῖς ἀποστόλοις, "Some were with the Jews; others were with the apostles."

92. Vocabulary

a. Perfect middle/passive indicative principal parts (translations are of the *passive* voice).

βέβλημαι	*I have been thrown*
βεβάπτισμαι	*I have been baptized*
ἔγνωσμαι	*I have been known*
γέγραμμαι	*I have been written*
λέλυμαι	*I have been loosed*
σέσωσμαι	*I have been saved*

b. Adverbs.

ἄχρι	*until, up to* (with gen.)
ἔτι	*still, yet*
ἕως	*until, up to* (with gen.)
καθώς	*just as, as*
καλῶς	*rightly, well* (cf. καλός)
νῦν	*now*
ὅπου	*where*
ὅτε	*when*
οὐκέτι	*no longer* (οὐκ + ἔτι)
οὐχί	*not* (emphatic form of οὐ)
σήμερον	*today* (cf. ἡμέρα)
τότε	*then*

c. Additional conjunctions.

γάρ	*for* (postpositive)
διό	*therefore*
ἤ	*or*
μὲν . . . δέ	*on the one hand . . . on the other hand* (postpositive)
οὐδέ	*and not, nor, not even* (οὐ + δέ)
οὐδὲ . . . οὐδέ	*neither . . . nor*
οὖν	*therefore, then* (postpositive)

93. Exercises

a. Read the lesson carefully. Learn by heart the paradigm of εἰμί in the future indicative. When you have completed this lesson, you may congratulate yourself. You have now covered half of this course!

b. Memorize the vocabulary to this lesson.

c. Translate the following sentences.

1. διὸ οἱ δοῦλοι λέλυνται ὑπὸ τοῦ κυρίου.

2. σήμερον βεβάπτισμαι ὑπὸ τοῦ ἀποστόλου τοῦ ἀγαθοῦ.

3. ὁ γὰρ Μεσσίας καλῶς ἔρχεται καθὼς γέγραπται περὶ αὐτοῦ ἐν ταῖς ἁγίαις γραφαῖς.

4. οὗτος οὐ βεβάπτισται εἰς τὸν Ἰησοῦν.

5. λυσόμεθα τοὺς δούλους τοὺς ἀγαθούς.

6. νῦν ἐστε ἁμαρτωλοί, ἀλλὰ τότε ἔσεσθε υἱοὶ θεοῦ.

7. οἱ δίκαιοι βλέψονται τὸν κύριον.

8. γινώσκω τὸν θεὸν καὶ ἔγνωσμαι ὑπ᾽ αὐτοῦ.

9. τὸ δαιμόνιον βέβληται ἐκ τοῦ ἀνθρώπου.

10. εἰμὶ μὲν ἁμαρτωλός, σέσωσμαι δέ.

11. οὐδὲ οἱ ἀπόστολοι διδάξονται τὴν ἀλήθειαν ὅτε ἔρχονται εἰς τὴν ἐκκλησίαν.

14

IMPERFECT MIDDLE AND PASSIVE, AORIST MIDDLE, AND PLUPERFECT MIDDLE AND PASSIVE INDICATIVE

This lesson continues our discussion of the middle and passive voices by introducing the various forms of the middle and passive in the secondary tenses.

94. The Imperfect Middle and Passive and Aorist Middle Indicative of λύω

As we have seen, Greek has separate sets of suffixes for the primary tenses and for the secondary tenses. It will be recalled that the *primary* middle/passive suffixes are -μαι, -σαι, -ται, -μεθα, -σθε, -νται (see §81). We may now give the *secondary* middle/passive suffixes:

	Singular	Plural
1.	-μην	-μεθα
2.	-σο	-σθε
3.	-το	-ντο

These suffixes are used to form the imperfect *middle* and *passive* indicative of λύω, which is given below. To facilitate comparison and contrast,

97

the first aorist *middle* indicative of λύω is also given. (The first aorist *passive* is formed on another stem and will be studied in Lesson 15.)

		Imperfect M/P	First Aorist Middle
	1.	ἐλυόμην	ἐλυσάμην
Sg.	2.	ἐλύου	ἐλύσω
	3.	ἐλύετο	ἐλύσατο
	1.	ἐλυόμεθα	ἐλυσάμεθα
Pl.	2.	ἐλύεσθε	ἐλύσασθε
	3.	ἐλύοντο	ἐλύσαντο

As with the imperfect active indicative, the imperfect middle and passive indicative is formed on the *present stem* (λυ). To this stem are added (a) the augment, (b) the connecting vowels o/ϵ, and (c) the secondary middle/passive suffixes. Notice that, in the imperfect system, one set of suffixes functions as both middle and passive, so that voice is distinguished by context alone.

The first aorist middle indicative is formed on the *first aorist active stem* (λυσα = verb stem λυ plus aoristic aspect morpheme σα). To this stem are added (a) the augment, and (b) the secondary middle/passive suffixes. *Notice that the main difference between the paradigms given above is the presence of the aoristic aspect morpheme σα in the aorist tense forms.*

Irregularities occur in the second person singular of both tenses. The form ἐλύου (imperfect) is from ἐλυεσο and is the result of the dropping of the σ and the contraction of the ϵ and o. The form ἐλύσω (first aorist) is from ἐλυσασο and is the result of the dropping of the σ of the suffix σο and the contraction of the α and o.

It will be recalled that the main difference between the *imperfect* tense and the *aorist* tense is the kind of action involved: the imperfect expresses imperfective aspect, while the aorist expresses aoristic aspect (see §15). In both tenses, past time is indicated by the past time morpheme (augment). The following chart indicates some of the possibilities for translation:

(a) ἐλυόμην (imperfect middle): "I was loosing myself"
"I was loosing for myself"
"I myself was loosing"

(b) ἐλυόμην (imperfect passive): "I was being loosed"

(c) ἐλυσάμην (aorist middle): "I loosed myself"
"I loosed for myself"
"I myself loosed"

Since the imperfect tense is built upon the present stem (derived from the first principal part), verbs that are deponent in the present tense will also be deponent in the imperfect tense. Thus ἔρχομαι ("I am coming") becomes ἠρχόμην ("I was coming"); πορεύομαι ("I am going") becomes ἐπορευόμην ("I was going"); etc. Similarly, γίνομαι has the 2 aor. form ἐγενόμην.

95. The Second Aorist Middle Indicative of λείπω

The second aorist middle indicative, like the second aorist active (see §52), is formed on the second aorist stem (derived from the third principal part). The second aorist middle indicative is conjugated exactly like the imperfect middle indicative, with the important exception that the second aorist is formed on the second aorist stem, while the imperfect is formed on the present stem. The second aorist middle indicative of λείπω is given below:

	Singular	Plural
1.	ἐλιπόμην	ἐλιπόμεθα
2.	ἐλίπου	ἐλίπεσθε
3.	ἐλίπετο	ἐλίποντο

On the translation of the aorist middle, see §94 above.

96. The Pluperfect Middle and Passive Indicative of λύω

The middle and passive voices of the pluperfect tense are identical. The pluperfect middle and passive is formed on the perfect middle stem (derived from the fifth principal part). To this reduplicated stem (λελυ) are added (a) the augment, and (b) the secondary middle/passive suffixes. As with the pluperfect active indicative (see §73), the augment is optional. The pluperfect middle and passive indicative of λύω is given below:

	Singular	Plural
1.	ἐλελύμην	ἐλελύμεθα
2.	ἐλέλυσο	ἐλέλυσθε
3.	ἐλέλυτο	ἐλέλυντο

As a middle, ἐλελύμην may be translated "I had loosed myself," "I had loosed for myself," "I myself had loosed," etc. As a passive, ἐλελύμην should be rendered "I had been loosed."

97. Vocabulary

Additional adverbs.

ἀμήν	*truly (Amen)*
ἀξίως	*worthily (cf. ἄξιος)*
ἐγγύς	*near*
ἐκεῖ	*there, in that place*
εὐθύς	*immediately, at once* (also appears as εὐθέως)
ἔξω	*outside (cf. ἐκ)*
οὕτως	*thus, in this manner* (cf. οὗτος)
πάντοτε	*always*
πότε	*when?*
ὧδε	*here, in this place*

98. Exercises

a. Read the lesson carefully. Learn by heart the secondary middle suffixes (§94). Review the paradigms in this lesson.

b. Memorize the vocabulary to this lesson.

c. Translate the following sentences.

1. οἱ γὰρ λόγοι τοῦ προφήτου ἐγράφοντο ἐν τῷ βιβλίῳ.

2. ἐκεῖ αἱ γραφαὶ τῶν ἀποστόλων ἠκούοντο ὑπὸ τῶν ἁμαρτωλῶν.

3. ἐν ἐκείναις ταῖς ἡμέραις καλῶς ἐδιδασκόμεθα ὑπὸ τῶν μαθητῶν τοῦ κυρίου.

4. τότε ἐξεπορεύετο ὁ ὄχλος πρὸς τὸν κύριον, νῦν δὲ οὐκέτι βλέπει αὐτόν.

5. τὰ δαιμόνια πάντοτε ἐξεβάλλετο ἐν τῷ λόγῳ τοῦ κυρίου.

6. οἱ ὄχλοι ἐξήρχοντο ἐκ τῆς ἐρήμου καὶ εἰσήρχοντο εἰς τὴν ἐκκλησίαν.

7. εὐθὺς οἱ μαθηταὶ ἐλύσαντο τοὺς δούλους τοῦ δικαίου ἀνθρώπου.

8. ἐλάβοντο οἱ ἀπόστολοι ἄρτον καὶ καρπὸν ἀπὸ τῶν μαθητῶν.

9. εἰδόμεθα τὸν κύριον καὶ ἐπιστεύσαμεν ἐν αὐτῷ.

10. ὧδε ἐλέλυντο οἱ δοῦλοι ὑπὸ τοῦ ἀγαθοῦ.

11. οὗτοι μὲν ἐγένοντο μαθηταὶ τοῦ κυρίου, ἐκεῖνοι δὲ ἔτι ἦσαν ἁμαρτωλοί.

12. ὁ κύριος ἦν ἐγγύς, ἀλλ᾽ οὐκ ἐβλέπετο ὑπὸ τῶν μαθητῶν αὐτοῦ.

15

AORIST AND FUTURE PASSIVE INDICATIVE

Both the aorist passive indicative and the future passive indicative are formed on the aorist passive stem. As in the active voice, Greek has both first and second aorist passives. These forms are introduced in this lesson.

99. The First Aorist Passive Indicative of λύω

The first aorist passive indicative of λύω is given below:

	Singular		Plural	
1.	ἐλύθην	I was loosed	ἐλύθημεν	we were loosed
2.	ἐλύθης	you were loosed	ἐλύθητε	you were loosed
3.	ἐλύθη	he was loosed	ἐλύθησαν	they were loosed

The forms of the first aorist passive indicative are obtained by (a) augmenting the present stem, (b) adding the *passive voice morpheme* θε (which is lengthened to θη throughout the conjugation), and (c) adding the secondary *active* endings -ν, -ς, none, -μεν, -τε, -σαν (see §48). The first person singular form ἐλύθην is the *sixth principal part*. The full principal parts of λύω have now been introduced: λύω, λύσω, ἔλυσα, λέλυκα, λέλυμαι, ἐλύθην.

As to function, the aorist passive indicative expresses undefined action received by the subject in past time. Compare the imperfect ἐλυόμην ("I was being loosed") with the aorist ἐλύθην ("I was loosed"). The ancient Christian hymn enshrined in 1 Timothy 3:16 provides a striking example of the aorist passive indicative:

"Ὅς   ἐφανερώθη ἐν σαρκί,

ἐδικαιώθη ἐν πνεύματι,

ὤφθη ἀγγέλοις.

ἐκηρύχθη ἐν ἔθνεσιν,

ἐπιστεύθη ἐν κόσμῳ,

ἀνελήμφθη ἐν δόξῃ.

"Who   **was manifested** in the flesh,

was vindicated in the spirit,

was seen by angels,

was proclaimed among the nations,

was believed in the world,

was received up in glory."

100. The Second Aorist Passive Indicative of γράφω

The second aorist passive indicative of γράφω is given below:

	Singular		Plural	
1.	ἐγράφην	*I was written*	ἐγράφημεν	*we were written*
2.	ἐγράφης	*you were written*	ἐγράφητε	*you were written*
3.	ἐγράφη	*he was written*	ἐγράφησαν	*they were written*

It will be observed that the θ, which is characteristic of the first aorist passive, is not found in the second aorist passive. Otherwise the endings of the two aorists are identical, as are their functions.

It is not possible to predict whether a verb will have a second aorist passive or a first aorist passive. The second aorist passive must simply be learned as an irregular principal part.

101. The First Future Passive Indicative of λύω

The first future passive indicative of λύω is given below:

	Singular		Plural	
1.	λυθήσομαι	*I will be loosed*	λυθησόμεθα	*we will be loosed*
2.	λυθήση	*you will be loosed*	λυθήσεσθε	*you will be loosed*
3.	λυθήσεται	*he will be loosed*	λυθήσονται	*they will be loosed*

The forms of the first future passive indicative are obtained from the sixth principal part (i.e., the aorist passive) by (a) removing the augment, (b) dropping the final ν, (c) adding the future time morpheme σ to this base, and (d) adding the primary middle/passive endings along with the ο/ε connecting vowels. Thus, from ἐλύθην we obtain λυθήσομαι by removing the augment (λυθην), dropping the ν (λυθη), adding σ (λυθησ), and then adding the first person singular primary middle/passive ending μαι with an ο connecting vowel (λυθήσομαι).

In function, the future passive indicative expresses action received by the subject in future time. Context and usage alone will determine whether the kind of action is aoristic or imperfective (see §15).

102. The Second Future Passive Indicative of γράφω

The second future passive indicative of γράφω is given below:

	Singular		Plural	
1.	γραφήσομαι	*I will be written*	γραφησόμεθα	*we will be written*
2.	γραφήση	*you will be written*	γραφήσεσθε	*you will be written*
3.	γραφήσεται	*he will be written*	γραφήσονται	*they will be written*

Like the first future passive, the forms of the second future passive indicative are obtained from the sixth principal part of the verb. If a verb has a second aorist passive, its future passive also has no θ.

103. Irregular Passive Forms

In the first aorist passive, as well as in the first future passive, the addition of θε (θη) to the stem causes certain phonological changes when the stem ends in a consonant. These modifications, analogous to those discussed in connection with the future and the aorist active indicative (§§20, 50), may be summarized as follows:

$$\kappa, \gamma, \chi + \theta = \chi\theta$$
$$\pi, \beta, \phi + \theta = \phi\theta$$
$$\tau, \delta, \theta + \theta = \sigma\theta$$

Note the following examples:

Lexical Form	Stem	Aorist Passive	Future Passive
ἄγω (I lead)	ἀγ	ἤχθην	ἀχθήσομαι
βαπτίζω (I baptize)	βαπτιδ	ἐβαπτίσθην	βαπτισθήσομαι
πείθω (I trust in)	πειθ	ἐπείσθην	πεισθήσομαι

104. Vocabulary

a. First aorist passive indicative principal parts.

ἤχθην	*I was led*
ἠκούσθην	*I was heard*
ἐβλήθην	*I was thrown*
ἐβαπτίσθην	*I was baptized*
ἐγενήθην	*I became* (deponent)
ἐγνώσθην	*I was known*
ἐδιδάχθην	*I was taught*
ἐδοξάσθην	*I was glorified*
ἡτοιμάσθην	*I was prepared*
ἐκηρύχθην	*I was preached*
ἐλήμφθην	*I was taken, I was received*
ἐλείφθην	*I was left*
ἐπείσθην	*I was trusted in*
ἐπέμφθην	*I was sent*
ἐπορεύθην	*I went* (deponent)
ἐσώθην	*I was saved*
ὤφθην	*I was seen* (from ὁράω; see §127)

b. Second aorist passive indicative principal parts.

ἀπεστάλην   *I was sent* (from ἀποστέλλω; see §127)

ἐγράφην   *I was written*

105. Exercises

a. Read the lesson carefully. Carefully note how the passive voice morpheme is used in the paradigms.

b. Memorize the vocabulary to this lesson.

c. Translate the following sentences.

1. οἱ μαθηταὶ ἐδιδάχθησαν ὑπὸ τῶν ἀποστόλων τοῦ κυρίου.

2. οἱ λόγοι τῶν προφητῶν ἐγράφησαν ἐν ταῖς γραφαῖς.

3. ἐπέμφθησαν οἱ ἀπόστολοι εἰς τὸν κόσμον.

4. διὰ τῆς ἀγάπης τοῦ θεοῦ ὁ ἁμαρτωλὸς ἐσώθη καὶ ἐγενήθη μαθητὴς τοῦ κυρίου.

5. τὸ εὐαγγέλιον ἐκηρύχθη ἐν τῷ κόσμῳ.

6. εἰσήλθομεν εἰς τὴν ἐκκλησίαν καὶ ἐβαπτίσθημεν.

7. ἐν ἐκείνῃ τῇ ἡμέρᾳ ἀκουσθήσεται ὁ λόγος τοῦ θεοῦ.

8. εἴδομεν τὸν κύριον καὶ ὤφθημεν ὑπ' αὐτοῦ.

9. ἐδιδάξατε τὰ τέκνα, ἐδιδάχθητε δὲ ὑπὸ τοῦ ἀποστόλου.

10. ἐλήμφθησαν οἱ ἁμαρτωλοὶ εἰς τὸν οὐρανόν.

11. τὰ δαιμόνια ἐξεβλήθη ἐκ τῶν πονηρῶν ὑπὸ τοῦ κυρίου.

12. ἐδοξάσθη ὁ θεὸς ὑπὸ τοῦ υἱοῦ αὐτοῦ, καὶ δοξασθήσεται ὑφ' ἡμῶν.

13. ἑτοιμασθήσονται ἡμῖν σωτηρία, χαρά, καὶ εἰρήνη ἐν οὐρανῷ.

14. φωνὴ ἠκούσθη ἐν τῇ ἐρήμῳ καὶ ἀκουσθήσεται ἐν τῇ γῇ.

15. ἀπεστάλησαν οἱ ἄγγελοι εἰς τὸν κόσμον.

16

REVIEW OF THE INDICATIVE MOOD

All the tenses and voices of the indicative mood have now been introduced. This lesson reviews the inflections learned thus far and provides a basis for the description of the inflections that remain to be discussed in the other moods.

106. Review of Verb Morphology

Much of your work in the past fifteen lessons has consisted of learning the various inflections that can occur in the Greek verb and the difference that is made to the meaning of the verb by inflecting it. We have seen that Greek verbs consist of a number of parts, each of which conveys a particular unit of meaning. Each such part is called a *morpheme*, and each morpheme is described according to the information it conveys. For example, λυ is classified as a lexical morpheme because it carries the lexical or dictionary meaning of the verb λύω. On the other hand, the prefix ἐ is classified as a grammatical or inflectional morpheme because it conveys information about the word's grammatical meaning—in this case that the action occurred in past time. Such prefixes and suffixes indicate the function of the word in each particular sentence where it is used.

The significance of inflectional morphemes can be illustrated by comparing them to a locomotive picking up boxcars in a freightyard. The locomotive is the lexical morpheme; the boxcars are the various grammatical morphemes, each carrying a particular load of meaning. To get the meaning conveyed by the entire train (verb form), we have to unload all the boxcars (morphemes). Likewise, to understand a Greek verb form, we must "unload" the meaning of each individual morpheme, since each morpheme carries its own piece of information.

In this lesson we will review the verb morphemes learned thus far, introducing new concepts only as necessary. The identification of the morphemes in any given form of a Greek verb is called *morphological analysis*. Morphological analysis allows us to obtain the significance of each morpheme and thus to understand the significance of the verb form. The morphemes encountered to this point may be classified as lexical morphemes, past time morphemes, perfective reduplication morphemes, passive voice morphemes, future time morphemes, aspect morphemes, final morphemes, and prepositional prefix morphemes.

(1) Every Greek verb contains a *lexical morpheme*, or verb stem, that carries the fundamental meaning of the word. The lexical morpheme may or may not be identical with the verb *root*—the basic nucleus upon which all the other forms of that verb are based. In the case of λύω, a regular verb, the stem λυ remains the same throughout the entire conjugation of the verb. Other verbs, such as γινώσκω, are irregular and can be mastered only by learning their principal parts. In Greek, the lexical morpheme of a verb is always a "bound" form because it cannot exist without a grammatical or inflectional morpheme attached to it. Hence the *lexical form* of a Greek verb is given in the present active indicative, first person singular (e.g., ἀκούω, βλέπω, γινώσκω).

The lexical morpheme is inherently either imperfective or aoristic. For imperfective stems such as λυ, an aoristic aspect morpheme is added in forming the aorist; for aoristic stems such as βαλ, an imperfective aspect morpheme is added in forming the present (see #6 below).

(2) The *past time morpheme*, or augment, indicates that the action of the verb refers to past time. The augment has several allomorphs: the syllabic augment (e.g., λύω, imperfect ἔλυον), the temporal augment (e.g., ἀκούω, imperfect ἤκουον), and the zero augment (e.g., εἰρηνεύω, imperfect εἰρήνευον). The augment is the only purely temporal element in the Greek verb system.

(3) Perfective aspect is indicated by *perfective reduplication*. Perfective reduplication usually involves the repetition of the initial consonant of the verb stem plus the vowel ε (e.g., λύω, perfect λέλυκα). Sometimes the reduplication takes the form of the syllabic augment (e.g., ζητέω, perfect ἐζήτηκα), the temporal augment (e.g., ἐλπίζω, perfect ἤλπικα), or the zero morpheme (e.g., ὑστερέω, perfect ὑστέρηκα). Perfective reduplication reflects an effort to express the idea of *completed* or *perfective* aspect in the Greek verb. Perfective reduplication is not, however, the only way that a Greek verb can show perfective aspect (see #6 below).

(4) The *passive voice morpheme* θє (θη) indicates that the verb is in the passive voice. This morpheme is usually aorist (e.g., ἐλύθην) but can be switched to the future passive if followed by the future time morpheme σ (e.g., λυθήσομαι).

(5) When the *future time morpheme* is present in a verb, it indicates that the action of the verb refers to future time. This morpheme contains several allomorphs. For most Greek verbs, the future stem is formed by adding σ to the present stem (as in λύσω). When, however, the present stem ends in a consonant, amalgamation takes place (e.g., πέμπω, future πέμψω).

(6) Greek verbs are capable of showing kind of action by means of certain *aspect morphemes*. *Aoristic* aspect is indicated by the addition of the *aoristic aspect morpheme* σα to the stem of the word (e.g., ἔλυσα). *Perfective* aspect is indicated by the addition of the *perfective aspect morpheme* κα to the verb stem (e.g., λέλυκα). This latter morpheme is found only in the active voice. In the middle and passive voices, perfective aspect is indicated by perfective reduplication alone (e.g., λέλυμαι). For *imperfective* verb stems, there is no *imperfective* aspect morpheme in Greek. Thus in the paradigm of λύω no morpheme is added to the verb to indicate imperfective aspect in the present and future tenses since the stem λυ is inherently imperfective. Instead, the *neutral morpheme* is used. The neutral morpheme is always o or є—o when the ending begins with μ or ν (e.g., λύομεν), є in all other cases (e.g., λύετє). If, however, a verb is inherently aoristic and an imperfective form is required, an *imperfective aspect morpheme* will be added. Most second aorist verbs are inherently aoristic and need to add an imperfective aspect morpheme to form the present tense. In the case of βάλλω, for example, this imperfective morpheme is the second λ (called an *infix*) that is added to the verb stem βαλ. Similarly, the verb μανθάνω (verb stem μαθ) contains two imperfective morphemes: the infix ν before the θ, and the additive morpheme αν. In some verbs an ι is inserted into the verb stem to form the present tense (e.g., βαίνω, verb stem βαν).

(7) Every verb must, of course, have an ending or a *final morpheme*. If the verb is indicative, subjunctive, imperative, or optative, this ending will be a *person-number suffix*. The person-number suffix has a wide range of forms and allomorphs (see §108 below). Person-number suffixes normally also indicate voice: -μεν, for example, indicates active voice, while -μεθα indicates middle or passive voice. Other person-number suffixes indicate past time or non-past time: -ντο is past time, while -νται is non-

past time (present or future). A morpheme that conveys multiple pieces of information is called a *multiple morpheme*.

(8) Finally, a large number of New Testament verbs are compound verbs—words composed of a simplex verb and a preposition that has been added to it. A compound verb is said to have a *prepositional prefix morpheme*.

In sum, there are altogether eight categories of morphemes that can occur in the indicative verb. The places where these morphemes can occur are called *morpheme slots*. The following selection of forms from λύω will help to illustrate these slots.

Verb	Prefix	Past	Perfective	Lexical	Passive	Future	Aspect	Final
λύομεν				λυ			ο	μεν
λύσομεν				λυ		σ	ο	μεν
ἐλύομεν		ἐ		λυ			ο	μεν
ἐλύσαμεν		ἐ		λυ			σα	μεν
λελύκαμεν			λε	λυ			κα	μεν
ἐλύθημεν		ἐ		λυ	θη			μεν
λυθησόμεθα				λυ	θη	σ	ο	μεθα
καταλύομεν	κατα			λυ			ο	μεν

107. Overview of λύω Based on the First Person Singular

The inflectional character of the Greek verb is seen particularly clearly when arranged according to the first person singular. The following overview of λύω in the indicative mood will serve as a handy summary of the basic tenses and voices of λύω learned thus far.

Tense	Voice	Form	Translation
Present	Active	λύω	*I loose*
	Middle	λύομαι	*I loose myself*
	Passive	λύομαι	*I am being loosed*
Future	Active	λύσω	*I will loose*
	Middle	λύσομαι	*I will loose myself*
	Passive	λυθήσομαι	*I will be loosed*
Imperfect	Active	ἔλυον	*I was loosing*
	Middle	ἐλυόμην	*I was loosing myself*
	Passive	ἐλυόμην	*I was being loosed*
Aorist	Active	ἔλυσα	*I loosed*
	Middle	ἐλυσάμην	*I loosed myself*
	Passive	ἐλύθην	*I was loosed*
Perfect	Active	λέλυκα	*I have loosed*
	Middle	λέλυμαι	*I have loosed myself*
	Passive	λέλυμαι	*I have been loosed*
Pluperfect	Active	ἐλελύκειν	*I had loosed*
	Middle	ἐλελύμην	*I had loosed myself*
	Passive	ἐλελύμην	*I had been loosed*

108. Overview of λύω Based on Principal Parts

The following chart is organized around the respective principal parts upon which the Greek tenses are constructed. These forms are basic and must be mastered before any further progress can be made.

(1) Present Active (λύω):

		Pres. Act.	Pres. M/P	Imperf. Act.	Imperf. M/P
	1.	λύω	λύομαι	ἔλυον	ἐλυόμην
Sg.	2.	λύεις	λύῃ	ἔλυες	ἐλύου
	3.	λύει	λύεται	ἔλυε(ν)	ἐλύετο
	1.	λύομεν	λυόμεθα	ἐλύομεν	ἐλυόμεθα
Pl.	2.	λύετε	λύεσθε	ἐλύετε	ἐλύεσθε
	3.	λύουσι(ν)	λύονται	ἔλυον	ἐλύοντο

(2) Future Active (λύσω):

		Fut. Act.	Fut. Middle
	1.	λύσω	λύσομαι
Sg.	2.	λύσεις	λύσῃ
	3.	λύσει	λύσεται
	1.	λύσομεν	λυσόμεθα
Pl.	2.	λύσετε	λύσεσθε
	3.	λύσουσι(ν)	λύσονται

(3) Aorist Active (ἔλυσα):

		Aor. Act.	Aor. Middle
	1.	ἔλυσα	ἐλυσάμην
Sg.	2.	ἔλυσας	ἐλύσω
	3.	ἔλυσε(ν)	ἐλύσατο
	1.	ἐλύσαμεν	ἐλυσάμεθα
Pl.	2.	ἐλύσατε	ἐλύσασθε
	3.	ἔλυσαν	ἐλύσαντο

(4) Perfect Active (λέλυκα):

		Perf. Act.	Pluperf. Active
	1.	λέλυκα	ἐλελύκειν
Sg.	2.	λέλυκας	ἐλελύκεις
	3.	λέλυκε(ν)	ἐλελύκει
	1.	λελύκαμεν	ἐλελύκειμεν
Pl.	2.	λελύκατε	ἐλελύκειτε
	3.	λελύκασι(ν)	ἐλελύκεισαν

(5) Perfect Middle (λέλυμαι):

		Perf. M/P	Pluperf. M/P
	1.	λέλυμαι	ἐλελύμην
Sg.	2.	λέλυσαι	ἐλέλυσο
	3.	λέλυται	ἐλέλυτο
	1.	λελύμεθα	ἐλελύμεθα
Pl.	2.	λέλυσθε	ἐλέλυσθε
	3.	λέλυνται	ἐλέλυντο

(6) Aorist Passive (ἐλύθην):

		Aor. Pass.	Fut. Passive
	1.	ἐλύθην	λυθήσομαι
Sg.	2.	ἐλύθης	λυθήσῃ
	3.	ἐλύθη	λυθήσεται
	1.	ἐλύθημεν	λυθησόμεθα
Pl.	2.	ἐλύθητε	λυθήσεσθε
	3.	ἐλύθησαν	λυθήσονται

113

109. Overview of εἰμί

		Present	Future	Imperfect
	1.	εἰμί	ἔσομαι	ἤμην
Sg.	2.	εἶ	ἔσῃ	ἦς
	3.	ἐστί(ν)	ἔσται	ἦν
	1.	ἐσμέν	ἐσόμεθα	ἦμεν
Pl.	2.	ἐστέ	ἔσεσθε	ἦτε
	3.	εἰσί(ν)	ἔσονται	ἦσαν

110. Guidelines for Verb Identification in the Indicative Mood

It is important for deciphering a verb to be able to identify all the morphemes of which it is composed. The following steps may be helpful:

(1) Check the beginning of the word for a past time morpheme or perfective reduplication. If the verb has a past time morpheme, it is either imperfect, aorist, or pluperfect. If it lacks a past time morpheme, it is either present, future, or perfect. If it has perfective reduplication, it is either perfect or pluperfect. Remember (a) to look for the past time morpheme *between* the preposition and the verb stem in compound verbs, and (b) that the past time morpheme may appear as an initial long vowel or diphthong.

(2) If the verb has both the past time morpheme and the aoristic aspect morpheme -σα- (or -σ-), it is a first aorist. Remove the past time morpheme, the aoristic aspect morpheme, and the ending, then add -ω, and you should be able to find the verb in the lexicon. If you can't, it is probably a dental stem verb and the dental has dropped out before the σ. Restore the dental (either ζ, δ, θ, or τ) until you find the word in the lexicon. Remember that some first aorists undergo amalgamation; in these instances the aoristic aspect morpheme will be disguised (e.g., ἔβλεψα).

(3) If the verb has a past time morpheme but no aoristic aspect morpheme or perfective reduplication, it is either a second aorist or an imperfect. Remove the past time morpheme and the ending, then add -ω, and if it is an imperfect you should find the word in the lexicon. If not, reattach the past time morpheme and add the first person singular ending -ον, and

see if the form is in the lexicon. If it is, the lexicon will tell you the corresponding present active indicative form.

(4) If the verb has a future time morpheme (-σ-), then it is a future. Strip off the -σ- and the ending, add -ω, and look the word up in the lexicon. Remember that some futures undergo amalgamation (e.g., βλέψω).

The following samples will illustrate the steps involved in verb identification in the indicative mood.

ἄγομεν	Remove person-number suffix
ἀγο-	Remove neutral morpheme
ἀγ-	Add -ω and look in lexicon (= ἄγω)
ἔλεγεν	Ignore movable -ν
ἐλεγε-	Remove neutral morpheme
ἐλεγ-	Remove past time morpheme
λεγ-	Add -ω and look in lexicon (= λέγω)
ἐγράψαμεν	Remove person-number suffix
ἐγραψα-	Remove aoristic aspect morpheme that has combined with either a π, φ or β to form ψ
ἐγραπ-	
or	Remove past time morpheme
ἐγραφ-	
γραπ-	
or	Add -ω and look in lexicon (= γράφω)
γραφ-	
ἐλάβετε	Remove person-number suffix
ἐλαβε-	Remove neutral morpheme
ἐλαβ-	Remove past time morpheme
λαβ-	Add -ω and look in lexicon (where λάβω does not appear); reattach augment and ending and look in lexicon (= ἔλαβον, second aorist of λαμβάνω)

111. Vocabulary

There is no new vocabulary for this lesson. This is a suitable point for a thorough review of the vocabularies you have learned thus far.

17

NOUNS OF THE THIRD DECLENSION

The third declension comprises a wide variety of stems. Hence the widest range of paradigms for different stems will be found in this declension. The third declension is to be analyzed by observing both the stem and the inflectional suffixes, which are distinctive for this declension.

112. Introducing the Third Declension

Third declension nouns are divided into classes depending on whether their stem ends in a consonant or a vowel. Consonant-stem nouns are further subdivided into paradigms by the nature of the last phoneme of the stem. Most of the paradigms of the third declension are considered regular since their forms can be predicted on the basis of regular phonological rules. Only in a small number of words are alternative ways used for handling the conjunction of stem and suffix.

Due to the great variety of their stems, third declension nouns are more difficult to master than either the first or second declension. There are, however, constant features in their endings. The genitive singular always ends in -ς (and -ος most frequently); the dative singular in -ι; the nominative, vocative, and accusative plural in -ς (and in -ες and -ας most frequently); the genitive plural in -ων; and the dative plural in -σι(ν). The most frequently encountered endings of the third declension may be conveniently summarized as follows:

		Masc./Fem.	Neuter
Sg.	N.	-ς, none	none
	G.	-ος	-ος
	D.	-ι	-ι
	A.	-α or -ν	none
Pl.	N.	-ες	-α
	G.	-ων	-ων
	D.	-σι	-σι
	A.	-ας	-α

113. Basic Paradigms of the Third Declension

Since the aim of most students is to be able to recognize (and not write) nouns of the third declension, it is not necessary to memorize all thirty or so third declension paradigms. Familiarity with the overall patterns of some basic paradigms will increase the likelihood of recognizing the case and number of most third declension nouns as they are encountered in the Greek New Testament. The vocative will not be given in this declension, since it is usually the same as the nominative.

(1) τὸ σῶμα (body), stem: σωματ-

Sg.	N.	σῶμα		σώματα
	G.	σώματος	Pl.	σωμάτων
	D.	σώματι		σώμασι(ν)
	A.	σῶμα		σώματα

(2) ἡ σάρξ (flesh), stem: **σαρκ-**

		Sg.		Pl.
	N.	σάρξ		σάρκες
Sg.	G.	σαρκός	Pl.	σαρκῶν
	D.	σαρκί		σαρξί(ν)
	A.	σάρκα		σάρκας

(3) ὁ ἄρχων (ruler), stem: **ἀρχοντ-**

	N.	ἄρχων		ἄρχοντες
Sg.	G.	ἄρχοντος	Pl.	ἀρχόντων
	D.	ἄρχοντι		ἄρχουσι(ν)
	A.	ἄρχοντα		ἄρχοντας

(4) τὸ γένος (race), stem: **γενεσ-**

	N.	γένος		γένη
Sg.	G.	γένους	Pl.	γενῶν
	D.	γένει		γένεσι(ν)
	A.	γένος		γένη

(5) ὁ βασιλεύς (king), stem: **βασιλ-ευ/ε-**

	N.	βασιλεύς		βασιλεῖς
Sg.	G.	βασιλέως	Pl.	βασιλέων
	D.	βασιλεῖ		βασιλεῦσι(ν)
	A.	βασιλέα		βασιλεῖς

(6) ἡ πόλις (city), stem: **πολ-ι/ε-**

	N.	πόλις		πόλεις
Sg.	G.	πόλεως	Pl.	πόλεων
	D.	πόλει		πόλεσι(ν)
	A.	πόλιν		πόλεις

114. More on the Third Declension

An exhaustive analysis of third declension nouns would require a treatment of greater length than is possible here. But it will be helpful to keep the following basic observations in mind:

(1) The nominative singular of third declension nouns takes various forms, and the gender of third declension nouns is not readily discernable. It is therefore necessary to learn the nominative singular, the genitive singular, the definite article, and the English definition all at once in order to have a complete knowledge of a third declension noun. It is best to memorize the nouns in the manner in which they are given in the vocabularies (e.g., ἐλπίς, ἐλπίδος, ἡ, *hope*).

(2) When σι(ν) is added to the stem to form the dative plural, the same modifications occur as in the formation of the future tense (see §20):

$$\pi, \beta, \phi + \sigma\iota(\nu) = \psi\iota(\nu)$$

$$\kappa, \gamma, \chi + \sigma\iota(\nu) = \xi\iota(\nu)$$

$$\tau, \delta, \theta + \sigma\iota(\nu) = \sigma\iota(\nu)$$

Examples:	Nom. Sg.	Gen. Sg.	Dat. Pl.
	ἐλπίς	ἐλπίδος	ἐλπίσι(ν)
	σάρξ	σαρκός	σαρξί(ν)

(3) Stems ending in αντ, εντ, or οντ delete the ντ and lengthen the remaining stem vowel:

$$\alpha\nu\tau + \sigma\iota(\nu) = \alpha\sigma\iota(\nu)$$

$$\epsilon\nu\tau + \sigma\iota(\nu) = \epsilon\iota\sigma\iota(\nu)$$

$$o\nu\tau = \sigma\iota(\nu) = ou\sigma\iota(\nu)$$

Examples:	Nom. Sg.	Gen. Sg.	Dat. Pl.
	ἄρχων	ἄρχοντος	ἄρχουσι(ν)

(4) The genitive singular ending -ος is identical to the nominative singular ending of second declension nouns (e.g., ἄνθρωπος). Where confusion between these declensions is possible, it is helpful to pay special attention to clues provided by articles or other modifiers.

Example:	ὁ ἄνθρωπος	(nominative singular)
	τοῦ ἄρχοντος	(genitive singular)

(5) As always in neuter nouns, the forms of the nominative and accusative cases are identical.

	σῶμα	σώματα
	σώματος	σωμάτων
Example:		
	σώματι	σώμασι(ν)
	σῶμα	σώματα

(6) Besides the nouns discussed above, there are a good number of third declension nouns in the New Testament that are so irregular as to defy definite classification. A few New Testament nouns have mixed declensions. Thus σάββατον ("Sabbath") has σαββάτῳ in the dative singular (second declension) but σάββασι(ν) in the dative plural (third declension). Irregular nouns of all three declensions are best treated as they are encountered in exegesis.

115. *Vocabulary*

a. Neuter nouns of the σῶμα type.

αἷμα, αἵματος, τό	*blood* (*hemat*ology)
θέλημα, θελήματος, τό	*will*
ὄνομα, ὀνόματος, τό	*name* (*onomat*opoeia)
πνεῦμα, πνεύματος, τό	*Spirit, spirit* (*pneumat*ic)
πῦρ, πυρός, τό	*fire* (*pyr*omaniac)
ῥῆμα, ῥήματος, τό	*word, saying* (*rhet*oric)
σπέρμα, σπέρματος, τό	*seed, descendant* (*sperm*)
στόμα, στόματος, τό	*mouth*
σῶμα, σώματος, τό	*body* (*somat*ic)

ὕδωρ, ὕδατος, τό   *water (hydra*tion)
φῶς, φωτός, τό   *light (phot*ography)

b. Feminine nouns of the σάρξ type.

ἐλπίς, ἐλπίδος, ἡ   *hope*
νύξ, νυκτός, ἡ   *night (noct*urnal)
σάρξ, σαρκός, ἡ   *flesh (sarc*ophagus)
χάρις, χάριτος, ἡ   *grace, favor* (cf. χαρά)
χείρ, χειρός, ἡ   *hand (chir*opractic)

c. Masculine nouns of the ἄρχων type.

αἰών, αἰῶνος, ὁ   *age (aeon;* εἰς τὸν αἰῶνα/εἰς
                          τοὺς αἰῶνας *= forever*)
ἀνήρ, ἀνδρός, ὁ   *man, husband (andr*ogenous)
ἄρχων, ἄρχοντος, ὁ   *ruler (olig*archy)
μάρτυς, μάρτυρος, ὁ   *witness (martyr)*
πατήρ, πατρός, ὁ   *father (patr*istics)

d. Neuter nouns of the γένος type.

γένος, γένους, τό   *race (genealogy)*
ἔθνος, ἔθνους, τό   *nation, Gentile (eth*nic)
ἔλεος, ἐλέους, τό   *mercy*
ἔτος, ἔτους, τό   *year*
μέρος, μέρους, τό   *part*
πλῆθος, πλήθους, τό   *multitude, crowd (pleth*ora)
σκότος, σκότους, τό   *darkness* (cf. σκοτία)
τέλος, τέλους, τό   *end (tele*ology)

e. Masculine nouns of the βασιλεύς type.

ἀρχιερεύς, ἀρχιερέως, ὁ   *high priest, chief priest*
βασιλεύς, βασιλέως, ὁ   *king* (cf. βασιλεία)
γραμματεύς, γραμματέως, ὁ *scribe, teacher of the law*
                          (cf. γράφω)
ἱερεύς, ἱερέως, ὁ   *priest (hier*archy)

121

f. Feminine nouns of the πόλις type.

ἀνάστασις, ἀναστάσεως, ἡ	*resurrection*
γνῶσις, γνώσεως, ἡ	*knowledge* (cf. γινώσκω)
δύναμις, δυνάμεως, ἡ	*power* (*dynamic*)
θλῖψις, θλίψεως, ἡ	*affliction, tribulation*
κλῆσις, κλήσεως, ἡ	*calling* (√ καλ)
κρίσις, κρίσεως, ἡ	*judgment* (*critic*)
παράκλησις, παρακλήσεως, ἡ	*encouragement, comfort* (*Paracle*te)
πίστις, πίστεως, ἡ	*faith* (cf. πιστεύω)
πόλις, πόλεως, ἡ	*city* (*metropolis*)

g. Feminine nouns of the ἄρχων type.

γυνή, γυναικός, ἡ	*woman, wife* (*gyneco*logy)
θυγάτηρ, θυγατρός, ἡ	*daughter*
μήτηρ, μητρός, ἡ	*mother* (*mater*nal)

116. Exercises

a. To be able to read New Testament Greek, all that matters is that you recognize a third declension noun when you encounter one and are able to find the word in a dictionary if you do not know its meaning. The first of these is fairly easily accomplished if you will learn by heart the basic endings of the third declension (§112) and observe how they function in the various paradigms given in this lesson. You must also have at least a passing acquaintance with the commonest nouns (in the nominative) if you want to acquire a facility in reading Greek.

b. Memorize the vocabulary to this lesson.

c. Translate the following.

1. ὁ λόγος σὰρξ ἐγένετο.

2. ὑμεῖς ἐστε τὸ φῶς τοῦ κόσμου.

3. τοῦτο ἐστι τὸ σῶμά μου.

4. οὐκ ἔχομεν ἐλπίδα ὅτι οὐ πιστεύομεν ἐν τῷ κυρίῳ.

5. ἐσώθημεν τῇ χάριτι διὰ πίστεως.

6. οὐκέτι γινώσκομεν τὸν Χριστὸν κατὰ τὴν σάρκα.

7. ἄρχων ἦλθε πρὸς τὸν Ἰησοῦν ἐν νυκτὶ καὶ ἐδιδάχθη ὑπ᾽ αὐτοῦ.

8. τὰ τέκνα ἔλαβεν ἀγαθὰ ἀπὸ τῆς μητρὸς αὐτῶν.

9. οἱ ἀρχιερεῖς καὶ οἱ γραμματεῖς ἔπεμψαν τοὺς δούλους αὐτῶν εἰς τὸ ἱερόν.

10. ὁ βασιλεὺς εἰσέρχεται εἰς τὴν πόλιν, ὁ δὲ γραμματεὺς ἐξέρχεται πρὸς τὴν ἔρημον.

11. ὁ υἱὸς τοῦ ἀνθρώπου ἕξει τὴν δύναμιν κρίσεως ἐν ἐκείνῃ τῇ ἡμέρᾳ.

12. οἱ ἱερεῖς ἔχουσι τὸν νόμον, ἀλλ᾽ οὐκ ἔχουσι τὴν ἀγάπην τοῦ θεοῦ ἐν ταῖς καρδίαις αὐτῶν.

13. ἐν τῇ ἀναστάσει οἱ ἅγιοι ἕξουσι ζωὴν καὶ εἰρήνην.

14. οἱ ἁμαρτωλοὶ ἤκουσαν τὰ ῥήματα τοῦ Χριστοῦ καὶ ἔλαβον τὸ ἔλεος αὐτοῦ.

15. τὰ ἔθνη οὐ γινώσκει τὸ θέλημα καὶ τὴν χάριν τοῦ θεοῦ.

16. ἐβάπτιζον οἱ μαθηταὶ ἐν τῷ ὀνόματι τοῦ Ἰησοῦ.

17. πονηροί εἰσιν ἐν τῷ σκότει ἁμαρτίας, πιστοὶ δὲ ἀκούουσι τοὺς λόγους τοῦ κυρίου καὶ γίνονται μαθηταὶ αὐτοῦ.

18. ἐγὼ μὲν ἐβάπτισα ὑμᾶς ἐν ὕδατι, αὐτὸς δὲ βαπτίσει ὑμᾶς ἐν τῷ πνεύματι.

19. ταῦτά ἐστι τὰ ῥήματα τοῦ ἁγίου πνεύματος.

20. ταῦτα εἶπεν ὁ ἀπόστολος περὶ τῶν ἀρχόντων τούτου τοῦ αἰῶνος.

21. ἐν ἐκείνῃ τῇ νυκτὶ τὰ ῥήματα τοῦ εὐαγγελίου ἐκηρύχθη τοῖς ἁμαρτωλοῖς.

22. μετὰ τὴν ἀνάστασιν τοῦ Χριστοῦ ὤφθησαν τὰ σώματα τῶν ἁγίων.

18

ADJECTIVES, PRONOUNS, AND NUMERALS OF THE FIRST AND THIRD DECLENSIONS

Several New Testament adjectives, pronouns, and numerals follow the third declension in the masculine and neuter and the first declension in the feminine. Others follow the third declension entirely. Common words of these types are presented in this lesson.

117. πᾶς

The adjective πᾶς, πᾶσα, πᾶν ("all") occurs a total of 1,226 times in the New Testament. The first declension feminine form πᾶσα has a sibilant stem and so follows the paradigm of δόξα (see §38). The stem of the third declension masculine and neuter forms is παντ-. The dative plural follows the rule stated in §114: αντ + σι(ν) = ασι(ν).

	Singular			Plural		
	M.	F.	N.	M.	F.	N.
N.	πᾶς	πᾶσα	πᾶν	πάντες	πᾶσαι	πάντα
G.	παντός	πάσης	παντός	πάντων	πασῶν	πάντων
D.	παντί	πάσῃ	παντί	πᾶσι(ν)	πάσαις	πᾶσι(ν)
A.	πάντα	πᾶσαν	πᾶν	πάντας	πάσας	πάντα

The following uses of πᾶς should be noted:

(1) When used in the *predicate* position, it usually means "all" (e.g., πᾶσα ἡ πόλις, "all the city"; πᾶν τὸ σῶμα, "all the body").

(2) When used in the *attributive* position, it usually means "whole" (e.g., ἡ πᾶσα πόλις, "the whole city"; τὸ πᾶν σῶμα, "the whole body").

(3) When used with an anarthrous noun, it usually means "every" in the singular (e.g., πᾶσα πόλις, "every city") and "all" in the plural (e.g., πᾶσαι πόλεις, "all cities").

(4) When standing alone, it functions as a substantive (e.g., πᾶς, "everyone"; πάντες, "all people"; πάντα, "all things").

These uses hardly exhaust the different meanings that πᾶς can have in the New Testament. Sometimes the sense of "full" or "pure" is found, as in James 1:2: Πᾶσαν χαρὰν ἡγήσασθε, "Consider it pure joy." Not a few New Testament examples exhibit hyperbole (overstatement), as in Matthew 4:24: προσήνεγκαν αὐτῷ πάντας τοὺς κακῶς ἔχοντας, "they brought to him all the sick [i.e., a great number of sick]." A particularly interesting problem arises in connection with the use of πᾶς in 2 Timothy 3:16. Scholars debate whether the words πᾶσα γραφὴ θεόπνευστος καὶ ὠφέλιμος should be rendered "All Scripture is God-breathed and profitable" or "Every God-breathed writing is also profitable." The difficulty arises partly from the meaning of πᾶσα, partly from the meaning of γραφή, and partly from the absence of the verb "is" in the Greek. If γραφή is taken in its normal sense of Holy Scripture, then the first rendering alone adequately expresses this truth. If γραφή is taken to mean writings in general, then the second rendering is both accurate and necessary. The matter is carefully discussed in the commentaries, but the clause nicely illustrates the complexity of Greek syntax and the bearing that grammar has on translation and interpretation.

118. εἷς, οὐδείς, and μηδείς

The numeral εἷς, μία, ἕν ("one") is given below. It will be observed that, unlike the prepositions εἰς ("into") and ἐν ("in"), the forms εἷς and ἕν are accented and take the rough breathing. The first declension feminine forms follow the paradigm of ἡμέρα (see §38). The masculine and neuter forms follow the paradigm of the third declension noun ἄρχων (see §113).

	Masculine	Feminine	Neuter
N.	εἷς	μία	ἕν
G.	ἑνός	μιᾶς	ἑνός
D.	ἑνί	μιᾷ	ἑνί
A.	ἕνα	μίαν	ἕν

The following examples illustrate the use of this numeral in the New Testament:

John 6:70: ἐξ ὑμῶν εἷς διάβολός ἐστιν.
"One of you is a devil."

Mark 10:8: ἔσονται οἱ δύο εἰς σάρκα μίαν.
"The two will be one flesh."

Sometimes εἷς occurs with ἕκαστος ("each"):

Eph 4:7: ἑνὶ ἑκάστῳ ἡμῶν ἐδόθη ἡ χάρις.
"To each one of us grace was given."

Declined exactly like εἷς are the pronouns οὐδείς and μηδείς ("no one," "nothing"). Οὐδείς is used with verbs in the indicative mood, while μηδείς occurs with verbs in the other moods (to be introduced). A New Testament example of οὐδείς is James 1:13: πειράζει δὲ αὐτὸς οὐδένα, "But he himself tempts no one." Since two negatives in Greek do not necessarily cancel each other out (as in English), οὐδείς and μηδείς may be used with a negative, as in Luke 4:2: οὐκ ἔφαγεν οὐδὲν ἐν ταῖς ἡμέραις ἐκείναις, "He did not eat anything [lit., He did not eat nothing] in those days."

119. πολύς and μέγας

These two irregular adjectives occur frequently enough in the New Testament to merit special attention. The feminine forms follow the declension of φωνή throughout. Πολύς ("much," plural "many," occurring 353 times) uses two stems, πολυ- and πολλο-. Μέγας ("great," occurring 194 times) also uses two stems, μεγα- and μεγαλο-. Only the underlined forms need be learned.

	Singular					
	M.	F.	N.	M.	F.	N.
N.	πολύς	πολλή	πολύ	μέγας	μεγάλη	μέγα
G.	πολλοῦ	πολλῆς	πολλοῦ	μεγάλου	μεγάλης	μεγάλου
D.	πολλῷ	πολλῇ	πολλῷ	μεγάλῳ	μεγάλῃ	μεγάλῳ
A.	πολύν	πολλήν	πολύ	μέγαν	μεγάλην	μέγα

	Plural					
	M.	F.	N.	M.	F.	N.
N.	πολλοί	πολλαί	πολλά	μεγάλοι	μεγάλαι	μεγάλα
G.	πολλῶν	πολλῶν	πολλῶν	μεγάλων	μεγάλων	μεγάλων
D.	πολλοῖς	πολλαῖς	πολλοῖς	μεγάλοις	μεγάλαις	μεγάλοις
A.	πολλούς	πολλάς	πολλά	μεγάλους	μεγάλας	μεγάλα

Note the following New Testament examples of πολύς:

Mark 1:34: δαιμόνια πολλὰ ἐξέβαλεν.
"He cast out many demons."

Matt 14:14: εἶδεν πολὺν ὄχλον.
"He saw a great crowd."

The masculine plural of πολύς may also be used substantivally:

Mark 13:6: πολλοὶ ἐλεύσονται ἐπὶ τῷ ὀνόματί μου.
"Many will come in my name."

120. ἀληθής

The adjective ἀληθής, ἀληθές ("true") is declined according to the third declension in the feminine as well as the masculine and neuter. Its declension is given below (cf. γένος):

	Singular		Plural	
	M./F.	N.	M./F.	N.
N.	ἀληθής	ἀληθές	ἀληθεῖς	ἀληθῆ
G.	ἀληθοῦς	ἀληθοῦς	ἀληθῶν	ἀληθῶν
D.	ἀληθεῖ	ἀληθεῖ	ἀληθέσι(ν)	ἀληθέσι(ν)
A.	ἀληθῆ	ἀληθές	ἀληθεῖς	ἀληθῆ

121. Comparison of Adjectives

Adjectives in Greek have three degrees: positive ("hard," "beautiful," "good"), comparative ("harder," "more beautiful," "better"), and superlative ("hardest," "most beautiful," "best"). To give the three degrees of an adjective is to *compare* it. Some adjectives in English compare regularly ("hard," "beautiful") and some irregularly ("good"). The same applies in Greek. With regular adjectives, the following forms are used:

Comparative: -τερος, -α, -ον
Superlative: -τατος, -η, -ον

These endings are added to the masculine stem of the positive degree of the adjective, and the resulting forms are declined like a regular adjective of the second (masculine and neuter) and first (feminine) declensions. Occasionally the o of the stem of the positive adjective is lengthened to ω in the comparative and superlative (see σοφός below). The following examples show the formation of the comparative and superlative degrees of some common Greek adjectives:

Positive	Comparative	Superlative
δίκαιος (righteous)	δικαιότερος (more righteous)	δικαιότατος (most righteous)
ἰσχυρός (strong)	ἰσχυρότερος (stronger)	ἰσχυρότατος (strongest)
νέος (new)	νεώτερος (newer)	νεώτατος (newest)
σοφός (wise)	σοφώτερος (wiser)	σοφώτατος (wisest)

To these may be added some very common irregular comparatives:

Positive	Comparative
ἀγαθός (good)	κρείσσων (better)
κακός (bad)	χείρων (worse)
μέγας (great)	μείζων (greater)
πολύς (much)	πλείων (more)

As in English, adjectives in Greek may be used to express a comparison between two or more substantives. In comparisons in English, we must place "than" after the comparative adjective: "he is stronger than his brother." Comparisons in Greek are expressed (1) by placing the noun or pronoun with which the comparison is made in the genitive case, as in John 13:16: οὐκ ἔστιν δοῦλος μείζων τοῦ κυρίου αὐτοῦ, "A slave is not greater than his lord"; this use is called the *genitive of comparison* and requires the English "than" to be supplied; or (2) by the particle ἤ ("than") and a noun or pronoun in the same case, as in John 3:19: ἠγάπησαν οἱ ἄνθρωποι μᾶλλον τὸ σκότος ἢ τὸ φῶς, "Men loved the darkness more than the light."

It should be noted that Greek comparatives and superlatives are not always to be understood as meaning "more of x" and "most of x." The comparative form is often used with a *superlative* function, as in 1 Corinthians 13:13: μείζων δὲ τούτων ἡ ἀγάπη, "But the greatest [lit. greater] of these is love." On the other hand, the superlative is often used in an *elative* sense, meaning "very" or "exceedingly," as in 2 Peter 1:4: τὰ τίμια καὶ μέγιστα ἡμῖν ἐπαγγέλματα δεδώρηται, "He has granted to us precious and exceedingly great [lit., greatest] promises."

122. Vocabulary

a. Adjectives, pronouns, and numerals of the first and third declensions.

ἅπας, ἅπασα, ἅπαν	each, every, all, whole (intensive form of πᾶς)
εἷς, μία, ἕν	one (henotheism)
μέγας, μεγάλη, μέγα	great, large (megaphone)

μηδείς, μηδεμία, μηδέν *no one, none, nothing, no* (with non-indicative moods)

οὐδείς, οὐδεμία, οὐδέν *no one, none, nothing, no* (with indicative mood)

πᾶς, πᾶσα, πᾶν *each, every, all, whole* (pan*oply*)

πολύς, πολλή, πολύ *much, many* (poly*theistic*)

b. Adjectives and numerals of the third declension.

ἀληθής, ἀληθές	*true* (cf. ἀλήθεια)
δύο	*two* (dat. δυσί [ν]; otherwise indeclinable)
δώδεκα	*twelve*
μείζων, μεῖζον	*greater, larger*
πέντε	*five* (Penta*gon*)
τέσσαρες, τέσσαρα	*four*
τρεῖς, τρία	*three*

123. Exercises

a. There are no new paradigms to be learned in this lesson. Instead, read the lesson carefully, noting the various uses of the adjectives given.

b. Memorize the vocabulary to this lesson.

c. Beginning with this lesson, all of your translation exercises will be taken directly from the Greek New Testament. In many cases only a part of the verse is set out to be translated, and in some cases the original sentences had to be altered slightly for purposes of simplification. You may be assured, however, that the thought and expressions are those of the original authors. Words and forms not yet encountered are explained in parentheses.

As you translate these passages, follow these simple instructions:

(1) Translate what is there, not what you may have memorized from an English translation. Try not to omit anything that is in the Greek or add anything into English, unless English idiom requires it. This means that at times your translation will be stilted, but it is desirable at this stage to convey what is being said in the Greek. As your familiarity with the language increases, it will be possible to produce a smoother and more idiomatic English translation.

(2) Be especially sensitive to the syntactical structure of your text. Note such matters as the presence or absence of the article, word order, verbal aspect, and the like. Learn something about the *style* of your author as you are translating.

(3) Once you have produced your own translation, feel free to check your conclusions against those in your commentaries and English translations. On the other hand, do not quit thinking for yourself. You will learn best by using these resources *critically*.

1. πάντες γὰρ ἥμαρτον καὶ ὑστεροῦνται (fall short) τῆς δόξης τοῦ θεοῦ (Rom 3:23).

2. τὰ πάντα δι' αὐτοῦ καὶ εἰς αὐτὸν ἔκτισται (have been created), καὶ αὐτός ἐστιν πρὸ πάντων (Col 1:16–17).

3. καὶ γὰρ ἐν ἑνὶ πνεύματι ἡμεῖς πάντες εἰς ἓν σῶμα ἐβαπτίσθημεν (1 Cor 12:13).

4. πάντες γὰρ ὑμεῖς εἷς ἐστε ἐν Χριστῷ Ἰησοῦ (Gal 3:28).

5. σὺ πιστεύεις ὅτι εἷς ἐστιν ὁ θεός; καλῶς ποιεῖς (you do). καὶ τὰ δαιμόνια πιστεύουσιν καὶ φρίσσουσιν (tremble) (Jas 2:19).

6. καὶ γὰρ τὸ σῶμα οὐκ ἔστιν ἓν μέλος (member) ἀλλὰ πολλά (1 Cor 12:14).

7. χαρὰν γὰρ πολλὴν ἔσχον καὶ παράκλησιν ἐπὶ τῇ ἀγάπῃ σου (Phlm 7).

8. καὶ εἶδον, καὶ ἤκουσα φωνὴν ἀγγέλων πολλῶν (Rev 5:11).

9. καὶ πολλοὶ τῶν ἀνθρώπων ἀπέθανον ἐκ τῶν ὑδάτων (Rev 8:11).

10. ὁ Ἰησοῦς εἶπεν αὐτῇ, Ὦ (O) γύναι, μεγάλη σου ἡ πίστις (Matt 15:28).

11. αὕτη ἐστὶν ἡ μεγάλη καὶ πρώτη ἐντολή (Matt 22:38).

12. οὗτος ἔσται μέγας καὶ υἱὸς ὑψίστου (of the Highest) κληθήσεται (will be called) (Luke 1:32).

13. καὶ εἶπεν αὐτοῖς ὁ ἄγγελος, εὐαγγελίζομαι ὑμῖν χαρὰν μεγάλην ἥτις (that) ἔσται παντὶ τῷ λαῷ (Luke 2:10).

14. τὸ μυστήριον τοῦτο μέγα ἐστίν, ἐγὼ δὲ λέγω εἰς Χριστὸν καὶ τὴν ἐκκλησίαν (Eph 5:32).

15. καὶ σημεῖον μέγα ὤφθη ἐν τῷ οὐρανῷ (Rev 12:1).

16. λέγει αὐτῷ ὁ Ἰησοῦς, Ἐγώ εἰμι ἡ ὁδὸς καὶ ἡ ἀλήθεια καὶ ἡ ζωή. οὐδεὶς ἔρχεται πρὸς τὸν πατέρα εἰ μὴ (except) δι᾽ ἐμοῦ (John 14:6).

17. βλέπετε (consider) γὰρ τὴν κλῆσιν (calling) ὑμῶν, ἀδελφοί, ὅτι οὐ πολλοὶ σοφοὶ κατὰ σάρκα (1 Cor 1:26).

18. διὰ τοῦτο ἐν ὑμῖν πολλοὶ ἀσθενεῖς (weak) (1 Cor 11:30).

19. καὶ πολλοὶ ἦλθον πρὸς αὐτὸν καὶ ἔλεγον ὅτι Ἰωάννης σημεῖον ἐποίησεν (did) οὐδέν (John 10:41).

20. μετὰ δὲ πολὺν χρόνον ἔρχεται ὁ κύριος τῶν δούλων ἐκείνων (Matt 25:19).

19

CONTRACT AND LIQUID VERBS

As noted in Lesson 3, there are two major conjugations in Greek: the -ω conjugation and the -μι conjugation. Contract verbs form a special class of the -ω conjugation. Contract verbs are introduced in this lesson, along with a unique but related class of verbs called liquid verbs.

124. The Present and Imperfect Tenses of Contract Verbs

Greek contains many verbs whose stems end in a short vowel (-α, -ε, or -o). When the connecting vowels o/ε used in the formation of the present and imperfect tenses are added to this stem, the two vowels combine and form either a long vowel or a diphthong. Thus, for example, φιλε + ετε becomes φιλεῖτε ("you love"). This process is called *contraction*, and verbs that are formed in this way are called *contract verbs*. These contractions take place in accordance with specific *rules of contraction*:

Rules of Contraction	Example
α + E-sound (ε or η) = α	τιμα + ετε = τιμᾶτε
α + O sound (o, ω, or ου) = ω	τιμα + ομεν = τιμῶμεν
α + any combination with ι = ᾳ	τιμα + ει = τιμᾷ
ε + ε = ει	φιλε + ετε = φιλεῖτε
ε + o = ου	φιλε + ομεν = φιλοῦμεν

Rules of Contraction (continued)	Example
ε before any long vowel or diphthong drops out	φιλε + ει = φιλεῖ
ο + long vowel = ω	δηλο + ω = δηλῶ
ο + short vowel or ου = ου	δηλο + ομεν = δηλοῦμεν
ο + any combination with ι = οι	δηλο + ει = δηλοῖ

The paradigms of τιμάω ("I honor"), φιλέω ("I love"), and δηλόω ("I show") are set forth below, showing the uncontracted forms in parentheses. The person-number suffixes are those already studied in connection with λύω. It should be noted that Greek-English dictionaries always give the first person singular of a contract verb in its *uncontracted* form so that its conjugation may be recognized at once. However, no uncontracted form ever occurs in the Greek New Testament.

		Present Active Indicative		
Sg.	1.	τιμῶ (ά-ω)	φιλῶ (έ-ω)	δηλῶ (ό-ω)
	2.	τιμᾷς (ά-εις)	φιλεῖς (έ-εις)	δηλοῖς (ό-εις)
	3.	τιμᾷ (ά-ει)	φιλεῖ (έ-ει)	δηλοῖ (ό-ει)
Pl.	1.	τιμῶμεν (ά-ομεν)	φιλοῦμεν (έ-ομεν)	δηλοῦμεν (ό-ομεν)
	2.	τιμᾶτε (ά-ετε)	φιλεῖτε (έ-ετε)	δηλοῦτε (ό-ετε)
	3.	τιμῶσι(ν) (ά-ουσι)	φιλοῦσι(ν) (έ-ουσι)	δηλοῦσι(ν) (ό-ουσι)

Imperfect Active Indicative			
Sg.	1.	ἐτίμων (α-ον)	ἐφίλουν (ε-ον)	ἐδήλουν (ο-ον)
	2.	ἐτίμας (α-ες)	ἐφίλεις (ε-ες)	ἐδήλους (ο-ες)
	3.	ἐτίμα (α-ε)	ἐφίλει (ε-ε)	ἐδήλου (ο-ε)
Pl.	1.	ἐτιμῶμεν (ά-ομεν)	ἐφιλοῦμεν (έ-ομεν)	ἐδηλοῦμεν (ό-ομεν)
	2.	ἐτιμᾶτε (ά-ετε)	ἐφιλεῖτε (έ-ετε)	ἐδηλοῦτε (ό-ετε)
	3.	ἐτίμων (α-ον)	ἐφίλουν (ε-ον)	ἐδήλουν (ο-ον)

Present Middle and Passive Indicative			
Sg.	1.	τιμῶμαι (ά-ομαι)	φιλοῦμαι (έ-ομαι)	δηλοῦμαι (ό-ομαι)
	2.	τιμᾷ (ά-η)	φιλῇ (έ-η)	δηλοῖ (ό-η)
	3.	τιμᾶται (ά-εται)	φιλεῖται (έ-εται)	δηλοῦται (ό-εται)
Pl.	1.	τιμώμεθα (α-όμεθα)	φιλούμεθα (ε-όμεθα)	δηλούμεθα (ο-όμεθα)
	2.	τιμᾶσθε (ά-εσθε)	φιλεῖσθε (έ-εσθε)	δηλοῦσθε (ό-εσθε)
	3.	τιμῶνται (ά-ονται)	φιλοῦνται (έ-ονται)	δηλοῦνται (ό-ονται)

135

Imperfect Middle and Passive Indicative			
Sg.	1.	ἐτιμώμην (α-όμην)	ἐφιλούμην (ε-όμην)	ἐδηλούμην (ο-όμην)
	2.	ἐτιμῶ (ά-ου)	ἐφιλοῦ (έ-ου)	ἐδηλοῦ (ό-ου)
	3.	ἐτιμᾶτο (ά-ετο)	ἐφιλεῖτο (έ-ετο)	ἐδηλοῦτο (ό-ετο)
Pl.	1.	ἐτιμώμεθα (α-όμεθα)	ἐφιλούμεθα (ε-όμεθα)	ἐδηλούμεθα (ο-όμεθα)
	2.	ἐτιμᾶσθε (ά-εσθε)	ἐφιλεῖσθε (έ-εσθε)	ἐδηλοῦσθε (ό-εσθε)
	3.	ἐτιμῶντο (ά-οντο)	ἐφιλοῦντο (έ-οντο)	ἐδηλοῦντο (ό-οντο)

125. The Other Tenses of Contract Verbs

In tenses of contract verbs other than the present and imperfect, there is no contraction of stem and ending since the suffix that is added to the verb stem begins with a consonant. With very few exceptions (e.g., καλέω), in the future and aorist tenses the final vowel of the stem is lengthened (α to η, ε to η, and o to ω). In the perfect stem, the final stem vowel is similarly lengthened, the stem is reduplicated, and the regular suffixes are added. It is only necessary to study the following first person singular forms, after which any form may be deduced from λύω.

Future Active Indicative	τιμήσω	φιλήσω	δηλώσω
Future Middle Indicative	τιμήσομαι	φιλήσομαι	δηλώσομαι
Future Passive Indicative	τιμηθήσομαι	φιληθήσομαι	δηλωθήσομαι

Aorist Active Indicative	ἐτίμησα	ἐφίλησα	ἐδήλωσα
Aorist Middle Indicative	ἐτιμησάμην	ἐφιλησάμην	ἐδηλωσάμην
Aorist Passive Indicative	ἐτιμήθην	ἐφιλήθην	ἐδηλώθην

Perfect Active Indicative	τετίμηκα	πεφίληκα	δεδήλωκα
Perfect Middle Indicative	τετίμημαι	πεφίλημαι	δεδήλωμαι
Perfect Passive Indicative	τετίμημαι	πεφίλημαι	δεδήλωμαι

126. Liquid Verbs

A special type of irregularity in the Greek verb system involves verbs whose stems end in one of the so-called liquid consonants (λ, μ, ν, or ρ). In the future of liquid verbs, an ε is inserted between the liquid consonant and the future time morpheme σ. Then the σ, as usual between two vowels, is dropped, and the ε is contracted with the vowel of the ending. For example, μενῶ, the future of μένω, is formed as follows: μένσω becomes μενέσω, μενέω, and finally μενῶ.

In the first aorist of liquid verbs, the σ of the aoristic aspect morpheme σα is dropped, and the stem undergoes compensatory lengthening, as in ἤγειρα, stem ἐγερ-, or as in ἔμεινα, stem μεν-. These forms are sometimes called *asigmatic aorists* since they do not contain the characteristic σ of the first aorist.

The present stems of liquid verbs are frequently lengthened. In stems ending in λ, this lengthening generally involves the doubling of the λ, as in ἀποστέλλω, stem στελ-. In ρ stems, an ι is generally added to the stem, as in αἴρω, stem αρ-.

The most important New Testament verbs that have liquid futures and liquid first aorists are given below:

Present		Future	First Aorist
ἀγγέλλω	(I announce)	ἀγγελῶ	ἤγγειλα
αἴρω	(I take up)	ἀρῶ	ἦρα
ἀποκτείνω	(I kill)	ἀποκτενῶ	ἀπέκτεινα
ἀποστέλλω	(I send)	ἀποστελῶ	ἀπέστειλα
ἐγείρω	(I raise)	ἐγερῶ	ἤγειρα
κρίνω	(I judge)	κρινῶ	ἔκρινα
μένω	(I abide)	μενῶ	ἔμεινα
σπείρω	(I sow)	σπερῶ	ἔσπειρα

127. Vocabulary

a. Contract verbs of the τιμάω type.

ἀγαπάω	*I love* (cf. ἀγάπη)
γεννάω	*I give birth to* (genealogy; cf. γένος)
ἐπιτιμάω	*I rebuke, I warn*
ἐρωτάω	*I ask, I request*
ζάω	*I live* (dep. fut. ζήσομαι)
μεριμνάω	*I worry, I am anxious*
νικάω	*I overcome*
ὁράω	*I see* (dep. fut. ὄψομαι)
πλανάω	*I deceive, I lead astray*
τιμάω	*I honor* (Timothy, "honoring God [θεός]")

b. Contract verbs of the φιλέω type.

αἰτέω	*I ask*
ἀκολουθέω	*I follow*
ἀσθενέω	*I am weak*
βλασφημέω	*I revile, I blaspheme*
δέω	*I bind, I tie*
διακονέω	*I serve, I minister to* (cf. διακονία)
δοκέω	*I think, I seem* (docetism)
ἐπικαλέω	*I call upon*
εὐλογέω	*I bless* (eulogy)
εὐχαριστέω	*I give thanks, I thank* (with dat.; Eucharist)
ζητέω	*I seek*
θεωρέω	*I see, I perceive* (theory)
καλέω	*I call* (fut. καλέσω; 1 aor. ἐκάλεσα)
κρατέω	*I grasp, I take hold of* (plutocratic [grasping wealth])
λαλέω	*I speak* (glossalalia)
μαρτυρέω	*I testify, I bear witness* (martyr)
μετανοέω	*I repent*
μισέω	*I hate* (misogynist [a woman-hater])
οἰκοδομέω	*I build up, I edify* (cf. οἶκος)

παρακαλέω	*I urge, I exhort, I comfort* (cf. παράκλησις)
περιπατέω	*I walk (peripat*etic)
ποιέω	*I do, I make (po*et)
προσκυνέω	*I worship*
τηρέω	*I keep*
φιλέω	*I love* (cf. φίλος)
φωνέω	*I call* (cf. φωνή)

c. Contract verbs of the δηλόω type.

δηλόω	*I show*
δικαιόω	*I justify* (cf. δικαιοσύνη)
πληρόω	*I fill, I fulfill*
σταυρόω	*I crucify* (cf. σταυρός)
τελειόω	*I perfect, I complete* (cf. τέλος)
φανερόω	*I reveal*

d. Liquid verbs.

ἀγγέλλω	*I announce* (cf. ἄγγελος)
αἴρω	*I take up, I take away*
ἀναβαίνω	*I go up, I ascend*
ἀποκτείνω	*I kill*
ἀποστέλλω	*I send* (cf. ἀπόστολος)
βαίνω	*I go* (always compounded in the NT; dep. fut. βήσομαι; 2 aor. ἔβην)
ἐγείρω	*I raise*
θέλω	*I want, I will* (fut. θελήσω; 1 aor. ἠθέλησα)
καταβαίνω	*I go down, I descend*
κρίνω	*I judge* (cf. κρίσις)
μένω	*I remain, I abide (perman*ent)
σπείρω	*I sow* (cf. σπέρμα)

128. Exercises

a. Study the lesson carefully. You are not expected to memorize any paradigms. Instead, become familiar with the various contractions that take place in the present and imperfect tenses of contract verbs.

b. Memorize the vocabulary to this lesson.

c. Translate the following.

1. καὶ καλέσεις τὸ ὄνομα αὐτοῦ Ἰησοῦν, αὐτὸς γὰρ σώσει τὸν λαὸν αὐτοῦ ἀπὸ τῶν ἁμαρτιῶν αὐτῶν (Matt 1:21).

2. τί (why) δέ με καλεῖτε, κυριε, κυρίε, καὶ οὐ ποιεῖτε ἃ (what) λέγω (Luke 6:46);

3. καὶ ἀγαπήσεις κύριον τὸν θεόν σου ἐξ ὅλης (all) καρδίας σου καὶ ἐξ ὅλης τῆς ψυχῆς σου (Mark 12:30).

4. οὕτως γὰρ ἠγάπησεν ὁ θεὸς τὸν κόσμον (John 3:16).

5. ἡμεῖς ἀγαπῶμεν, ὅτι αὐτὸς πρῶτος ἠγάπησεν ἡμᾶς (1 John 4:19).

6. γράφω ὑμῖν, νεανίσκοι (young men), ὅτι νενικήκατε τὸν πονηρόν (1 John 2:13).

7. μακάριοι οἱ καθαροὶ (pure) τῇ καρδίᾳ, ὅτι αὐτοὶ τὸν θεὸν ὄψονται (Matt 5:8).

8. δικαιοσύνη γὰρ θεοῦ ἐν αὐτῷ ἀποκαλύπτεται (is being revealed) ἐκ πίστεως εἰς πίστιν, καθὼς γέγραπται, ὁ δὲ δίκαιος ἐκ πίστεως ζήσεται (Rom 1:17).

9. ἐν ἐκείνῃ τῇ ἡμέρᾳ ἐν τῷ ὀνόματί μου αἰτήσεσθε, καὶ οὐ λέγω ὑμῖν ὅτι ἐγὼ ἐρωτήσω τὸν πατέρα περὶ ὑμῶν (John 16:26).

10. Ὁ οὖν ἀρχιερεὺς ἠρώτησεν τὸν Ἰησοῦν περὶ τῶν μαθητῶν αὐτοῦ καὶ περὶ τῆς διδαχῆς αὐτοῦ (John 18:19).

11. Εὐχαριστοῦμεν τῷ θεῷ πάντοτε περὶ πάντων ὑμῶν (1 Thess 1:2).

12. αὐτὸς γὰρ ὁ πατὴρ φιλεῖ ὑμᾶς, ὅτι ὑμεῖς ἐμὲ πεφιλήκατε καὶ πεπιστεύκατε ὅτι ἐγὼ παρὰ τοῦ θεοῦ ἐξῆλθον (John 16:27).

13. ἀλλὰ τοῦτο ἔχεις, ὅτι μισεῖς τὰ ἔργα τῶν Νικολαϊτῶν (Rev 2:6).

14. ἐγὼ δέδωκα (have given) αὐτοῖς τὸν λόγον σου, καὶ ὁ κόσμος ἐμίσησεν αὐτούς, ὅτι οὐκ εἰσὶν ἐκ τοῦ κόσμου καθὼς ἐγὼ οὐκ εἰμὶ ἐκ τοῦ κόσμου (John 17:14).

15. Οἱ οὖν στρατιῶται ὅτε ἐσταύρωσαν τὸν Ἰησοῦν ἔλαβον τὰ ἱμάτια αὐτοῦ καὶ ἐποίησαν τέσσαρα μέρη (John 19:23).

16. Ἀβραὰμ ὁ πατὴρ ἡμῶν οὐκ ἐξ ἔργων ἐδικαιώθη; (Jas 2:21).

17. καὶ οὓς (those whom) ἐκάλεσεν, τούτους καὶ ἐδικαίωσεν· οὓς δὲ ἐδικαίωσεν, τούτους καὶ ἐδόξασεν (Rom 8:30).

18. οὐδὲ γὰρ ὁ πατὴρ κρίνει οὐδένα, ἀλλὰ τὴν κρίσιν πᾶσαν δέδωκεν (has given) τῷ υἱῷ (John 5:22).

19. νυνὶ δὲ μένει πίστις, ἐλπίς, ἀγάπη, τὰ τρία ταῦτα· μείζων δὲ τούτων ἡ ἀγάπη (1 Cor 13:13).

20. καὶ ἀποκτενοῦσιν αὐτόν, καὶ τῇ τρίτῃ (third) ἡμέρᾳ ἐγεθήσεται (Matt 17:23).

21. καθὼς ἐμὲ ἀπέστειλας εἰς τὸν κόσμον, κἀγὼ ἀπέστειλα αὐτοὺς εἰς τὸν κόσμον (John 17:18).

20

PARTICIPLES (VERBAL ADJECTIVES)

The Greek participle is a grammatical hybrid. As its name implies, the participle shares ("takes part" or "participates") in the nature of both a verb and an adjective, just as the infinitive (Lesson 21) shares in the characteristics of both a verb and a noun. The main uses of the participle are listed below, together with a description of how the participle is formed. This lesson is undoubtedly formidable, and an attempt to absorb it in its entirety on first reading could lead to severe indigestion. A better plan is to get a general idea of the formation of the participle, then observe its various uses. Finally, work through the examples found in §132 until translation comes easily and quickly.

129. The Nature of Greek Participles

The participle is a declinable verbal adjective. It is used to attach a verbal idea to a noun (or pronoun), as in John 4:10: "He would have given you *living* water." Here the participle translated "living" is the equivalent of an adjective, qualifying the noun "water." But the participle may also modify a verbal idea rather than a noun, and thus may exhibit predominantly verbal characteristics. An example is Matthew 2:10: "*Seeing* the star, they rejoiced." Here the participle translated "seeing" is adjectival to the extent that it qualifies "they." Yet it is verbal in that it emphasizes the action of seeing, and as a verb it takes an object ("the star"). The words "seeing the star" are, in fact, the equivalent of a clause with a main verb and could also be translated "When they saw the star" or "Because they saw the star." We will see that a Greek participle is often best translated into English by either a temporal ("when" or "while") or a causal ("because" or "since") clause.

Being adjectival, the participle in Greek is fully inflected to permit agreement of gender, number, and case. And being verbal, the participle has tense and voice. Greek has three basic tense forms of the participle: present, aorist, and perfect—that is, one for each aspect. The present participle expresses imperfective aspect, the aorist participle expresses aoristic aspect, and the perfect participle expresses perfective aspect (see §15). (The rarely used future participle need not be studied.) English, on the other hand, does not have a full complement of participles and instead uses auxiliary verbs to round out the number. The participles of the verb "love" may be set forth as follows:

Tense	Active Voice	Passive Voice
Present	loving	being loved
Past	having loved	loved

The Greek participle is used in much the same way as the English participle, but it is used more frequently and with greater flexibility. The most common participles in Greek are the present and the aorist.

130. The Formation of Greek Participles

At first sight, the formation of Greek participles may seem rather daunting; in fact, the forms already learned in connection with the three major declensions of nouns provide us with the basic inflectional patterns. Participles may be divided into two basic groups: (1) those with first and third declension endings, and (2) those with first and second declension endings. The former division may be further divided into four subgroups according to their endings, the nominative and genitive of which are given below:

Group	Masculine	Feminine	Neuter
I.	-ων	-ουσα	-ον
	-οντος	-ουσης	-οντος
II.	-σας	-σασα	-σαν
	-σαντος	-σασης	-σαντος
III.	-θεις	-θεισα	-θεν
	-θεντος	-θεισης	-θεντος

Group	Masculine	Feminine	Neuter
IV.	-κως	-κυια	-κος
	-κοτος	-κυιας	-κοτος

Although the forms of the Greek participle are spelled out in greater detail below, it is only necessary to learn the nominative and genitive singular forms of a given paradigm of the participle to be able to recognize any form of that participle. All participles decline their feminine forms in accordance with the first declension; these differ according to whether the stem ends in σ, another consonant, or a vowel. All active participles in the masculine and neuter are declined in accordance with the third declension, while the masculine and neuter of middle and passive participles follow the second declension.

(1) Participles with First and Third Declension Endings

Group I:	-ων	-ουσα	-ον
	-οντος	-ουσης	-οντος

This group includes (a) the present active participle of verbs like λύω and φιλέω, (b) the second aorist active participle of verbs like λείπω, and (c) the present participle of εἰμί. The masculine and neuter inflections follow the paradigm of ἄρχων (see §113), while the feminine inflections follow the paradigm of δόξα (see §38). (Translations given in parentheses are approximations of the general English equivalents.)

(a) The Present Active Participle of λύω ("loosing"):

	Singular		
	Masculine	**Feminine**	**Neuter**
N.	λύων	λύουσα	λῦον
G.	λύοντος	λυούσης	λύοντος
D.	λύοντι	λυούσῃ	λύοντι
A.	λύοντα	λύουσαν	λῦον

144

	Plural		
	Masculine	**Feminine**	**Neuter**
N.	λύοντες	λύουσαι	λύοντα
G.	λυόντων	λυουσῶν	λυόντων
D.	λύουσι(ν)	λυούσαις	λύουσι(ν)
A.	λύοντας	λυούσας	λύοντα

i. The stem of the present active participle for the masculine and neuter is λυοντ-. The dative plural of these genders is λύουσι(ν) (cf. ἄρχων, dative plural ἄρχουσι(ν), §113). The context must determine whether λύουσι(ν) is an indicative verb or a participle.

ii. With contract verbs ending in -εω, the rules of contraction (see §124) are applied:

φιλῶν	φιλοῦσα	φιλοῦν
φιλοῦντος	φιλούσης	φιλοῦντος
etc.		

(b) The Second Aorist Active Participle of λείπω ("having left"):

λιπών	λιποῦσα	λιπόν
λιπόντος	λιπούσης	λιπόντος
etc.		

The second aorist active participle is built on the second aorist stem. It is declined exactly like the present participle; see (a) above. It will be recalled that the augment occurs only in the indicative mood. Thus λείπω ("I leave") has the second aorist active indicative ἔλιπον ("I left") and the second aorist active participle λιπών ("having left"). Note that the second aorist stem of εἶπον ("I said") remains εἰπ- in the participle εἰπών, "having said."

(c) The Present Participle of εἰμί ("being"):

ὤν	οὖσα	ὄν
ὄντος	οὔσης	ὄντος
etc.		

The forms of the present participle of εἰμί are identical to the endings of the present active participle of λύω; see (a) above.

145

Group II:	-σας	-σασα	-σαν
	-σαντος	-σασης	-σαντος

The inflections in this group are the same as those of πᾶς, πᾶσα, πᾶν (see §117). They cover the first aorist active participle of λύω ("having loosed"):

	Singular		
	Masculine	**Feminine**	**Neuter**
N	λύσας	λύσασα	λῦσαν
G.	λύσαντος	λυσάσης	λύσαντος
D.	λύσαντι	λυσάσῃ	λύσαντι
A.	λύσαντα	λύσασαν	λῦσαν

	Plural		
N	λύσαντες	λύσασαι	λύσαντα
G.	λυσάντων	λυσασῶν	λυσάντων
D.	λύσασι(ν)	λυσάσαις	λύσασι(ν)
A.	λύσαντας	λυσάσας	λύσαντα

The first and second aorists differ only in form (see §52). Note again the absence of the augment in the aorist participle. Thus λύω ("I loose") has the first aorist active indicative ἔλυσα ("I loosed") and the first aorist active participle λύσας ("having loosed"). The σα that characterizes the first aorist system is found throughout the declension of the participle. When the σ is not found in the liquid first aorist stem, neither is it found in the participle. Thus ἀγγέλλω ("I announce") has the first aorist active indicative ἤγγειλα ("I announced") and the first aorist active participle ἄγγειλας ("having announced").

Group III:	-θεις	-θεισα	-θεν
	-θεντος	-θεισης	-θεντος

This group covers (a) the first aorist passive of verbs like λύω, and (b) the second aorist passive of verbs like γράφω:

(a) The First Aorist Passive Participle of λύω ("having been loosed"):

	Singular		
	Masculine	**Feminine**	**Neuter**
N	λυθείς	λυθεῖσα	λυθέν
G.	λυθέντος	λυθείσης	λυθέντος
D.	λυθέντι	λυθείσῃ	λυθέντι
A.	λυθέντα	λυθεῖσαν	λυθέν

	Plural		
N	λυθέντες	λυθεῖσαι	λυθέντα
G.	λυθέντων	λυθεισῶν	λυθέντων
D.	λυθεῖσι(ν)	λυθείσαις	λυθεῖσι(ν)
A.	λυθέντας	λυθείσας	λυθέντα

The first aorist passive participle is built on the sixth principal part. Thus λύω ("I loose") has the first aorist passive indicative ἐλύθην ("I was loosed") and the first aorist passive participle λυθείς ("having been loosed").

(b) The Second Aorist Passive Participle of γράφω ("having been written"):

γραφείς	γραφεῖσα	γραφέν
γραφέντος	γραφείσης	γραφέντος
etc.		

Note the absence of the θ in the second aorist passive system.

Group IV:	-κως	-κυια	-κος
	-κοτος	-κυιας	-κοτος

This group includes the perfect active participle of λύω ("having loosed"). The masculine and neuter inflections generally correspond to the paradigm of ἄρχων (see §113), while the feminine inflections follow the paradigm of ἡμέρα (see §38).

	Singular		
	Masculine	**Feminine**	**Neuter**
N.	λελυκώς	λελυκυῖα	λελυκός
G.	λελυκότος	λελυκυίας	λελυκότος
D.	λελυκότι	λελυκυίᾳ	λελυκότι
A.	λελυκότα	λελυκυῖαν	λελυκός

	Plural		
N.	λελυκότες	λελυκυῖαι	λελυκότα
G.	λελυκότων	λελυκυιῶν	λελυκότων
D.	λελυκόσι(ν)	λελυκυίαις	λελυκόσι(ν)
A.	λελυκότας	λελυκυίας	λελυκότα

Note the presence of the characteristic κ of the perfect system. In second perfects the κ is not found. Thus γράφω ("I write") has the second perfect active indicative γέγραφα ("I have written") and the second perfect active participle γεγραφώς ("having written"). The feminine in the perfect active participle, having a stem ending in ε, ι, or ρ, is declined like ἡμέρα (see §38).

(2) Participles with First and Second Declension Endings

All the participles in this group have the endings -μενος, -μενη, -μενον and follow the declension of ἀγαθός (see §43). There is no need to set out the paradigms of these participles in detail.

(a) The Present Middle and Passive Participle of λύω ("loosing oneself" or "being loosed"):

λυόμενος	λυομένη	λυόμενον
λυομένου	λυομένης	λυομένου
etc.		

(b) The First Aorist Middle Participle of λύω ("having loosed oneself"):

λυσάμενος	λυσαμένη	λυσάμενον
λυσαμένου	λυσαμένης	λυσαμένου
etc.		

(c) The Perfect Middle and Passive Participle of λύω ("having loosed oneself" or "having been loosed"):

λελυμένος   λελυμένη   λελυμένον

λελυμένου   λελυμένης   λελυμένου

etc.

(d) The Second Aorist Middle Participle of λείπω ("having left oneself"):

λιπόμενος   λιπομένη   λιπόμενον

λιπομένου   λιπομένης   λιπομένου

etc.

131. Uses of the Greek Participles

Greek participles can be used in three basic ways. These uses are best learned by observing the following model sentences:

(1) ὁ ἄνθρωπος **ὁ λέγων** ταῦτα βλέπει τὸν δοῦλον.

"The man **who is saying** these things sees the servant."

or "The man **who says** these things sees the servant."

(2) **ὁ λέγων** ταῦτα βλέπει τὸν δοῦλον.

"**The one who is saying** these things sees the servant."

or "**The man who is saying** these things sees the servant."

or "**The one who says** these things sees the servant."

(3) **λέγων** ταῦτα ὁ ἄνθρωπος βλέπει τὸν δοῦλον.

"**While saying** these things, the man sees the servant."

or "**While he is saying** these things, the man sees the servant."

or "**Saying** these things, the man sees the servant."

It is obvious that the syntactic functions of participles in Greek are similar in many ways to those of participles in English. In practice, however, participles need to be paraphrased appropriately in the light of the context.

The following discussion of the three uses of Greek participles will make this clear:

149

(1) Like an adjective, the participle may be used attributively, that is, it may attribute a quality to a noun (cf. ὁ ἄνθρωπος ὁ ἀγαθός, "The good man"). In sentence (1), λέγων is used attributively in that it attributes a quality to the noun ἄνθρωπος, with which it agrees in gender, number, and case. Typically, a participle used attributively stands in the attributive position (i.e., it is immediately preceded by the article). The best way to translate an attributive participle is by means of a relative clause. A relative clause is one that begins with a relative pronoun ("who," "which," or "that"). Thus ὁ ἄνθρωπος ὁ λέγων ταῦτα may be translated "the man **who is saying** these things" or "the man **who says** these things." Similar model sentences could be constructed for plurals (οἱ ἄνθρωποι **οἱ λέγοντες** ταῦτα, "the men **who are saying** these things"), for all genders (τὰ τέκνα **τὰ λέγοντα** ταῦτα, "the children **that are saying** these things"), and for the other voices (ὁ δοῦλος **ὁ λυόμενος** ὑπὸ τοῦ ἀποστόλου, "the servant **who is being loosed** by the apostle").

(2) Like an adjective, the participle may also be used substantively, that is, as a substantive or noun, as in sentence (2). Just as ὁ ἀγαθός means "the good one" or "the good man," so **ὁ λέγων** means "**the one who is saying**," "**the man who is saying**," or "**the one who says**." Compare **οἱ λέγοντες** ταῦτα, "**the ones who are saying** these things"; **αἱ λέγουσαι** ταῦτα, "**the women who are saying** these things"; **τὰ βλεπόμενα** ὑπὸ τοῦ ἀποστόλου, "**the things that are being seen** by the apostle"; etc.

(3) In addition to being used adjectivally and substantivally, the participle may also be used adverbially to indicate some circumstance under which the action of the main verb takes place. The adverbial participle is anarthrous and stands in the predicate position, as in sentence (3). Most adverbial participles may be translated by means of a dependent clause introduced by such words as "while," "when," "having," "after," "because," depending on the context. It is important to understand that participles do not, properly speaking, have "tense." That is, they do not refer to past, present, or future time. It turns out, however, that the present participle most frequently denotes *contemporaneous* action, that is, action taking place at the *same time* as the action of the main verb, while the aorist participle most frequently denotes *antecedent* action, that is, action that took place *before* the action of the main verb. In translation, therefore, the present participle may generally be rendered by a phrase consisting of "while" plus an English present participle, and the aorist participle by a phrase consisting of "having" or "after" plus an English past participle. A few examples will make this clear:

(a) **λέγων** ταῦτα ὁ ἄνθρωπος βλέπει τὸν δοῦλον.
   "**While saying** these things, the man sees the servant."
or "**While he is saying** these things, the man sees the servant."

(b) **εἰπὼν** ταῦτα ὁ ἄνθρωπος βλέπει τὸν δοῦλον.
   "**Having said** these things, the man sees the servant."
or "**After he said** these things, the man sees the servant."

It should also be noted that this relationship of participle to main verb remains the same regardless of the tense of the main verb. In (c) and (d) below, the present participle λέγων is translated in such a way as to show that it is *contemporaneous* with the action of the main verb:

(c) **λέγων** ταῦτα ὁ ἄνθρωπος βλέπει τὸν δοῦλον.
   "**While he is saying** these things, the man sees the servant."

(d) **λέγων** ταῦτα ὁ ἄνθρωπος ἔβλεψε τὸν δοῦλον.
   "**While he was saying** these things, the man saw the servant."

Again, similar models could be constructed with plural nouns and with nouns in other genders:

(e) **λέγοντες** ταῦτα οἱ ἄνθρωποι βλέπουσι τὸν δοῦλον.
   "**While they are saying** these things, the men see the servant."

(f) **λέγοντες** ταῦτα οἱ ἄνθρωποι ἔβλεψαν τὸν δοῦλον.
   "**While they were saying** these things, the men saw the servant."

(g) **λέγουσαι** ταῦτα αἱ ἀγαθαὶ ἔβλεψαν τὸν δοῦλον.
   "**While they were saying** these things, the good women saw the servant."

Examples (f) and (g) show why no *imperfect* form of the participle is needed in Greek. Imperfective aspect is achieved by using a present participle with a past tense main verb.

(4) As explained in §15 and illustrated in the examples of the participle studied thus far, the *present* participle denotes imperfective aspect, while the *aorist* participle denotes aoristic aspect. This distinction should normally be observed when translating participles:

(a) ὁ δοῦλος **ὁ λυόμενος** ὑπὸ τοῦ κυρίου βλέπει τὸν ἀπόστολον.
"The servant **who is being loosed** by the Lord sees the apostle."

(b) ὁ δοῦλος **ὁ λυθεὶς** ὑπὸ τοῦ κυρίου βλέπει τὸν ἀπόστολον.
"The servant **who was loosed** by the Lord sees the apostle."

The *perfect* participle, on the other hand, denotes completed action whose results are still felt. New Testament examples of the perfect participle include:

Luke 9:35:   οὗτός ἐστιν ὁ υἱός μου, **ὁ ἐκλελεγμένος**.
"This is my Son, **the one who has been chosen**."

Here the perfect passive participle of ἐκλέγω ("I choose") emphasizes the Father's permanent choice of the Son.

Rev 5:12:   ἄξιόν ἐστιν τὸ ἀρνίον **τὸ ἐσφαγμένον**.
"Worthy is the lamb **that has been slain**."

Here the perfect passive participle of σφάζω ("I slay") shows that the author has in mind a state of affairs resultant upon an earlier action.

John 11:44:   ἐξῆλθεν **ὁ τεθνηκώς**.
"**The one who had been dead** came forth."

Here the perfect active participle of θνήσκω ("I die") describes completed action. This latter example also shows why no *pluperfect* form of the participle is needed in Greek, since this sense may be gained by using a perfect participle with a past tense main verb.

(5) The usual negative with the participle is μή (there are only seventeen New Testament instances of οὐ with the participle):

ὁ ἄνθρωπος **ὁ μὴ λέγων** ταῦτα βλέπει τὸν δοῦλον.
"The man **who is not saying** these things sees the servant."

(6) Verbs that are deponent in the indicative mood are also deponent in the participle. Thus, for example, ἔρχομαι ("I come") has the present deponent participle ἐρχόμενος ("coming"). Remember that participles of deponent verbs have an *active* meaning even though they have a middle or passive form:

οἱ ἐρχόμενοι ἐκ τοῦ οἴκου βλέπουσι τὸν δοῦλον.
"**The ones who are coming** out of the house see the servant."

(7) Present participles are occasionally used with some forms of the verb εἰμί, and the resulting *periphrastic construction* is equivalent to the English present progressive or past progressive:

    (a) **εἰμὶ λύων** τὸν δοῦλον.
          "**I am loosing** the servant."

    (b) **ἦν βλέπων** τὸν ἀπόστολον.
          "**He was seeing** the apostle."

The periphrastic construction usually emphasizes the duration of an action, as in Luke 2:51: **ἦν ὑποτασσόμενος** αὐτοῖς, "**He was submitting himself** to them." Here the periphrastic construction (the imperfect indicative of εἰμί plus the present middle participle of ὑποτάσσω, "I submit") emphasizes the continuance of Jesus' obedience to his parents. Luke stresses this point because the previous context implies that Jesus may have been irresponsible to his earthly parents when he stayed behind in Jerusalem.

(8) As already noted, aorist participles employ the unaugmented stems in their formation. Since it is not always evident what these forms are, the aorist participles of some important irregular verbs are given below:

Verb	Act. Ind.	Act. Part.	Pass. Ind.	Pass. Part.
ἄγω	ἤγαγον	ἀγαγών	ἤχθην	ἀχθείς
λέγω	εἶπον	εἰπών	ἐρρήθην	ῥηθείς
ἔρχομαι	ἦλθον	ἐλθών		
λαμβάνω	ἔλαβον	λαβών	ἐλήμφθην	λημφθείς
ὁράω	εἶδον	ἰδών	ὤφθην	ὀφθείς

(9) To *parse* a participle, it is necessary to give its tense, voice, mood ("participle" is placed in the mood slot), gender, number, case, and source (the participle has no *person*). Thus λύοντες is parsed: "present active participle, masculine plural nominative, from λύω."

132. Mastering Greek Participles

New Testament exegesis is impossible without a thorough understanding of the participle. The most helpful way of mastering Greek participles is by working through a number of examples. In translating Greek participles into idiomatic English, one must usually resort to paraphrase. In the following illustrative sentences, no more than three translations are given for each example. Practice reading the following Greek sentences, keeping the English translation covered up. Then test your translation by reference to the next line(s).

1. ὁ ἀπόστολος ὁ λέγων ταῦτα γινώσκει τὸν κύριον.
    "The apostle who is saying these things knows the Lord."
    "The apostle who says these things knows the Lord."

2. ὁ λέγων ταῦτα γινώσκει τὸν κύριον.
    "The one who is saying these things knows the Lord."
    "The man who is saying these things knows the Lord."
    "The one who says these things knows the Lord."

3. βλέπομεν τὸν ἀπόστολον τὸν λέγοντα ταῦτα.
    "We see the apostle who is saying these things."
    "We see the apostle who says these things."

4. βλέπομεν τὸν λέγοντα ταῦτα.
    "We see the one who is saying these things."
    "We see the man who is saying these things."
    "We see the one who says these things."

5. βλέπομεν τὴν λέγουσαν ταῦτα.
    "We see the woman who is saying these things."
    "We see the woman who says these things."

6. ἐβλέψαμεν τὴν λέγουσαν ταῦτα.
    "We saw the woman who was saying these things."

7. λέγων ταῦτα ὁ ἀπόστολος βλέπει τὸν δοῦλον.
    "While saying these things, the apostle sees the servant."
    "While he is saying these things, the apostle sees the servant."

8. εἰπὼν ταῦτα ὁ ἀπόστολος βλέπει τὸν δοῦλον.
    "Having said these things, the apostle sees the servant."
    "After he said these things, the apostle sees the servant."

9. εἰπὼν ταῦτα ὁ ἀπόστολος ἔβλεψε τὸν δοῦλον.
    "Having said these things, the apostle saw the servant."
    "After he had said these things, the apostle saw the servant."

10. ὁ δοῦλος ὁ βλεπόμενος ὑπὸ τοῦ ἀποστόλου ἀγαθός ἐστιν.
    "The servant who is being seen by the apostle is good."

11. ὁ δοῦλος ὁ βλεπόμενος ὑπὸ τοῦ ἀποστόλου ἀγαθὸς ἦν.
    "The servant who was being seen by the apostle was good."

12. τὰ βλεπόμενα μένει εἰς τοὺς αἰῶνας.
    "The things that are being seen abide forever."

13. τὰ μὴ βλεπόμενα οὐ μένει εἰς τοὺς αἰῶνας.
    "The things that are not being seen do not abide forever."

14. οἱ βλεπόμενοι ὑπὸ τοῦ κυρίου σώζονται.
    "The ones who are being seen by the Lord are being saved."
    "The men who are being seen by the Lord are being saved."

15. οἱ βλεπόμενοι ὑπὸ τοῦ κυρίου ἐσώθησαν.
    "The ones who were being seen by the Lord were saved."
    "The men who were being seen by the Lord were saved."

16. ὁ μένων ἐν αὐτῷ ἐλπίδα ἔχει.
    "The one who is abiding in him has hope."
    "The man who is abiding in him has hope."
    "The man who abides in him has hope."

17. ὁ μὴ μένων ἐν αὐτῷ ἐλπίδα οὐκ ἔχει.
    "The one who is not abiding in him does not have hope."
    "The man who is not abiding in him does not have hope."
    "The man who does not abide in him does not have hope."

18. οἱ ἀκούοντες τὸ εὐαγγέλιον ἐπίστευσαν ἐν τῷ θεραπεύοντι
    τοὺς ἀνθρώπους.
    "The ones who were hearing the gospel believed in the one who
    was healing the men."

19. πιστεύομεν ἐν τῷ πέμποντι αὐτόν.
"We believe in the one who is sending him."

20. ἐπιστεύσαμεν ἐν τῷ πέμποντι αὐτόν.
"We believed in the one who was sending him."

21. πορευόμενοι οἱ ἀπόστολοι ἐκήρυσσον τὸ εὐαγγέλιον.
"While going, the apostles were preaching the gospel."
"While they were going, the apostles were preaching the gospel."

22. ὁ ἄνθρωπος ὁ πέμψας τοὺς ἀποστόλους δίκαιός ἐστιν.
"The man who sent the apostles is righteous."

23. ὁ πέμψας τοὺς ἀποστόλους δίκαιός ἐστιν.
"The one who sent the apostles is righteous."
"The man who sent the apostles is righteous."

24. ἀκούσας ταῦτα ὁ ἀπόστολος ἐκήρυξε τὸ εὐαγγέλιον.
"After hearing these things, the apostle preached the gospel."
"When he had heard these things, the apostle preached the gospel."

25. ἐλέγομεν ταῦτα τοῖς πορευομένοις εἰς τὸ ἱερόν.
"We were saying these things to the ones who were going into the temple."

26. τοῦτό ἐστιν τὸ πνεῦμα τὸ σῶζον τοὺς ἀνθρώπους τοὺς σω-ζομένους.
"This is the spirit that is saving the men who are being saved."

27. ὁ ἀπόστολος ὁ ἐξελθὼν ἐκ τῆς ἐκκλησίας ἦλθεν εἰς τὸν οἶκον.
"The apostle who had gone out of the church went into the house."

28. ὁ ἀπόστολος ἐξελθὼν ἐκ τῆς ἐκκλησίας ἦλθεν εἰς τὸν οἶκον.
"The apostle, after going out of the church, went into the house."
"The apostle, after he had gone out of the church, went into the house."

29. οἱ μὴ ἰδόντες τὸν κύριον οὐ πιστεύουσιν εἰς αὐτόν.
"The ones who did not see the Lord do not believe in him."
"The men who did not see the Lord do not believe in him."

30. οὗτοί εἰσιν οἱ ἀκούσαντες τὸν λόγον ἐν ταῖς ἡμέραις ταῖς πονηραῖς.
"These are the ones who heard the word in the evil days."
"These are the men who heard the word in the evil days."

31. τὰ τέκνα τὰ δεξάμενα τὸν κύριον ἤγαγε τοὺς ἀδελφοὺς εἰς τὴν ἐκκλησίαν.
"The children that had received the Lord led the brothers into the church."

32. οἱ διδαχθέντες τὴν ἀλήθειαν ἐβαπτίσθησαν καὶ εἰσῆλθον εἰς τὸν οἶκον τοῦ θεοῦ.
"The ones who had been taught the truth were baptized and went into the house of God."
"The men who had been taught the truth were baptized and went into the house of God."

33. ἰδοῦσαι τὸν κηρύξαντα τὸ εὐαγγέλιον αἱ ἀγαθαὶ ἦλθον εἰς τὸν οἶκον.
"After they had seen the one who had preached the gospel, the good women went into the house."

34. ἔτι ὄντες ἐν τῷ ἱερῷ ἐκήρυξαν οἱ ἀπόστολοι τοῖς μαθηταῖς τὴν βασιλείαν.
"While they were still in the temple, the apostles preached the kingdom to the disciples."

133. The Genitive Absolute

When the subject of a participle is different than the subject of the main verb of the sentence, the participle and any noun or pronoun accompanying it are placed in the genitive case. The clause containing the participle is therefore "loosed" from the rest of the sentence, and the construction is called the *genitive absolute* (from Lat. *absolutus*, "loosed"). Compare the following sentences:

εἰπόντες ταῦτα ἐξῆλθον οἱ ἀπόστολοι.
"**When they had said** these things, the apostles went out."

εἰπόντων τῶν μαθητῶν ταῦτα ἐξῆλθον οἱ ἀπόστολοι.
"**When the disciples had said** these things, the apostles went out."

157

The genitive absolute may also be used with a pronoun:

εἰπόντων αὐτῶν ταῦτα ἐξῆλθεν ὁ ἀπόστολος.
"**When they had said** these things, the apostle went out."

134. Exercises

a. Read the lesson carefully. Study closely the various ways in which the Greek participle is inflected and translated. Though not inherently difficult, the participle tends to cause beginning students as much trouble as any other thing in the Greek verb system. A little extra effort invested in mastering these forms and uses will pay rich dividends in your reading of New Testament Greek.

b. Translate the following sentences.

1. ἦλθεν ὁ Ἰησοῦς εἰς τὴν Γαλιλαίαν κηρύσσων τὸ εὐαγγέλιον τοῦ θεοῦ (Mark 1:14).

2. Εὐχαριστῶ τῷ θεῷ μου πάντοτε, ἀκούων σου τὴν ἀγάπην καὶ τὴν πίστιν ἣν (that) ἔχεις πρὸς τὸν κύριον Ἰησοῦν καὶ εἰς πάντας τοὺς ἁγίους (Phlm 4–5).

3. βλέπει τὸν Ἰησοῦν ἐρχόμενον πρὸς αὐτὸν καὶ λέγει, Ἴδε (Look!) ὁ ἀμνὸς τοῦ θεοῦ ὁ αἴρων τὴν ἁμαρτίαν τοῦ κόσμου (John 1:29).

4. Καὶ εἶδον ἄλλον ἄγγελον ἰσχυρὸν καταβαίνοντα ἐκ τοῦ οὐρανοῦ (Rev 10:1).

5. μακάριος ὁ ἀναγινώσκων καὶ οἱ ἀκούοντες τοὺς λόγους τῆς προφητείας (prophecy) καὶ τηροῦντες τὰ ἐν αὐτῇ γεγραμμένα (Rev 1:3).

6. οὗτός ἐστιν ὁ ἄρτος ὁ ἐκ τοῦ οὐρανοῦ καταβαίνων (John 6:50).

7. Καὶ ἦν ἐκβάλλων δαιμόνιον (Luke 11:14).

8. καὶ ἐλθόντες λέγουσιν αὐτῷ, Διδάσκαλε (teacher), οἴδαμεν ὅτι ἀληθὴς εἶ (Mark 12:14).

9. καὶ αὐτὸς ἐδίδασκεν ἐν ταῖς συναγωγαῖς αὐτῶν, δοξαζόμενος ὑπὸ πάντων (Luke 4:15).

10. καὶ ὄψονται τὸν υἱὸν τοῦ ἀνθρώπου ἐρχόμενον ἐπὶ τῶν νεφελῶν (clouds) τοῦ οὐρανοῦ (Matt 24:30).

11. Ταῦτα αὐτοῦ λαλοῦντος πολλοὶ ἐπίστευσαν εἰς αὐτόν (John 8:30).

12. ἀσπάζομαι ὑμᾶς ἐγὼ Τέρτιος ὁ γράψας τὴν ἐπιστολὴν ἐν κυρίῳ (Rom 16:22).

13. Δικαιωθέντες οὖν ἐκ πίστεως εἰρήνην ἔχομεν πρὸς τὸν θεὸν διὰ τοῦ κυρίου ἡμῶν Ἰησοῦ Χριστοῦ (Rom 5:1).

21

INFINITIVES
(VERBAL NOUNS)

The infinitive, like the participle (Lesson 20), is a hybrid. But while the participle is a verbal adjective, the infinitive is a verbal noun. Verbal aspect is more easily studied in the infinitive than in the other moods of the verb.

135. Introducing the Infinitive

Finite verbs, as we have seen, show by their endings the person and number of their subject. For example, we translate λύομεν "we loose" because the ending -μεν indicates that the verb is first person plural. Verbal forms that are not limited by person and number are called *infinitives* (from Lat. *infinitivus*, "not limited"). Hence an infinitive is an indeclinable verbal noun whose meaning is not limited by person and number, although it does show different endings according to whether it is present, future, aorist, or perfect tense, and active, middle, or passive voice.

In English, the infinitive is normally formed by placing the preposition "to" before the verb, as in "they wanted *to go*." Sometimes the "to" does not occur, as in "they can *go*," that is, "they are able *to go*." Similarly, the Greek infinitive was originally a noun in the dative case (λύειν, the present infinitive of λύω, originally meant "for loosing" or "in loosing"). In both English and Greek, the infinitive may be used as a noun. An example is Philippians 1:21: "*To die* is gain." Here the infinitive "to die" is the *subject* of the verb "is" and is therefore the equivalent of a noun. Another example is Luke 16:3: "I am ashamed *to beg*." Again, the infinitive "to beg" is the equivalent of a noun, although here it is the *object* of the verb in the sentence. Sometimes English uses the suffix *-ing* instead of "to" in translating the infinitive. The above sentences might just as well have been translated "*Dying* is gain" and "I am ashamed of *begging*."

The Greek infinitive occurs most frequently in the present, aorist, and perfect tenses. (The future infinitive occurs only five times in the New Testament and need not concern us.) The distinction between these tenses, as we have frequently observed (see §15), is not one of *time* of action but rather one of *kind* of action. Compare the following uses of λύω in the active infinitive:

Aorist	λῦσαι	"to loose"	(aoristic aspect)
Present	λύειν	"to be loosing"	(imperfective aspect)
Perfect	λελυκέναι	"to have loosed"	(perfective aspect)

Here the true nature of the Greek tense system is clearly seen:

(1) The *aorist* infinitive is the least marked form and is used to refer to an action without defining its nature or extent (see Acts 25:11: "I do not refuse to die"). In general, the aorist infinitive was used by the New Testament writers unless some reason existed for using the present or perfect.

(2) The *present* infinitive is used to refer to action that is ongoing or progressive. A New Testament example is John 21:3, where Peter says "I am going to fish." Here the present infinitive implies that Peter and his fellow disciples were contemplating a return to their former occupation while they waited for Jesus to appear in Galilee.

(3) The *perfect* infinitive is used to express the existing results of an action or the continuation of a state. For example, in Acts 26:32 Agrippa says of Paul, "This man may have been able to have been set free." Presumably Agrippa thought that Paul could have remained a free man had he not appealed to Caesar. Notice also these examples:

Matt 14:22:	"He required the disciples *to get into* [aorist infinitive] the boat and *to go ahead* [present infinitive] of him to the other side."
Acts 15:37–38:	"Barnabas wanted *to take* [aorist infinitive] John . . . , but Paul thought it best not *to take* [present infinitive] him along."
Phil 3:4:	"If anyone else has a mind *to put confidence* [perfect infinitive] in the flesh, I far more."

1 Cor 2:2:   "For I determined not *to know* [perfect infinitive] anything among you except Jesus Christ and him crucified."

The use of the infinitive in these examples is obviously best explained on the basis of verbal aspect. These examples suffice to show that tense in the Greek infinitive has to do with kind of action rather than with time of action.

136. The Infinitives of λύω

The infinitives of λύω, in its various aspects and voices, are given below. In the translations an attempt has been made to express the aspectual significance of the present and perfect infinitives, though it should be remembered that such translations are usually "over-translations."

Active	Present	λύειν	"to be loosing"
	Aorist	λῦσαι	"to loose"
	Perfect	λελυκέναι	"to have loosed"
Middle	Present	λύεσθαι	"to be loosing oneself"
	Aorist	λύσασθαι	"to loose oneself"
	Perfect	λελύσθαι	"to have loosed oneself"
Passive	Present	λύεσθαι	"to be being loosed"
	Aorist	λυθῆναι	"to be loosed"
	Perfect	λελύσθαι	"to have been loosed"

Here one can easily recognize the various tense markers encountered earlier in connection with the indicative mood:

(1)   The first aorist active infinitive contains the aoristic aspect morpheme σα (or σ).

(2)   The first aorist passive infinitive contains the passive voice morpheme θη (lengthened from θε).

(3)   Perfect infinitives show reduplication, and the perfect *active* infinitive contains the perfective aspect morpheme κ (shortened from κα).

The above forms also illustrate the basic suffixes of the infinitive:

(1)   -ειν in the present active infinitive.

(2)   -αι in the aorist active infinitive.

(3)   -ναι in the perfect active and aorist passive infinitive.

(4)   -σθαι elsewhere.

Note that aorist infinitives, like aorist participles, do not contain the augment.

137. The Infinitives of Other Verbs

The above analysis of λύω is applicable to the infinitives of other verbs, including contract verbs, verbs with second aorists, and deponent verbs. The following points should especially be noted:

(1) The σ of the first aorist infinitive often amalgamates with a preceding consonant, as in πέμπω, first aorist active infinitive πέμψαι (to send). (On the rules of amalgamation, see §20.)

(2) Verbs that have second aorists also have second aorist infinitives. These infinitives are formed by adding the suffix -ειν to the unaugmented second aorist stem. Second aorist infinitives may be illustrated by the following forms:

Verb		Second Aorist Ind.		Second Aorist Inf.	
ἄγω	(I lead)	ἤγαγον	(I led)	ἀγαγεῖν	(to lead)
βάλλω	(I throw)	ἔβαλον	(I threw)	βαλεῖν	(to throw)
ἔρχομαι	(I come)	ἦλθον	(I went)	ἐλθεῖν	(to come)
ἐσθίω	(I eat)	ἔφαγον	(I ate)	φαγεῖν	(to eat)
λαμβάνω	(I receive)	ἔλαβον	(I received)	λαβεῖν	(to receive)
λέγω	(I say)	εἶπον	(I said)	εἰπεῖν	(to say)
ὁράω	(I see)	εἶδον	(I saw)	ἰδεῖν	(to see)

(3) Second aorist middle infinitives are formed by adding the connecting vowel -ε- and the suffix -σθαι to the unaugmented second aorist stem:

Second Aor. Act. Inf.		Second Aor. Mid. Inf.	
βαλεῖν	(to throw)	βαλέσθαι	(to throw oneself)
λαβεῖν	(to receive)	λαβέσθαι	(to receive oneself)

(4) Second aorist passive infinitives are formed by adding the suffix -ναι to the unaugmented second aorist passive stem:

Verb		Second Aor. Pass. Ind.		Second Aor. Pass. Inf.	
γράφω	(I write)	ἐγράφην	(I was written)	γραφῆναι	(to be written)

(5) In the present active infinitive of contract verbs, the suffix -εν is used instead of -ειν. Hence the contracted forms of the model verbs used in Lesson 19 appear as τιμᾶν (to be honoring), φιλεῖν (to be loving), and δηλοῦν (to be showing).

(6) Verbs that are deponent in the aorist indicative are also deponent in the aorist infinitive. For example, γίνομαι has the aorist infinitives γενέσθαι (aorist middle form) and γενηθῆναι (aorist passive form). Both infinitives are translated "to become."

(7) The present infinitive of εἰμί is εἶναι (to be).

(8) To parse the infinitive, it is necessary to give its tense, voice, and source, along with the word "infinitive" in the mood slot. Thus λύειν is parsed "present active infinitive, from λύω." (Remember that there is no person or number in the infinitive.)

138. Uses of the Infinitive

Infinitives can be divided into two major functional categories: adverbial and substantival uses. Before discussing these uses, however, the following features of the infinitive should be noted:

(1) The infinitive may be used with or without the article. Only the neuter singular article is used (τό, τοῦ, and τῷ).

(2) When the infinitive is used with the article, it may also be used with a preposition. In the New Testament, the following prepositions occur most frequently with infinitives: διά (33 occurrences), εἰς (72 occurrenc-

es), ἐν (55 occurrences), μετά (15 occurrences), πρό (9 occurrences), and πρός (12 occurrences). Most of these prepositions have their usual meaning when used with infinitives, but some take on a specialized meaning and must be translated accordingly.

(3) Although infinitives do not have subjects in the same sense that finite verbs do, the infinitive often contains a "subject" that indicates who or what produces the action expressed in the infinitive. This "subject" is usually put in the accusative case and is an exception to the rule stated in Lesson 4 that the subject of a Greek verb is put in the nominative case (see §28). This use of the accusative as the "subject" of the infinitive is called the *accusative of general reference*. A similar phenomenon occurs in English when we say "I know *him to be* good" for "I know *he is* good." The former sentence is exactly the same as the Greek accusative-and-infinitive construction. The clause "he is good" has been converted into an infinitival phrase by putting its subject ("he") into the accusative ("him") and by changing its finite verb "is" to the infinitive "to be." In Greek, "I know him to be good" becomes γινώσκω αὐτὸν εἶναι ἀγαθόν.

(4) Anarthrous infinitives may occur with impersonal verbs such as δεῖ ("it is necessary") and ἔξεστι(ν) ("it is lawful").

(5) Infinitives (like participles) are negated by μή.

We may now discuss the two uses of the infinitive. We begin with the *adverbial* infinitive—so called because its verbal aspects are primary. The adverbial infinitive usually makes a further assertion about the main verb. It may also function as an adverbial phrase modifying the main verb. The following uses of the adverbial infinitive are the ones most frequently encountered in the New Testament:

(1) The infinitive of *purpose*. Here the infinitive indicates the purpose of the action expressed by the main verb. Purpose is most frequently expressed by (a) the infinitive alone, (b) the infinitive with τοῦ, and (c) the infinitive with εἰς τό:

Matt 2:2:   "We have come *to worship* [προσκυνῆσαι] him."

Phil 3:10:   *"To know* [τοῦ γνῶναι] him."

1 Thess 3:5: "I sent him *to know about* [εἰς τὸ γνῶναι] your faith."

(2) The infinitive of *result*. Here the infinitive is introduced by ὥστε and used to express the result of the action of the main verb:

1 Thess 1:8: *"So that we do not have a need* [ὥστε μὴ . . . χρείαν ἔχειν] to say anything."

(3) The infinitive of *time* (temporal infinitive). In this use of the infinitive, three viewpoints are possible. An event that sets the main clause in antecedent time (the event in the main clause will happen before the event in the infinitive clause) is expressed by πρίν or πρὶν ἤ and the infinitive; contemporaneous time is expressed by ἐν τῷ and the infinitive; and subsequent time is expressed by μετὰ τό and the infinitive:

Matt 26:34: *"Before the cock crows* [πρὶν ἀλέκτορα φωνῆσαι], you will deny me three times."

Luke 24:51: *"While he was blessing* [ἐν τῷ εὐλογεῖν αὐτὸν] them, he departed from them."

Matt 26:32: *"After I have been raised* [μετὰ τὸ ἐγερθῆναι με], I will go before you into Galilee."

Of the uses of the infinitive, this one is the most foreign to English speakers. It is impossible to translate infinitives of time literally into English. They are best translated by converting them into subordinate clauses and changing the infinitives into finite verbs. For example, ἐν τῷ εὐλογεῖν αὐτόν is literally "in the to be blessing him." Less literally, the clause could be rendered "in the process of his blessing." But the best translation is "while he was blessing."

(4) The infinitive of *cause* (causal infinitive). Here διὰ τό is regularly used with the infinitive to express the idea of cause:

Matt 13:6: "It withered *because it did not have a root* [διὰ τὸ μὴ ἔχειν ῥίζαν]."

(5) The infinitive of *command* (imperatival infinitive). On rare occasions, the infinitive may be used to express a command:

Rom 12:15: *"Rejoice* [χαίρειν] with those who rejoice; **weep** [κλαίειν] with those who weep."

Turning now to the *substantival* use of the infinitive, we note that here the noun aspect of the infinitive is primary. The following are the most frequently encountered categories of the substantival infinitive:

(1) The infinitive as *subject*:

Phil 1:21:   "*To live* [τὸ ζῆν] is Christ, and *to die* [τὸ ἀποθανεῖν] is gain."

(2) The infinitive as *object*:

Phil 2:13:   "God is the one who is working in you both *to will* [τὸ θέλειν] and *to work* [τὸ ἐνεργεῖν] his good pleasure."

(3) The infinitive as *modifier*. Here the infinitive is used to modify or to complete the sense of nouns, adjectives, or verbs:

Rev 11:18:   "The time has come for the dead *to be judged* [κριθῆναι]."
1 Cor 7:39:   "She is free *to be married* [γαμηθῆναι] to whom she wishes."
Luke 10:40:   "My sister has forsaken me *to serve* [διακονεῖν] alone."

139. Vocabulary

a. Additional verbs.

δεῖ	*it is necessary* (impers. verb; takes the acc. and inf.)
ἔξεστι(ν)	*it is lawful* (impers. verb; takes the dat. and inf.)
μέλλω	*I am about to, I will* (takes the inf.)

b. Additional adverb.

πρίν	*before*

c. Conjunction.

ὥστε	*so that*

140. Exercises

a. Read the lesson carefully. Thoroughly review the forms of the infinitive and its various uses. Note that all forms of the infinitive end in either -αι or -ειν.

b. Memorize the vocabulary to this lesson.

c. Translate the following sentences.

1. πιστεύετε ὅτι δύναμαι (I am able) τοῦτο ποιῆσαι; (Matt 9:28).

2. ἐγὼ χρείαν (need) ἔχω ὑπὸ σοῦ βαπτισθῆναι, καὶ σὺ ἔρχῃ πρός με; (Matt 3:14).

3. ἔδωκεν (he gave) αὐτοῖς ἐξουσίαν τέκνα θεοῦ γενέσθαι (John 1:12).

4. ἄξιος εἶ λαβεῖν τὸ βιβλίον (Rev 5:9).

5. μέλλει γὰρ Ἡρῴδης ζητεῖν τὸ παιδίον τοῦ ἀπολέσαι (to destroy) αὐτό (Matt 2:13).

6. Πολλὰ εἶχον γράψαι σοι, ἀλλ' οὐ θέλω διὰ μέλανος καὶ καλάμου (ink and pen) σοι γράφειν (3 John 13).

7. ἔλεγεν γὰρ ὁ Ἰωάννης αὐτῷ, Οὐκ ἔξεστίν σοι ἔχειν αὐτήν (Matt 14:4).

8. καὶ λέγουσίν μοι, Δεῖ σε πάλιν (again) προφητεῦσαι (to prophesy) ἐπὶ λαοῖς καὶ ἔθνεσιν καὶ γλώσσαις καὶ βασιλεῦσιν πολλοῖς (Rev 10:11).

9. Παρακαλῶ οὖν ὑμᾶς ἐγὼ ὁ δέσμιος (prisoner) ἐν κυρίῳ ἀξίως περιπατῆσαι τῆς κλήσεως ἧς (with which) ἐκλήθητε (Eph 4:1).

10. ἦλθεν ἐκ τῶν περάτων (ends) τῆς γῆς ἀκοῦσαι τὴν σοφίαν Σολομῶνος (Luke 11:31).

11. εἶπεν αὐτοῖς Ἰησοῦς, Ἀμὴν ἀμὴν λέγω ὑμῖν, πρὶν Ἀβραὰμ γενέσθαι ἐγὼ εἰμί (John 8:58).

12. οὐ δύναται (he is able) εἶναί μου μαθητής (Luke 14:26).

22

ADDITIONAL PRONOUNS

> This lesson introduces several classes of Greek pronouns in addition to those studied earlier in Lessons 9, 11, and 18.

141. Interrogative Pronouns

As in English, questions may be introduced by interrogative words, either pronouns (e.g., "who?", "what?") or adverbs (e.g., "where?", "how?", "when?"). The interrogative pronoun in Greek is τίς ("who?")/ τί ("what?"):

τίς λέγει τοῦτο;   "Who says this?"
τί ἐστι τοῦτο;   "What is this?"

The declension of the interrogative pronoun is as follows:

	Singular		Plural	
	Masc./Fem.	Neut.	Masc./Fem.	Neut.
N.	τίς	τί	τίνες	τίνα
G.	τίνος	τίνος	τίνων	τίνων
D.	τίνι	τίνι	τίσι(ν)	τίσι(ν)
A.	τίνα	τί	τίνας	τίνα

Note the following New Testament examples:

Matt 12:48: τίς ἐστιν ἡ μήτηρ μου;
"**Who** is my mother?"

Matt 22:20: τίνος ἡ εἰκὼν αὕτη;
"**Whose** image is this?"

Matt 11:16: τίνι ὁμοιώσω τὴν γενεὰν ταύτην;
"**To whom** shall I compare this generation?"

John 18:4: τίνα ζητεῖτε;
"**Whom** do you seek?"

Rom 9:30: τί ἐροῦμεν;
"**What** will we say?"

i. It should be noted that the neuter accusative singular (τί) is often used adverbially to mean "why": τί ποιεῖτε τοῦτο; "Why are you doing this?"

ii. Questions in Greek expecting an *affirmative* answer ("Yes") have οὐ with the indicative, while questions expecting a *negative* answer ("No") or implying hesitation have μή with the indicative:

Luke 4:22: οὐχὶ υἱός ἐστιν Ἰωσὴφ οὗτος;
"This is Joseph's son, isn't it?"

1 Cor 12:30: μὴ πάντες γλώσσαις λαλοῦσιν;
"All do not speak in tongues, do they?"

John 6:67: μὴ καὶ ὑμεῖς θέλετε ὑπάγειν;
"Surely you do not want to go away, do you?"

iii. The interrogative pronoun may also be used in indirect questions: ἐρωτᾷ αὐτὸν τίς ἐστιν, "He asks him who he is" (from the direct question, "Who is he?").

142. Indefinite Pronouns

The Greek indefinite pronoun is τις/τι. This pronoun is the equivalent of the English "someone," "anyone," "something," "anything," "a certain one," and the like. Its forms are identical to those of the interrogative pronoun apart from accentuation: the indefinite pronoun is an enclitic, throwing its accent back onto the preceding word (on enclitics, see Appendix 1). Note the following examples:

Matt 12:29: πῶς δύναταί τις εἰσελθεῖν;
"How can **anyone** enter?"

Luke 9:49:   εἴδομέν **τινα**
               "We saw **someone**."

The indefinite pronoun may also be used adjectivally:

Luke 1:5:   ἐγένετο ἱερεύς **τις**
               "There was **a certain** priest."

143. Relative Pronouns

The relative pronoun is so named because it "relates" to a noun or pronoun in another clause of the sentence. This noun or pronoun is called the *antecedent* because it is logically prior to the relative (though it is not always *written* first). The clause in which the relative pronoun stands is called a *relative clause*. In the following sentences, the relative clauses are set off in italics:

"The Spirit *who gives life* has been given."

"The words *that I speak* are life."

"The one *whom the Father sent* is here."

In these sentences the pronouns "who," "that," and "whom" relate back to an antecedent noun or pronoun. In British English, the word *which* is frequently used as the relative pronoun in place of *that*:

"The words *which I speak* are life."

English sometimes omits the relative pronoun altogether:

"The words I speak are life."

The forms of the relative pronoun are given below. Its declension follows the endings of οὗτος (see §77).

	Singular			Plural		
	M.	F.	N.	M.	F.	N.
N.	ὅς	ἥ	ὅ	οἵ	αἵ	ἅ
G.	οὗ	ἧς	οὗ	ὧν	ὧν	ὧν
D.	ᾧ	ᾗ	ᾧ	οἷς	αἷς	οἷς
A.	ὅν	ἥν	ὅ	οὕς	ἅς	ἅ

The relative pronoun agrees with its antecedent in *gender* and *number*, but its *case* is determined by its function in the relative clause. Compare the following sentences:

(1) ὁ ἄνθρωπος **ὅς** εἶδε τὸν κύριόν ἐστιν ἀπόστολος.
     "The man **who** saw the Lord is an apostle."

(2) ὁ ἄνθρωπος **ὅν** εἴδομέν ἐστιν ἀπόστολος.
     "The man **whom** we saw is an apostle."

Here the pronouns ὅς and ὅν are masculine and singular because their antecedent (ἄνθρωπος) is masculine and singular. However, ὅς is *nominative* because it is the *subject* of its relative clause, while ὅν is *accusative* because it is the *object* of its relative clause. The relative pronoun may also take the *genitive* and *dative* cases:

(3) ὁ ἄνθρωπος **οὗ** λόγους ἠκούσαμέν ἐστιν ἀπόστολος.
     "The man **whose** words we heard is an apostle."

(4) ὁ ἄνθρωπος **ᾧ** εἴπομεν τὸν λόγον ἐστὶν ἀπόστολος.
     "The man **to whom** we spoke the word is an apostle."

The uses of the relative pronoun are clearly indicated in the following New Testament examples:

Col 2:10:   ἐν αὐτῷ, **ὅς** ἐστιν ἡ κεφαλή.
            "In him, **who** is the head."

Matt 2:9:   ἰδοὺ ὁ ἀστήρ, **ὅν** εἶδον ἐν τῇ ἀνατολῇ.
            "Behold, the star, **which** they saw in the east."

Eph 3:7: διὰ τοῦ εὐαγγελίου, **οὗ** ἐγενήθην διάκονος.

"Through the gospel, **of which** I became a minister."

Matt 17:5: οὗτός ἐστιν ὁ υἱός μου ὁ ἀγαπητός, ἐν **ᾧ** εὐδόκησα.

"This is my beloved son, **in whom** I am well pleased."

Sometimes the antecedent of the relative pronoun is not expressed:

Matt 10:38: **ὃς** οὐ λαμβάνει τὸν σταυρὸν αὐτοῦ οὐκ ἔστιν μου ἄξιος.

"[He] **who** does not take his cross is not worthy of me."

144. Indefinite Relative Pronouns

The indefinite relative pronoun is so named because it is a combination of the relative ὅς and the indefinite τις. Both forms experience inflection. In the New Testament, the indefinite relative pronoun occurs almost exclusively in the nominative singular and plural:

Singular	ὅστις, ἥτις, ὅτι
Plural	οἵτινες, αἵτινες, ἅτινα

The indefinite relative pronoun is usually translated "who," but its meaning sometimes involves a qualitative idea: "who is of such a nature." A possible New Testament example of this is Romans 1:25:

οἵτινες μετήλλαξαν τὴν ἀλήθειαν τοῦ θεοῦ ἐν τῷ ψεύδει.

"**Who** [were of such nature that they] exchanged the truth of God for a lie."

Normally, however, ὅστις is used without any significant difference in meaning from ὅς. In relative clauses, ὅς is the rule (1,395 occurrences) and ὅστις the exception (153 occurrences).

145. Reciprocal Pronouns

From ἄλλος ("other, another") is formed the reciprocal pronoun. In the New Testament, the reciprocal pronoun occurs only in the following forms (all plurals):

ἀλλήλων	"of one another"
ἀλλήλοις	"to one another"
ἀλλήλους	"one another"

146. Reflexive Pronouns

The reflexive pronoun refers back to the subject of the sentence (e.g., "Jesus does not save *himself*"). There is therefore no nominative of the reflexive pronoun. The third person reflexive pronoun is declined just like αὐτός: ἑαυτοῦ, ἑαυτῷ, ἑαυτόν, etc. The first and second persons are made up of a combination of ἐμέ and σέ with αὐτός: ἐμαυτοῦ, ἐμαυτῷ, ἐμαυτόν; σεαυτοῦ, σεαυτῷ, σεαυτόν. In the plural, ἑαυτῶν/-οῖς/ούς does duty for all persons: e.g., μαρτυρεῖτε ἑαυτοῖς, "You bear witness to yourselves" (Matt 23:31).

147. Possessive Pronouns (Adjectives)

The possessive pronouns ἐμός ("my"), σός ("your"), ἴδιος ("his"), ἡμέτερος ("our"), and ὑμέτερος ("your") are sometimes used instead of the genitive case of the personal pronouns when emphasis is desired. These possessive pronouns are declined (and function) like regular adjectives of the first and second declensions. They stand in the attributive position:

	ὁ ἐμὸς λόγος	"my word"
or		
	ὁ λόγος ὁ ἐμός	"my word"

Normally, however, "my word" is ὁ λόγος μου.

148. Vocabulary

a. Additional pronouns.

ἀλλήλων	*one another* (*al*ien)
ἑαυτοῦ, -ῆς	*himself, herself*
ἐμαυτοῦ, -ῆς	*myself*
ἐμός, -ή, -όν	*my, mine*
ἡμέτερος, -α, -ον	*our*
ἴδιος, -α, -ον	*his, one's own* (*idio*syncrasy)

174

ὅς, ἥ, ὅ	who, which, that, what
ὅστις, ἥτις, ὅτι	who, whoever, what, whatever
σεαυτοῦ, -ῆς	yourself
σός, σή, σόν	your (singular)
τίς, τί	who?, which?, what?, why?
τις, τι	one, a certain one, someone, anyone
ὑμέτερος, -α, -ον	your (plural)

149. Exercises

a. Read the lesson carefully. Review the pronouns introduced earlier (Lessons 9, 11, and 18).

b. Memorize the vocabulary to this lesson.

c. Translate the following sentences.

1. σὺ τίς εἶ; (John 1:19).

2. Καὶ ἔστιν αὕτη ἡ ἀγγελὶα (message) ἣν ἀκηκόαμεν ἀπ' αὐτοῦ (1 John 1:5).

3. μὴ σὺ μείζων εἶ τοῦ πατρὸς ἡμῶν Ἀβραάμ, ὅστις ἀπέθανεν; (John 8:53).

4. κοινωνίαν (fellowship) ἔχομεν μετ' ἀλλήλων (1 John 1:7).

5. καὶ ἡ κοινωνία δὲ ἡ ἡμετέρα μετὰ τοῦ πατρὸς καὶ μετὰ τοῦ υἱοῦ Ἰησοῦ Χριστοῦ (1 John 1:3).

6. σὺ περὶ σεαυτοῦ μαρτυρεῖς (John 8:13).

7. οὐ τῷ σῷ ὀνόματι ἐπροφητεύσαμεν (we prophesied); (Matt 7:22).

8. καὶ ἡ κρίσις ἡ ἐμὴ δικαία ἐστίν (John 5:30).

9. ἀλλ' οὐ τί θέλω ἀλλὰ τί σύ (Mark 14:36).

10. τί οὖν βαπτίζεις εἰ (if) σὺ οὐκ εἶ ὁ Χριστός; (John 1:25).

11. ἀπαγγέλλομεν (we announce) ὑμῖν τὴν ζωὴν τὴν αἰώνιον ἥτις ἦν πρὸς τὸν πατέρα (1 John 1:2).

23

THE SUBJUNCTIVE MOOD

The subjunctive is the mood of contingency. While the indicative assumes reality, the subjunctive assumes unreality. Because it is a mood of potential action, the subjunctive usually has a future orientation. This lesson introduces the basic idea of the subjunctive and its most common uses.

150. Introducing the Subjunctive

As mentioned in §13, mood indicates the *manner* in which the action of a verb is regarded by the speaker. There are four basic moods in Greek, two of which we have already encountered: the *indicative* mood, which makes an assertion, and the *infinitive* mood, which expresses an action generally and without reference to a particular person or thing. The other two moods to be studied are the *subjunctive* mood, which expresses a thought or wish rather than an actual fact, and the *imperative* mood, which expresses a command (Lesson 24). Compare the following sentences:

> Indicative: "*I loose* the servant."
>
> Infinitive: "*To loose* the servant is difficult."
>
> Subjunctive: "*Though he loose* the servant, I will not go."
>
> Imperative: "*Loose* the servant!"

Note that the subjunctive expresses a condition in which there is an element of doubt. The subjunctive may therefore be called the *mood of contingency*. Morphologically, the subjunctive mood is nearly obsolete in English. It is most frequently indicated by the deletion of the -*s* in the third person singular:

Indicative:	"Heaven *helps* us."
Subjunctive:	"Heaven *help* us!"

Occasionally the subjunctive of the verb "be" is found:

Infinitive:	"My teacher asked me *to be* prompt."
Subjunctive:	"My teacher asked that *I be* prompt."

Generally, however, English tends to substitute alternative forms of "be" for the subjunctive: "My teacher asked that *I would be* prompt."

At one time the Greek subjunctive was related to the future indicative. Thus, it is not surprising that the subjunctive generally refers to future events. Except for some rare occurrences of the perfect tense, the subjunctive is found only in the present and the aorist in the New Testament. As with the other non-indicative moods, only the *kind of action* (verbal aspect) is in view in the subjunctive: the present subjunctive expresses imperfective action, while the aorist subjunctive expresses aoristic action. As with the infinitive, the normal tense of the subjunctive is the aorist.

151. The Forms of the Subjunctive

The forms of the Greek subjunctive are, happily, very simple. Those of λύω are given below. Note that (a) the stem in the subjunctive is always the same as the corresponding stem of the indicative; (b) there is never an augment; (c) the vowel in the ending is always ω or η (lengthened from ο and ε); and (d) the primary endings are employed even in the aorist.

			Present Act.	Present M/P
		1.	λύω	λύωμαι
Sg.		2.	λύῃς	λύῃ
		3.	λύῃ	λύηται
		1.	λύωμεν	λυώμεθα
Pl.		2.	λύητε	λύησθε
		3.	λύωσι(ν)	λύωνται

177

		Aorist Active	Aorist Middle	Aorist Passive
Sg.	1.	λύσω	λύσωμαι	λυθῶ
	2.	λύσῃς	λύσῃ	λυθῆς
	3.	λύσῃ	λύσηται	λυθῇ
Pl.	1.	λύσωμεν	λυσώμεθα	λυθῶμεν
	2.	λύσητε	λύσησθε	λυθῆτε
	3.	λύσωσι(ν)	λύσωνται	λυθῶσι(ν)

Note carefully:

(1) The endings given above are also used with the second aorist:

Second Aorist Active: λίπω, λίπῃς, λίπῃ, etc.

Second Aorist Middle: λίπωμαι, λίπῃ, λίπηται, etc.

Second Aorist Passive: γραφῶ, γραφῇς, γραφῇ, etc.

(2) Verbs that are deponent in the indicative mood are deponent in the corresponding paradigm of the subjunctive:

γίνομαι has the present subjunctive γίνωμαι, γίνῃ, γίνηται, etc.

γίνομαι has the aorist subjunctive γένωμαι, γένῃ, γένηται, etc.

ἔρχομαι has the present subjunctive ἔρχωμαι, ἔρχῃ, ἔρχηται, etc.

(3) The present subjunctive of contract verbs in -εω follows the regular pattern given above (e.g., η is substituted for ει, and ω for ου). The present subjunctive of contract verbs in -αω is identical with the indicative forms, owing to the rules of contraction (see §124). The present subjunctive of verbs in -οω follows the pattern of the indicative.

(4) Like the participle and the infinitive, the subjunctive is negated by μή.

(5) The present subjunctive of εἰμί is: ὦ, ᾖς, ᾖ, ὦμεν, ἦτε, ὦσι(ν).

152. Uses of the Subjunctive

Being a potential mood, the subjunctive expresses action that is possible but not necessarily occurring. By the nature of the case, then, the subjunctive is related to the future (i.e., what may be or what may have been). As a result, the English future indicative is often used to convey the idea of the Greek subjunctive (whether present or aorist).

There are seven main uses of the subjunctive in the New Testament, four of which involve main clauses, and three of which involve subordinate clauses.

The Subjunctive in Main Clauses

(1) *The Hortatory Subjunctive.* The term *hortatory* is derived from the Latin *hortor*, "I exhort." In this construction, the subjunctive is used in the *first person plural* when the speaker is urging others to join in some action. In English, the words "let us" are required to complete the translation.

Heb 12:1: **τρέχωμεν** τὸν προκείμενον ἡμῶν ἀγῶνα.
"**Let us run** the race that is set before us."

1 John 4:7: ἀγαπητοί, **ἀγαπῶμεν** ἀλλήλους.
"Beloved, **let us love** one another."

The present tense of both τρέχωμεν and ἀγαπῶμεν suggests the idea "keep on doing" or "make it your habit to do."

(2) *The Subjunctive of Prohibition.* The negative μή is sometimes used with the *aorist* subjunctive to forbid the initiation or occurrence of an action. In translation, the word "ever" may be supplied when the context warrants such a rendering.

Matt 6:34: **μὴ μεριμνήσητε** εἰς τὴν αὔριον.
"**Don't worry** about tomorrow."
or "**Don't ever worry** about tomorrow."

Prohibition may also be expressed by μή with the *present imperative* (see §158). However, the present imperative is normally used when the command is to *stop* doing something, whereas the aorist subjunctive is normally used when the command is *not to start* doing something. "Normally" is an important qualifier: "Do not marvel" in John 3:7 clearly does not mean "Do not start to marvel." In this instance, as in many others, the aorist adds *urgency* to the prohibition.

(3) *The Deliberative Subjunctive.* The subjunctive is commonly used in deliberative questions, that is, questions in which a person deliberates about what to do before acting. When the question is rhetorical, no an-

swer is expected. In this construction, the English future tense is generally used in translation.

John 19:15:   τὸν βασιλέα ὑμῶν **σταυρώσω**;
                "**Shall I crucify** your king?"

(4) *The Subjunctive of Emphatic Negation.* The double negative οὐ μή may be used with the *aorist* subjunctive to strongly deny that something will happen. In this instance, οὐ μή is rendered "certainly not" or "never." Again, the English future is generally used to convey the idea of the Greek construction.

Matt 5:20:   **οὐ μὴ εἰσέλθητε** εἰς τὴν βασιλέαν τῶν οὐρανῶν.
               "**You will certainly not enter** the kingdom of heaven."
or   "**You will never enter** the kingdom of heaven."

Emphatic negation is sometimes (though rarely) expressed by οὐ μή with the *future indicative* (see Matt 16:22: οὐ μὴ ἔσται σοι τοῦτο, "This will never happen to you").

The Subjunctive in Subordinate Clauses

(1) *Purpose Clauses.* Purpose clauses indicate the purpose or intent of the action of the main verb. Purpose clauses are most frequently introduced by ἵνα or ὅπως, both of which may be rendered "in order that" or "that." In the case of negative purpose, ἵνα μή and ὅπως μή may be rendered "in order that . . . not" or "lest."

John 1:7:   οὗτος ἦλθεν εἰς μαρτυρίαν **ἵνα μαρτυρήσῃ** περὶ τοῦ
              φωτός.
              "He came for a witness **in order that he might testify**
              about the light."

As is to be expected, this verse uses the unmarked aorist subjunctive. An interesting example of the juxtaposition of the *aorist* and *present* subjunctive in a final clause is John 10:38: ἵνα γνῶτε καὶ γινώσκητε ὅτι ἐν ἐμοὶ ὁ πατήρ, "that you might know and keep on knowing that the Father is in me." The difference here seems to be between the fact of knowing and the continuing process of knowing.

The tense of the subjunctive in a purpose clause must always be carefully noted. At the same time, overinterpretation is to be avoided (e.g., the purpose of John's Gospel cannot be decided merely on the basis of the tense of the subjunctive found in John 20:31 [either the present πιστεύητε or the aorist πιστεύσητε]).

(2) *Indefinite Clauses.* The subjunctive may be used in clauses introduced by a relative pronoun that does not refer to a definite person or thing. In these clauses, the relative pronoun is followed by the particle ἄν, which adds an element of indefiniteness to the clause.

Matt 20:27: καὶ **ὃς ἂν θέλῃ** ἐν ὑμῖν εἶναι πρῶτος ἔσται ὑμῶν δοῦλος.
"And **whoever wants** to be first among you will be your slave."

(3) *Conditional Clauses.* This use of the subjunctive involves the particle ἐάν ("if") in the protasis of a conditional sentence (see below).

153. Conditional Sentences

As its name indicates, a conditional sentence is a statement of an event that is conditioned upon something else happening (e.g., "If he is an apostle, he will be saved"). A complete conditional sentence has two clauses: an "if" clause ("If he is an apostle") and a main clause ("he will be saved"). The "if" clause is called the *protasis* (from πρότασις, "a putting forward"), and the main clause is called the *apodosis* (from ἀπό-δοσις, "a giving back"). The protasis is grammatically dependent upon the apodosis. Only the apodosis can stand alone grammatically as a complete sentence.

Greek has two general types of conditional sentences: real and potential. A real condition expresses a plain, though conditioned, fact: "If God loves us, we must love." A potential condition expresses a contingency: "If God permits, we will do this." Real conditions have the indicative mood in the protasis, while for the most part potential conditions have the subjunctive in the protasis. The negative is οὐ with the indicative and μή with the subjunctive.

The following treatment of conditional sentences gives only the simplest and most common constructions that appear in the New Testament. When these have been mastered, the less common constructions will present little difficulty.

Conditions with the Indicative Mood in the Protasis

(1) *Simple Condition.* This condition is used when the speaker assumes the reality of the premise. Simple conditions are expressed by εἰ ("if") with the indicative mood in the protasis and usually the indicative mood

181

in the apodosis. The premise in the protasis may or may not be actually true. If the premise is objectively true, it may be rendered "since."

Gal 5:18: εἰ δὲ πνεύματι ἄγεσθε, οὐκ ἐστὲ ὑπὸ νόμον.
"But if you are being led by the Spirit, you are not under law."

or possibly "But since you are being led by the Spirit, you are not under law."

This is the most common class of New Testament conditional sentences, occurring some 300 times. An example of a "real" condition in which the "reality" is only assumed for the sake of argument is Matt 12:26: "If [εἰ] Satan casts out Satan . . ."

(2) *Contrary-to-Fact Condition.* This condition is used when the speaker assumes the premise to be untrue. Contrary-to-fact conditions are expressed by εἰ with a secondary tense of the indicative in the protasis and the particle ἄν with a secondary tense of the indicative in the apodosis. The premise may be actually contrary to fact (see John 5:46), or it may be contrary to what the speaker believes to be the facts (see Luke 7:39).

John 11:32: εἰ ἦς ὧδε οὐκ ἄν μου ἀπέθανεν ὁ ἀδελφός.
"If you had been here, my brother would not have died."

The thought here is, "If you had been here [and you weren't!], my brother would not have died [but he did!]." Here the conditional sentence is being used as a mild rebuke.

Conditions with the Subjunctive Mood in the Protasis

(1) *Probable Future Condition.* This construction is used to express a condition believed by the speaker to be a realizable fact in the future. Probable future conditions are expressed by ἐάν ("if" = εἰ + ἄν) with the subjunctive in the protasis and the *future* indicative in the apodosis. The subjunctive is appropriate because of the element of doubt in this type of condition.

Heb 6:3: καὶ τοῦτο ποιήσομεν ἐὰν ἐπιτρέπῃ ὁ θεός.
"And this we will do, if God permits."

(2) *Present General Condition.* This construction is used to express a condition that is believed by the speaker to be generally true in the pres-

ent. Present general conditions are expressed by ἐάν with the subjunctive in the protasis and the *present* indicative in the apodosis.

1 John 1:8:   ἐὰν εἴπωμεν ὅτι ἁμαρτίαν οὐκ ἔχομεν, ἡ ἀλήθεια οὐκ ἔστιν ἐν ἡμῖν.
"If we say that we do not have sin, the truth is not in us."

The following chart summarizes the most commonly occurring Greek conditional sentences:

Name	Protasis	Apodosis
Simple	εἰ + indicative	indicative (usually)
Contrary-to-fact	εἰ + indicative	ἄν + indicative
Probable Future	ἐάν + subjunctive	future indicative
Present General	ἐάν + subjunctive	present indicative

154. Vocabulary

a. Additional conjunctions, adverbs, and particles.

ἄν	A particle adding an element of indefiniteness to a clause
ἐάν	*if* (εἰ + ἄν; used with subj.)
ἐὰν μή	*except, unless* (used with subj.)
εἰ	*if* (used with indicative)
ἵνα	*that, in order that* (used with subj.)
ὅπως	*that, in order that* (used with subj.)
ὅταν	*whenever, when* (ὅτε + ἄν; used with subj.)
πάλιν	*again*
πῶς	*how?*
ὡς	*as, about*

155. Exercises

a. Read the lesson carefully. Learn by heart the present active subjunctive of λύω—its suffixes are used throughout the subjunctive. Remember that the key to recognizing the subjunctive is the long vowel in its ending.

b. Memorize the vocabulary to this lesson.

c. Translate 1 John 1:5–10. If there are any words that have not appeared in the vocabularies to this point, look them up in a Greek lexicon. For guidance on the choice of a lexicon, see the Epilogue (§176). (Note: the verb form ἀφῇ in verse nine is the second aorist active subjunctive, third singular, from ἀφίημι ["I forgive"], a verb of the -μι conjugation [see Lesson 25]).

24

THE IMPERATIVE AND OPTATIVE MOODS

All languages have means of expressing commands, entreaties, and prohibitions. Greek most commonly expresses these functions by means of the imperative mood. This lesson introduces the imperative mood as well as the final mood to be studied, the optative.

156. Introducing the Imperative

The basic function of the imperative mood is to express action that can be realized only by the exercise of the will of one person upon that of another (e.g., "please *go*"; "*run* quickly"; "*be* quiet"). The imperative mood can occur in the present, aorist, and perfect tenses. However, the perfect active imperative is not found in the New Testament, and the perfect passive imperative occurs only in Mark 4:39. There is no first person imperative. The negative with the imperative is μή.

All imperatives refer to future time, since a command by its very nature refers to a time subsequent to that of the command itself. However, the imperative, as a mood, is timeless. The essential distinction is rather between the kinds of action being described (see §15). The aorist imperative generally denotes an urgent command without regard to its continuation or frequency, while the present imperative generally denotes a command to continue to do an action or to do it repeatedly. This difference is well illustrated in the parallel versions of a petition in the so-called Lord's Prayer. Matthew uses an aorist imperative, whereas Luke uses a present imperative:

Matt 6:11: τὸν ἄρτον ἡμῶν τὸν ἐπιούσιον **δὸς** ἡμῖν
σήμερον.

Luke 11:3: τὸν ἄρτον ἡμῶν τὸν ἐπιούσιον **δίδου** ἡμῖν καθ᾿
ἡμέραν.

Here Matthew's aorist emphasizes the simple act: "give [today]," whereas Luke's present implies duration: "keep on giving [each day]." Note that the aorist imperative serves to indicate *that* something is to be done, whereas the present imperative specifies *how* or *when* something is to be done.

Another important distinction between the present and the aorist imperative is the difference between general precepts and specific commands. A general precept is a moral regulation that is broadly applicable in many situations, while a specific command is a request for action to be done in a particular situation. As a rule of thumb, general precepts in the New Testament employ the *present* imperative, and specific commands the *aorist* imperative. Note the following examples:

Rom 12:14: "*Bless* those who persecute you." (present imperative)

Luke 6:8: "*Arise* and *come forward.*" (aorist imperatives)

Hence, in addition to meaning "keep on doing," in certain contexts the present imperative is to be understood in a *customary* sense: "make it your habit to do" or "do whenever the situation arises." As might be expected, in books where narrative is predominant (such as the Gospels), the aorist imperative tends to occur more frequently than the present. On the other hand, in books that are mainly didactic or hortatory (such as the Pauline epistles), the present imperative is used more often than the aorist.

157. The Forms of the Imperative

The forms of the *present* imperative are given below. Forms given in bold type are identical to those of the indicative mood. These forms can be distinguished from each other only by the context.

(1) Present active imperative.

	Singular		Plural	
2.	λῦε	*loose*	**λύετε**	*loose*
3.	λυέτω	*let him loose*	λυέτωσαν	*let them loose*

186

(2) Present middle imperative.

2.	λύου	loose yourself	**λύεσθε**	loose yourselves
3.	λυέσθω	let him loose himself	λυέσθωσαν	let them loose themselves

(3) Present passive imperative.

2.	λύου	be loosed	**λύεσθε**	be loosed
3.	λυέσθω	let him be loosed	λυέσθωσαν	let them be loosed

The forms of the *first aorist* imperative are as follows. Note the absence of the augment in the aorist imperative.

(1) First aorist active imperative.

2.	λῦσον	loose	λύσατε	loose
3.	λυσάτω	let him loose	λυσάτωσαν	let them loose

(2) First aorist middle imperative.

2.	λῦσαι	loose yourself	λύσασθε	loose yourselves
3.	λυσάσθω	let him loose himself	λυσάσθωσαν	let them loose themselves

(3) First aorist passive imperative

2.	λύθητι	be loosed	λύθητε	be loosed
3.	λυθήτω	let him be loosed	λυθήτωσαν	let them be loosed

The forms of the *second aorist* imperative are as follows:

(1) Second aorist active imperative.

2.	λίπε	leave	λίπετε	leave
3.	λιπέτω	let him leave	λιπέτωσαν	let them leave

Compare the forms of the *present* active imperative: λῦε, λυέτω, etc.

(2) Second aorist middle imperative.

2.	λιποῦ	leave yourself	λίπεσθε	leave yourselves
3.	λιπέσθω	let him leave himself	λιπέσθωσαν	let them leave themselves

(3) Second aorist passive imperative.

2.	ἀποστάληθι	be sent	ἀποστάλητε	be sent
3.	ἀποσταλήτω	let him be sent	ἀποσταλήτωσαν	let them be sent

The forms of the *present imperative* of εἰμί are as follows:

2.	ἴσθι	be	ἔστε	be
3.	ἔστω	let him be	ἔστωσαν	let them be

It should also be noted that verbs that are deponent in the indicative mood will be deponent in the imperative. For example, γίνομαι has the following forms:

2.	γίνου	become	γίνεσθε	become
3.	γινέσθω	let him become	γινέσθωσαν	let them become

158. Uses of the Imperative

The following are the basic uses of the imperative mood:

(1) *The Imperative of Command.* This is the fundamental use of the imperative. It makes a direct demand upon the will of another.

1 Thess 5:16–18: πάντοτε **χαίρετε**, ἀδιαλείπτως **προσεύχεσθε**, ἐν παντὶ **εὐχαριστεῖτε**.
"Always **rejoice**, unceasingly **pray**, in everything **give thanks**."

Two imperatival forms of ὁράω, namely, ἴδε (2 aor. act. impv.) and ἰδού (2 aor. mid. impv.), merit special attention. Owing to Septuagintal usage, both terms function as interjections and may be rendered "See!", "Look!", "Behold!", etc. They may be used either absolutely (e.g., Matt 11:10) or with the nominative (e.g., Rev 4:1). Another common New Testament interjection is οὐαί, "Woe!", "How terrible!"

(2) *The Imperative of Prohibition.* μή with the present imperative is generally used to prohibit the continuance of an action in progress. The word "stop" may be used in translation when the context suggests this sense.

1 Thess 5:19–20: τὸ πνεῦμα **μὴ σβέννυτε**, προφητείας **μὴ ἐξουθενεῖτε**.
"**Don't quench** the Spirit; **don't despise** prophecies."

or perhaps   "**Stop quenching** the Spirit; **stop despising** prophecies."

The *context*, of course, has to determine whether the particular action being proscribed is actually occurring or lies in the future. Generally, in *specific commands* the present imperative has the sense of "stop doing," while in *general precepts* the present imperative means "make it your habit *not* to do." Contrast μή plus the present imperative with μή plus the aorist subjunctive; the latter generally prohibits the beginning of an action (see §152).

(3) *The Imperative of Entreaty.* This is the use of the imperative to express a request rather than a direct command. This sense is sometimes expressed by using the word "please" in translation.

John 17:11: πάτερ ἄγιε, **τήρησον** αὐτούς.
"Holy Father, **preserve** them."

or   "Holy Father, **please preserve** them."

159. The Optative Mood

The optative mood was a common feature in Classical Greek but was gradually lost, its functions being taken over by the indicative and subjunctive moods. The main New Testament use of the optative is to express a wish (hence its name, from Lat. *opto*, "I wish"). The optative is found only 67 times in the New Testament and only in the present and aorist tenses. The negative is μή. The most common example of the optative is

Paul's μὴ γένοιτο, "May it not be!" Optatives can often be recognized by the presence of οι, ει, or αι after the verb stem:

1 Thess 5:23:   ὁ θεὸς τῆς εἰρήνης **ἁγιάσαι** ὑμᾶς.
   "**May** the God of peace **sanctify** you."

160. Vocabulary

a. Interjections.

ἰδού	*See!, Look!, Behold!* (cf. ἴδε)
οὐαί	*Woe!, How terrible!*

b. Additional -ω verbs.

ἀγοράζω	*I buy* (*agora*phobia [fear of the marketplace])
ἐγγίζω	*I come near* (cf. ἐγγύς)
ἐλπίζω	*I hope* (cf. ἐλπίς)
θαυμάζω	*I am amazed* (*thauma*turge [a magician])
καθαρίζω	*I cleanse* (*cathar*sis)
καθίζω	*I seat, I sit* (*cath*edral [a bishop's "seat"])
πειράζω	*I test, I tempt*
σκανδαλίζω	*I cause to stumble, I cause to sin*

161. Exercises

a. Read the lesson carefully. The key to learning the imperative forms is the second person plural, since it is the same as the corresponding form in the indicative mood (without, of course, the augment). Note that -ω and -ωσαν for the third person singular and plural (respectively) are present in all forms. The second person singular of all tenses and voices of the imperative calls for special study. Learn by heart (1) the present active imperative and (2) the present middle imperative of λύω.

b. Memorize the vocabulary to this lesson.

c. Translate 1 John 2:1–6.

25

THE CONJUGATION OF
-μι VERBS

This lesson introduces a unique but important class of Greek verbs called -μι verbs. The New Testament contains only a small number of -μι verbs, but those that do occur appear frequently. Reading the New Testament in Greek is impossible without a working knowledge of this class of verbs.

162. Introducing -μι Verbs

Greek contains two basic conjugations: the -ω conjugation, and the -μι conjugation. The -μι verbs are so named because their dictionary forms (present active indicative, first singular) end in -μι rather than -ω. These verbs have endings differing from those of the -ω conjugation in the *present*, *imperfect*, and *second aorist* tenses. In these tenses the -μι verbs do not use the connecting vowels ο/ε before their personal endings. Otherwise their endings are the same as those of -ω verbs.

The most common -μι verb is εἰμί (see §109). The most important -μι verbs other than εἰμί are δίδωμι ("I give"), τίθημι ("I put"), and ἵστημι ("I stand"). In the case of -μι verbs, it is especially important to remember the distinction made in §20 between the *verb* stem, from which most of the tenses of the verb are formed, and the *present* stem, from which the present and imperfect tenses are formed. The stems of the three principal -μι verbs are as follows:

-μι verb	Verb stem	Present stem
δίδωμι	δο	διδο
τίθημι	θε	τιθε
ἵστημι	στα	ἱστα

It will be observed that the present stem is a *reduplicated* form of the verb stem. (τιθε stands for θιθε, the first θ having been deaspirated to τ. ἱστα stands for σιστα, the initial σ having been replaced by the rough breathing.) This is called *present reduplication* since it occurs in the present and imperfect tenses of the verb. Present reduplication serves to indicate *imperfective* aspect in verb stems that are inherently aoristic (see §106). The reduplicated present stem is *lengthened* in the singular: διδο becomes διδω; τιθε becomes τιθη; and ἱστα becomes ἱστη.

163. The Forms of -μι Verbs

The paradigms of the three principal -μι verbs are given below. Forms other than those given here are regular enough to be recognized as they are encountered (these include participles, imperatives, and subjunctive forms). Other -μι verbs are so infrequent that it has been deemed wisest to omit them altogether.

(1) Present active indicative.

	1.	δίδωμι	τίθημι	ἵστημι
Sg.	2.	δίδως	τίθης	ἵστης
	3.	δίδωσι(ν)	τίθησι(ν)	ἵστησι(ν)
	1.	δίδομεν	τίθεμεν	ἵσταμεν
Pl.	2.	δίδοτε	τίθετε	ἵστατε
	3.	διδόασι(ν)	τιθέασι(ν)	ἱστᾶσι(ν)

(2) Present middle and passive indicative.

	1.	δίδομαι	τίθεμαι	ἵσταμαι
Sg.	2.	δίδοσαι	τίθεσαι	ἵστασαι
	3.	δίδοται	τίθεται	ἵσταται
	1.	διδόμεθα	τιθέμεθα	ἱστάμεθα
Pl.	2.	δίδοσθε	τίθεσθε	ἵστασθε
	3.	δίδονται	τίθενται	ἵστανται

(3) Imperfect active indicative.

	1.	ἐδίδουν	ἐτίθην	ἵστην
Sg.	2.	ἐδίδους	ἐτίθεις	ἵστης
	3.	ἐδίδου	ἐτίθει	ἵστη
	1.	ἐδίδομεν	ἐτίθεμεν	ἵσταμεν
Pl.	2.	ἐδίδοτε	ἐτίθετε	ἵστατε
	3.	ἐδίδοσαν	ἐτίθεσαν	ἵστασαν

(4) Imperfect middle and passive indicative.

	1.	ἐδιδόμην	ἐτιθέμην	ἱστάμην
Sg.	2.	ἐδίδοσο	ἐτίθεσο	ἵστασο
	3.	ἐδίδοτο	ἐτίθετο	ἵστατο
	1.	ἐδιδόμεθα	ἐτιθέμεθα	ἱστάμεθα
Pl.	2.	ἐδίδοσθε	ἐτίθεσθε	ἵστασθε
	3.	ἐδίδοντο	ἐτίθεντο	ἵσταντο

193

(5) Aorist active indicative.

	1.	ἔδωκα	ἔθηκα	ἔστησα
Sg.	2.	ἔδωκας	ἔθηκας	ἔστησας
	3.	ἔδωκε(ν)	ἔθηκε(ν)	ἔστησε(ν)
	1.	ἐδώκαμεν	ἐθήκαμεν	ἐστήσαμεν
Pl.	2.	ἐδώκατε	ἐθήκατε	ἐστήσατε
	3.	ἔδωκαν	ἔθηκαν	ἔστησαν

i. Note that δίδωμι and τίθημι have κ instead of σ in the aorist tense stem.

ii. The first aorist form ἔστησα is *transitive*, that is, it takes a direct object in the accusative case, as in Matt 4:5: "*He stood* [ἔστησεν] him upon the pinnacle of the temple." ἵστημι also has a second aorist form ἔστην, which is *intransitive*, that is, it does not take a direct object. An example is John 20:19: "Jesus *stood* [ἔστη] in the midst."

(6) Future active indicative.

	1.	δώσω	θήσω	στήσω
Sg.	2.	δώσεις	θήσεις	στήσεις
		etc.	etc.	etc.

(7) Future middle indicative.

	1.	δώσομαι	θήσομαι	στήσομαι
Sg.	2.	δώσῃ	θήσῃ	στήσῃ
		etc.	etc.	etc.

(8) Future passive indicative.

	1.	δοθήσομαι	τεθήσομαι	σταθήσομαι
Sg.	2.	δοθήσῃ	τεθήσῃ	σταθήσῃ
		etc.	etc.	etc.

(9) Aorist passive indicative.

	1.	ἐδόθην	ἐτέθην	ἐστάθην
Sg.	2.	ἐδόθης	ἐτέθης	ἐστάθης
		etc.	etc.	etc.

(10) Present active infinitive.

διδόναι	τιθέναι	ἱστάναι

(11) Present middle and passive infinitive.

δίδοσθαι	τίθεσθαι	ἵστασθαι

(12) Aorist active infinitive.

δοῦναι	θεῖναι	στῆναι

(13) Aorist passive infinitive.

δοθῆναι	τεθῆναι	σταθῆναι

164. Vocabulary

a. -μι verbs.

ἀνίστημι	*I raise, I rise* (cf. ἀνάστασις)
ἀποδίδωμι	*I give back, I repay*
ἀπόλλυμι	*I destroy*
ἀφίημι	*I send away, I forgive*
δείκνυμι	*I show*
δίδωμι	*I give* (√ δο; *donate*)
δύναμαι	*I am able, I can* (dep. verb; cf. δύναμις)
ἐπιτίθημι	*I put on*
ἵστημι	*I stand, I cause to stand* (√ στα; *static*)

195

κάθημαι	*I sit* (dep. verb)
παραδίδωμι	*I betray, I hand over, I pass on*
τίθημι	*I place, I put* (√ θε; *the*sis)
φημί	*I say* (√ φα; *pha*tic)

165. Exercises

a. Read the lesson carefully, noting the various morphemes used to form -μι verbs. Learn by heart the present and the imperfect active indicative of δίδωμι.

b. Memorize the vocabulary to this lesson.

c. Translate 1 John 2:7–14.

26

READING YOUR GREEK
NEW TESTAMENT
SIX AREAS OF APPLICATION

166. Introduction

In the previous twenty-five lessons, you have spent a significant amount of time with grammar. It is now time to summarize how this knowledge affects your understanding of Scripture. Grammatical study will help you see how the parts of a passage are related to each other, provide you with insights into what the text is actually saying, and even help you organize your sermons and Bible lessons. There are at least six critical areas where a knowledge of Greek grammar plays a major role in exegesis: aspect; voice; the article; word, phrase, and clause order; syntactical structure; and discourse structure. Other areas could be pointed out. A section on phonology, for example, might have been included. The importance of phonology is seen, for instance, in Hebrews 1:1 in the recurrence of the consonant π in πολυμερῶς ("in many parts"), πολυτρόπως ("in many ways"), πάλαι ("long ago"), πατράσιν ("fathers"), and προφήταις ("prophets"). This device, known as alliteration, both contributes to the aesthetic appeal of the text and indicates prominence. But phonology is not all that germane at this level of exegesis. Care has been taken to limit our discussion to the areas of greatest application for the beginning student. As with previous lessons, the aim is to present numerous examples to show you just what to look for.

167. Observe the Aspect

Aspect, it will be recalled, refers to the view of the action that the speaker chooses to present to the hearer (see §15). The three categories of aspect in Greek are aoristic, imperfective, and perfective. Generally speaking, aoristic aspect is the unmarked aspect, with imperfective aspect the more heavily marked, and perfective aspect the most heavily marked.

Aoristic aspect is also the "background" aspect, used as a backdrop against which other actions may be viewed. Imperfective aspect is the "foreground" aspect, standing out against the aorist, while perfective aspect is the "frontground" aspect, prominent wherever it is used. The three aspects in Greek may be visualized as follows:

Aoristic aspect	Unmarked	Emphasizes the verbal idea
Imperfective aspect	Marked	Emphasizes the process
Perfective aspect	Marked	Emphasizes the effects

Aspect must not be confused with time of action. English asks: "*When* did it happen?" Greek asks: "*How* did it happen?"

Aspect is best illustrated in an extended analysis. Romans 6:7–11 is a good example: "For *the one who has died* [aoristic aspect] is *freed* [perfective aspect] from sin. Now if *we have died* [aoristic aspect] with Christ, *we believe* [imperfective aspect] that *we will also live* [aoristic aspect] with him, *knowing* [perfective aspect] that if Christ *was raised* [aoristic aspect] from the dead, then *he no longer dies* [imperfective aspect] and death *no longer dominates* [imperfective aspect] him. For the death that *he died* [aoristic aspect] he died [aoristic aspect] to sin once for all. But the life that *he lives* [imperfective aspect] *he lives* [imperfective aspect] to God. So *you also must consider* [imperfective aspect] yourselves dead to sin and *alive* [imperfective aspect] to God." Although many other details could be examined in this text, the above analysis demonstrates how verbal aspect helps us to establish the meaning of a text. Note also the following examples:

a. Colossians 1:16: "For in him all things *were created* [aoristic aspect] . . . , and all things *have been created* [perfective aspect] through him and for him." Here the aorist points to the historical fact of creation, whereas the more heavily marked perfect stresses Christ's continuing sovereignty over his creation.

b. 1 Corinthians 15:4: "Christ *died* [aoristic aspect] . . . and *was raised* [perfective aspect]." The aorist "died" calls attention to the fact of Christ's death—"he did, in fact, die." However, by using the perfect "was raised," Paul deliberately highlights an essential aspect of the gospel account: "the Christ who died was raised and is still alive today!"

c. Romans 6:13: "*Present* yourselves [aoristic aspect] to God as those *alive* [imperfective aspect] from the dead." Typically, the aorist here has been interpreted to mean "present yourselves *once and for all.*" The aorist, however, is not concerned with *how often* the action is to take place, but *that* it is to take place. Hence we cannot conclude *from the aorist* that one can make a single offering, never to be repeated. The stress on kind of action is found only in the word "alive," where Paul uses a present participle to show that believers share in Christ's resurrection life (see also v 4).

168. Observe the Voice

As we have seen, voice refers to the manner in which the speaker chooses to relate the subject to the action of the verb (see §14). The three categories of voice in Greek are active, middle, and passive. The active represents the subject as simply acting without any further comment on its involvement in the action. The middle and passive voices, on the other hand, highlight the grammatical subject. This may be visualized as follows:

Active voice	Unmarked	Emphasizes the action
Middle voice	Marked	Emphasizes the subject
Passive voice	Marked	Emphasizes the subject

Note, for example, 3 John 12: "Demetrius *has received* a good testimony from everyone." Here the Greek passive form of the verb "receive" facilitates the focus on Demetrius by emphasizing the person affected. Note also these examples:

a. 1 Corinthians 13:12: "Now *I know* [active voice] in part, but then *I will fully know* [middle voice], even as *I have been fully known* [passive]."

b. 1 Thessalonians 1:2: "*We give thanks* [active voice] to God always for all of you as *we make* [middle voice] mention of you in our prayers."

c. Matthew 5:4: "Blessed are they who *mourn* [active voice], for they *will be comforted* [passive voice]."

169. Observe the Article

The presence or absence of the Greek article is often important in exegesis. The sheer frequency of the article in the Greek New Testament (some 19,700 occurrences) makes it a significant feature of syntax. The general function of the article may be outlined as follows (see also §33):

Presence: (1) *Definite stress.* Galatians 3:8: "*the* Scripture [i.e., not any writing, but the Old Testament itself] foresaw that God would justify the Gentiles."

(2) *Anaphoric stress* (from ἀναφορά, "a carrying back"). James 2:14: "Can *that* faith [i.e., the works-less faith just mentioned] save him?"

Absence: (1) *Indefinite stress.* 1 Timothy 6:10: "The love of money is *a* root [i.e., one of many roots] of all kinds of evil."

(2) *Qualitative stress.* Galatians 1:1: "Paul, *an* apostle [i.e., an authoritative representative, but not the only one] of Jesus Christ."

Two other uses of the article call for discussion. The Granville Sharp Rule (formulated in 1798) states that when two nouns of the same case are connected by καί, a single article before the first noun denotes conceptual unity, whereas the repetition of the article denotes particularity. An example of two nouns connected by a single article is Titus 2:13: **τοῦ** μεγάλου **θεοῦ** καὶ **σωτῆρος** ἡμῶν Ἰησοῦ Χριστοῦ, "our great God and Savior Jesus Christ." Here the single article shows that the author viewed Christ as God. An example of a repeated article to denote particularity is Revelation 1:8: Ἐγώ εἰμι **τὸ** ἄλφα καὶ **τὸ** ὦ, "I am the Alpha and the Omega," that is, Jesus is both *the* beginning and *the* end.

The Granville Sharp Rule could be extended to include prepositional phrases. Two nouns connected by καί and governed by a single preposition usually imply conceptual unity. An example is John 3:5: ἐὰν μή τις γεννηθῇ ἐξ ὕδατος καὶ πνεύματος, "unless one is born of water and Spirit." This clause has usually been interpreted to refer to two distinct births. However, since "water" and "Spirit" are both governed by one preposition, it could be argued that only one birth is in view, the "water" emphasizing the cleansing work of the "Spirit."

Colwell's Rule (published in 1933) states that anarthrous predicate nominatives that precede the copula (the verb "to be") are usually definite in meaning. The implications of this rule are especially notable in John 1:1: θεὸς ἦν ὁ λόγος, "the Word was God." θεός, the predicate nominative, is anarthrous and precedes the copula ἦν. The result is that θεός is

almost certainly definite in meaning: "the Word was *God*"—not merely
"*a* god."

170. Observe the Word, Phrase, and Clause Order

Word, phrase, and clause order in New Testament Greek are fairly
well-defined, and variations from the norm are often used for purposes of
conveying emphasis (see §35). In English, emphasis is often conveyed by
tone of voice or by italics:

"This man was God's Son" (no emphasis—a simple statement of fact).
"*This* man was God's Son" (i.e., "He, and no other, was God's Son").
"This man was *God's* Son" (i.e., "He was God's, not a human being's, Son").
"This man was God's *Son*" (emphasizing sonship).

In Greek, emphasis is generally conveyed by placing a word out of its
usual order. Thus, in Matthew 27:54, ἀληθῶς θεοῦ υἱὸς ἦν οὗτος ("Truly this man was *God's* Son"), the position of the possessive genitive θεοῦ
before its noun is emphatic. Notice also that ἀληθῶς conveys emphasis,
as do adverbs generally. Finally, observe that the subject οὗτος follows
the verb ἦν. This order—verb first, then the subject—is a common one
in the New Testament and is probably due to the influence of the Septua-
gint (the Greek Old Testament). Frequently, however, the subject comes
before the verb, especially when it introduces a new topic or is being
contrasted to something else in the near context.

The norms of Greek word, phrase, and clause order are given below.
Any departure from the customary order, whether by pre-positioning or
post-positioning, may be exegetically significant. Also listed are word
classes that intrinsically convey emphasis.

(1) *Customary Word/Phrase Order*

(a)	Copulative clauses:	Verb	Subject	Complement
(b)	Non-copulative clauses:	Verb	Subject	Object	Indirect Object

Prep. Phrase

(2) *Customary Clause Order*

Temporal (ὅταν)	**MAIN CLAUSE**	Temporal (ἕως, ἀχρί)
Conditional (εἰ, ἐάν)		Neg. Conditional
		(ἐὰν μή)
		Local (ὅπου)
		Comparative (καθῶς)
		Purpose (ἵνα)
		Causal (ὅτι)
		Content (ὅτι)

(3) *Intrinsically Emphatic Word Classes*

    (a) Adverbs (e.g., ἀληθῶς, εὐθύς)
    (b) Emphatic personal pronouns (ἐμοῦ, ἐμοί, ἐμέ, etc.)
    (c) Emphatic possessive adjectives (σός, ἡμέτερος, etc.)
    (d) Nominative personal pronouns (ἐγώ, ἡμεῖς, etc.)
    (e) Intensive pronouns (αὐτός, αὐτή, etc.)
    (f) Intensive adverbs (οὐχί, νυνί)
    (g) Double negatives (οὐ μή)

To summarize, emphatic words, phrases, and clauses normally belong to the following classes (including some classes discussed in previous lessons):

    (a) Direct objects preceding the verb
    (b) Subjects preceding the verb (except where a new topic or contrast is in view)
    (c) Predicate adjectives/nominatives preceding their subject and/or verb
    (d) Genitive nouns/pronouns preceding the noun they modify
    (e) Attributive adjectives following the noun they modify
    (f) Attributive demonstratives following the nouns they modify
    (g) Imperative verbs following their subject and/or object
    (h) Prepositional phrases preceding their verb
    (i) Indirect objects preceding their verb
    (j) Temporal (ἕως, ἀχρί), negative conditional, local, comparative, purpose, causal, and content clauses preceding the main clause
    (k) Temporal (ὅταν) and conditional clauses following the main clause

(l) Word classes that intrinsically imply prominence (adverbs, emphatic pronouns, etc.)

When reading Greek, pay special attention to nominative complements and accusative objects at the beginning of sentences. Watch, moreover, for the splitting of a syntactic unit. Such grammatical discontinuity generally conveys emphasis. In 3 John 4, for example, the adjective "greater" is separated from its noun "joy" by four Greek words. This device is especially common in Luke, Paul, and Hebrews. Finally, the "nominative absolute" construction, in which the subject is placed at the head of its clause without regard to the syntax, focuses attention on the subject. An example is John 1:33: "But *the one who sent me* to baptize in water, *he* said to me . . ." This is more emphatic than "But the one who sent me to baptize in water said to me . . ." This is a common Semitic idiom and a notable feature of John's Gospel.

Study the following sentences:

a. 1 John 1:5: ὁ θεὸς **φῶς** ἐστιν.
    "God is **light**."

b. John 19:18: **αὐτὸν** ἐσταύρωσαν.
    "They crucified **him**."

c. 1 John 1:8: ἐὰν εἴπωμεν ὅτι **ἁμαρτίαν** οὐχ ἔχομεν,
    ἑαυτοὺς πλανῶμεν.
    "If we say that we do not have **sin**, we deceive **ourselves**."

d. 1 Cor 1:24: Χριστὸν, **θεοῦ** δύναμιν καὶ **θεοῦ** σοφίαν.
    "Christ, **God's** power and **God's** wisdom."

e. John 1:46: **ἐκ Ναζαρὲτ** δύναταί τι ἀγαθὸν εἶναι;
    "Can anything good come **out of Nazareth**?"

f. Gal 3:29 ἄρα **τοῦ Ἀβραὰμ** σπέρμα ἐστέ, **κατ'** **ἐπαγγελίαν** κληρονόμοι.
    "Therefore you are **Abraham's** seed, heirs **according to promise**."

g.   1 Thess 3:8   νῦν ζῶμεν, **ἐὰν ὑμεῖς** στήκετε ἐν κυρίῳ.
"Now we live, **if you** stand firm in the Lord."

h.   John 8:45   **ἐγὼ** δὲ **ὅτι τὴν ἀλήθειαν** λέγω, οὐ πιστεύετέ μοι.
"But **because I** speak **the truth**, you do not believe me."

i.   Phil 2:22   **σὺν ἐμοὶ** ἐδούλευσεν εἰς τὸ εὐαγγέλιον.
"He served **with me** in the gospel."

j.   Matt 2:16   Ἡρῴδης ἐθυμώθη **λίαν**.
"Herod was **exceedingly** angry."

k.   Matt 1:21   **αὐτὸς** γὰρ σώσει τὸν λαὸν αὐτοῦ ἀπὸ τῶν ἁμαρτιῶν αὐτῶν.
"For he **himself** will save his people from their sins."

l.   John 10:11   Ἐγώ εἰμι ὁ ποιμὴν ὁ **καλός**.
"**I** am the **good** shepherd."

m.   John 5:22   **τὴν κρίσιν** δέδωκεν τῷ υἱῷ.
"He has given **judgment** to the Son."

n.   John 1:14   ὁ λόγος **σὰρξ** ἐγένετο.
"The Word became **flesh**."

o.   2 Cor 7:1   **ταύτας** οὖν ἔχοντες τὰς ἐπαγγελίας.
"Having, therefore, **these** promises."

p.   John 6:27   **τοῦτον** γὰρ ὁ πατὴρ ἐσφράγισεν ὁ θεός.
"For the Father, even God, has set his seal on **this one**."

q.   Mark 14:31   **οὐ μή** σε ἀπαρνήσομαι.
"I will **never** deny you!"

These are but a few specimens taken from a larger number of instances, and selected for their brevity. You will be able to find many more examples for yourself as you read the Greek New Testament.

171. Observe the Syntactical Structure

One of the most satisfying (and challenging) aspects of exegesis is tracing an author's argument. A weakness in many commentaries is their failure to explain how each proposition relates to preceding and following propositions. A proposition is simply a statement about something, usually represented by a clause (e.g., "Christ died") or a phrase (e.g., "for our sins").

In studying the relationships that exist between propositions, we can assume that the choices an author makes are *meaningful* choices. The use of a main clause instead of a participial clause, for example, is not a matter of random variation but one of meaningful (though not necessarily conscious) choice. And it is a fair assumption that the New Testament authors took it for granted that their readers would make a reasonable effort to see how an argument developed.

Relationships between propositions are of two types: coordinate or subordinate (see §34). Coordinate propositions are independent and can stand alone, whereas subordinate propositions are related in some supporting way to the main proposition. If I say, "I studied Greek and I went to seminary," both "I studied Greek" and "I went to seminary" are independent propositions, since there is no syntactically dependent relationship between them. But if I say, "I studied Greek when I went to seminary," the clause "when I went to seminary" is a subordinate proposition since it is dependent upon the main clause "I studied Greek." In the New Testament, coordinating propositions are generally signaled by coordinating conjunctions such as καί, δέ, ἀλλά, οὖν, and διό, and by simple juxtaposition with no connecting word (asyndeton). Subordinating propositions are usually signaled by subordinating conjunctions such as γάρ, ἵνα, ὅτι, and ὥστε, by non-finite verbs (participles and infinitives), by relative pronouns, and by prepositions.

In narrative texts, such as the Gospels and Acts, propositions are frequently represented by a single clause or sentence. In the epistles, on the other hand, a group of clauses is more often used (see, e.g., Eph 1:3–14). In studying the propositional arrangement of a text, it is helpful to arrange subordinate clauses under the main clause in the following manner:

MAIN CLAUSE

    SUBORDINATE CLAUSE A

    SUBORDINATE CLAUSE B

    SUBORDINATE CLAUSE C.

In this way we can see what the key supporting clauses are and how they relate to the main clause. Consider the following examples:

(1) Ephesians 5:18–21:

Be filled with the Spirit
   a. **speaking** to each other in psalms
   b. **singing and making melody** in your hearts
   c. **giving thanks** for all things
   d. **submitting yourselves** to one another in the fear of Christ.

(2) Matthew 28:19–20:

Make disciples of all the nations
   a. **baptizing** them . . .
   b. **teaching** them . . .

In both of these examples, participial clauses support the main clause and tell us *how* to fulfill the content of the command. It should be noted that the main clause will not always come first in the Greek text. Because it is central, however, you will still want to display the main clause before setting off any subordinate clauses that may be present. In the following analysis of Hebrews 12:1–2, the main clause is given first, even though it is actually the third clause of the paragraph:

Therefore **let us run** (τρέχωμεν) with endurance the race set before us
   a. **having** (ἔχοντες) so great a cloud of witnesses surrounding us
   b. **laying aside** (ἀποθέμενοι) every encumbrance and the easily entangling sin
   c. **fixing** (ἀφορῶντες) our eyes on Jesus the author and perfecter of faith
      who endured the cross
         for the joy set before him
      and sat down at the right hand of the throne of God
         despising the shame.

Notice that the first line of the analysis alone contains an independent finite verb (τρέχωμεν, "let us run"). This clause expresses the author's main point: *running the race with endurance*. Now observe how this clause is modified by three participial clauses that qualify "the race": (a) those who have already completed the race are a great encouragement to us; (b) we cannot, however, hope to attain the goal without an abhorrence of personal sin; and (c) in view of our own weaknesses, we must look to Jesus, "the author and perfecter of faith." The remaining items in the paragraph are a striking description of Jesus, showing how the theme of "running the race" climaxes in "Jesus and who he is." By reducing these elements to an outline, we can move directly from theory to practice:

Text: Hebrews 12:1–2

Title: Run to Win!

Theme: The Christian is called upon to follow the example of Jesus into a life of submission and obedience ("let us run with endurance. . . .")

Outline:

    I. Our Encouragement ("having so great a cloud of witnesses")

    II. Our Entanglements ("laying aside every encumbrance . . .")

    III. Our Example ("fixing our eyes on Jesus...")

This simple outline clearly demonstrates how by analyzing the structure of a text we can move from interpretation to application. In shaping our interpretation by the text's internal structure, we can emphasize the dominant thoughts of the author without majoring on the minors or reading into the text our favorite subjects.

Now notice how the author's focus on Jesus is confirmed by the rhetorical device known as "chiasmus" (the following diagram is a paraphrase):

A having SEATED around us such a great cloud of witnesses

   B SETTING ASIDE every weight and clinging sin

      C with PATIENT ENDURANCE

         D let us run the race THAT IS SET BEFORE US

            E fixing our eyes on Jesus, the author and perfecter of faith

         D´ who for the joy THAT WAS SET BEFORE HIM

      C´ PATIENTLY ENDURED the cross

   B´ SCORNING the shame

A´ and HAS TAKEN HIS SEAT at the right hand of the throne of God

A chiasmus is simply an inverted parallelism in which the center line receives the emphasis. Discovery of this pattern is not only an indication of the author's literary artistry, but also calls attention to the centerpiece of the entire paragraph: Jesus!

To summarize, careful analysis of syntactical structure may provide increased understanding of individual words, sentences, and even entire paragraphs. The New Testament is filled with significant structures that often go completely ignored by beginning exegetes and scholars alike. For your convenience, the following analysis of Galatians 1:1–5 is provided in the hope that it will serve as a model for analyzing the structure of a New Testament passage.

(1) Paul (is writing) to the churches of Galatia [*"A to B"*]

   an apostle [*this fact was being challenged by the Judaizers*]
   not from men [*not a human source*]
   nor through man [*no individual human served as agent*]
   but through Jesus Christ and God the Father [*a divine source*]
         who raised him from the dead [*it was the risen Christ who called Paul*]
   and all the brothers with me [*Paul's gospel was not an oddity but the received message by all those with him*]

(2) Grace (be) to you and peace [*"Greeting"*]

   from God our Father and the Lord Jesus Christ [*a divine source*]
      who gave himself for our sins [*substitutionary atonement: nothing more needed*]
            that he might deliver us from this present evil age [*salvation involves holy living*]
                  according to the will of our God and Father [*Paul's gospel—not the Judaizers'—is according to God's plan*]
                        to whom be the glory forever. Amen. [*God therefore gets all the glory for salvation*]

Notice that Paul's opening greeting breathes something of the tone and contents of the entire letter. The usual elements of a letter are present ("A to B, Greeting"), but the reader is plunged immediately into the heart of Paul's theme:

(1) The source of Paul's apostolic authority (treated in chaps. 1–2)
(2) The gospel of grace (treated in chaps. 3–4)
(3) Deliverance from sin's power (treated in chaps. 5–6)

172. Observe the Discourse Structure

It has already been pointed out that meaning operates on different levels: words, clauses, sentences, paragraphs, and whole books. The linguistic discipline that tries to integrate the information deduced from all these levels is called *discourse analysis*. The aim of discourse analysis is to get at the total meaning of a text (discourse). Only then can the meaning of the individual words and sentences be fully understood. This method of analysis contrasts significantly with older methods of exegesis, in which the word was considered the central unit of study.

A discourse analysis of any given text usually starts with trying to divide it into major and minor sections and the sections into paragraphs. Then it is possible to tackle the meaning of sentences and words. In studying discourse, the interpreter looks closely at the structural features that bind the text together and that give it cohesion. These features include:

(a) Terminal features that mark the beginning and end of the discourse
(b) Features that mark major internal transitions
(c) Features that mark spatial, temporal, and logical relations
(d) Features that identify participants
(e) Features that foreground or background successive participants and events

Such elements as conjunctions, order of events, sentence length, and indications of time and place all play an important role in determining cohesion and progression of thought. For example, in Matthew's Gospel the adverb τότε often starts a new section (see 4:1, 5, 11), though it does not always have this function (4:10). Likewise, the phrase καὶ ἐγένετο (traditionally rendered "and it came to pass") often introduces a new section in Luke's Gospel. The phrase μετὰ ταῦτα ("after these things") normally begins a new section in John's Gospel. In Paul's letters, vocatives such as "brothers" often occur at the beginning of a new paragraph (e.g., 1 Thess 4:1, 13; 5:1, 12, 25). Paul also uses περὶ δέ ("Now about . . .") to indicate both unity and transition between larger sections of a text. περὶ δέ appears five times in 1 Corinthians (7:1, 25; 8:1; 12:1; 16:1), and in each instance Paul is introducing a new subject, probably in answer to questions posed to him by the Corinthians (see 7:1). Paul uses the same construction in 1 Thessalonians (4:9, 13; 5:1) to introduce significant topics in the letter: "brotherly love" (4:9–12), "the dead in Christ" (4:13–18), and "steadfast hope" (5:1–11).

These are but a few markers of cohesion and progression that are found in the New Testament. If you desire to pursue the relation between discourse analysis and Bible study in greater detail, there are several studies that you may find helpful (see the Epilogue). This lesson is only a beginning in your study of discourse structure. If you are now a bit more sensitive to transitional markers, paragraph structure, and relationships that exist between units of discourse, then you are off to a good start.

173. Exercises

a. Romans 1:1–7 reveals much about Paul's purpose(s) in writing Romans. Using the previous analysis of Galatians 1:1–5 as a model, indicate how the various parts of the paragraph relate to the whole.

(1) Paul (is writing) to those who are in Rome

beloved of God
called saints

    a servant of Jesus Christ
    called an apostle
    separated unto the gospel of God

which he announced beforehand
    through the prophets
    in the Holy Scriptures
    concerning his Son
        who came

from the seed of David
according to the flesh

who was powerfully declared the Son of God
    according to the Spirit of holiness
    from the resurrection of the dead

Jesus Christ our Lord

through whom we have received grace
and apostleship

> unto the obedience of faith
> among all the Gentiles for his
> name's sake
>> among whom you also
>> are called of Jesus Christ

(2) Grace (be) to you and peace
from God our Father and the Lord Jesus Christ.

b. Reread 1 John 1:5–2:6. This will involve you in nearly every phase of exegesis discussed in this lesson. Get a feel for the author's use of aspect, voice, the article, and techniques that convey emphasis, syntactical structure, and cohesion. These critical skills will be useful whenever you are reading your Greek New Testament.

EPILOGUE
THE NEXT STEP

174. Introduction

You have now covered the elements of New Testament Greek and have laid a foundation for reading and understanding the Greek New Testament. But if you are to retain the skills you have gained, you must use them and add to them. The following are some books and other helps that you may find useful in your further studies. For the most part, these are standard texts that have served Greek students for some time.

175. Concordances

A concordance is an alphabetically arranged index of Scripture words. W. F. Moulton and A. S. Geden's *A Concordance to the Greek Testament* (5th ed.; Edinburgh: T. & T Clark, 1897) is still very useful, even though it is based on an outdated Greek text. Moulton and Geden has now been completely revised: *A Concordance to the Greek New Testament,* edited by I. Howard Marshall (6th ed.; Edinburgh: T. & T. Clark, 2002). Another useful concordance is *The Greek-English Concordance to the New Testament,* edited by J. R. Kohlenberger III, E. Goodrick, and J. Swanson (Grand Rapids: Zondervan, 1997).

176. Lexicons and Translation Aids

For translation, every serious student of the New Testament should have W. Bauer, *A Greek-English Lexicon of the New Testament and Other Early Christian Literature* (3rd ed. Chicago: University of Chicago Press, 2000). In addition to providing definitions, BDAG includes information on the history of words and suggests translations of difficult words. A user-friendly alternative to Bauer is G. Abbott-Smith, *A Manual Greek Lexicon of the New Testament* (3rd ed.; Edinburgh: T & T. Clark, 1937), which, in addition to providing corresponding Hebrew words, contains a helpful appendix of irregular verb forms.

For rapid reading, an excellent resource is C. L. Rogers Jr. and C. L. Rogers III's *New Linguistic and Exegetical Key to the Greek New Testament* (Grand Rapids: Zondervan, 1998). This book proceeds through the New Testament in canonical order, listing under the appropriate chapter and verse any difficult form or grammatical construction. It also includes references culled from the leading lexicons, grammars, and commentaries. It is based on UBS⁴.

177. Textual Criticism

We have said little about New Testament textual criticism, but not because this field is unimportant. On the principles and methods of textual criticism, the standard introduction is still B. M. Metzger's *The Text of the New Testament* (3rd ed.; Oxford: Oxford University Press, 1991), though D. A. Black's *New Testament Textual Criticism* (Grand Rapids: Baker, 1994) is a less technical alternative. To see why the UBS editors preferred one reading over another, Metzger's *A Textual Commentary on the Greek New Testament* (2nd ed.; New York: United Bible Societies, 1994) is indispensable. For an overview of modern approaches to textual criticism, see D. A. Black (ed.), *Rethinking New Testament Textual Criticism* (Grand Rapids: Baker, 2002).

178. Intermediate Grammars

As you continue your studies of New Testament Greek, you would do well to have any one of the following intermediate grammars:

H. E. Dana and J. R. Mantey, *A Manual Grammar of the Greek New Testament* (New York: Macmillan, 1927).

J. H. Greenlee, *A Concise Exegetical Grammar of New Testament Greek* (3rd ed.; Grand Rapids: Eerdmans, 1963).

J. A. Brooks and C. L. Winbery, *Syntax of New Testament Greek* (Lanham, MD: University Press of America, 1979).

D. A. Black, *It's Still Greek to Me* (Grand Rapids: Baker, 1998).

D. B. Wallace, *Greek Grammar Beyond the Basics* (Grand Rapids: Zondervan, 1996).

179. Linguistic Analysis

There are several helpful works on New Testament Greek linguistics available, including:

J. P. Louw, *Semantics of New Testament Greek* (Philadelphia: Fortress, 1982).

M. Silva, *Biblical Words and Their Meaning: An Introduction to Lexical Semantics* (Grand Rapids: Zondervan, 1983).

D. A. Black, *Linguistics for Students of New Testament Greek: A Survey of Basic Concepts and Applications* (Grand Rapids: Baker, 1988).

P. Cotterell and M. Turner, *Linguistics and Biblical Interpretation* (Downers Grove: IVP, 1989).

On the relatively new field of Greek discourse analysis, see J. Beekman and J. Callow, *The Semantic Structure of Written Communication* (Dallas: SIL, 1981), and, more recently, D. A. Black (ed.), *Linguistics and New Testament Interpretation: Essays on Discourse Analysis* (Nashville: B&H, 1992). The earlier work of J. P. Louw, "Discourse Analysis and the Greek New Testament," *The Bible Translator* 24 (1973): 101–18, is still very useful.

180. New Testament Exegesis

On moving from text to sermon, the following works will be helpful:

G. D. Fee, *New Testament Exegesis: A Handbook for Students and Pastors* (3rd ed.; Philadelphia: Westminster, 2002).

W. L. Liefeld, *New Testament Exposition* (Grand Rapids: Zondervan, 1984).

N. Windham, *New Testament Greek for Preachers and Teachers* (Lanham, MD: University Press of America, 1991).

D. A. Black, *Using New Testament Greek in Ministry: A Practical Guide for Students and Pastors* (Grand Rapids: Baker, 1993).

R. J. Erickson, *A Beginner's Guide to New Testament Exegesis* (Downers Grove, Ill.: IVP, 2005).

On the various methods employed in New Testament interpretation, see I. H. Marshall (ed.), *New Testament Interpretation: Essays on Principles and Methods* (Grand Rapids: Eerdmans, 1977); D. A. Black and D. S. Dockery (eds.), *Interpreting the New Testament: Essays on Methods and Issues* (Nashville: B&H, 2001).

181. The History of Greek

On the nature of New Testament Greek and the history of the Greek language, see J. H. Greenlee, "The Language of the New Testament," in *The Expositor's Bible Commentary* (ed. F. E. Gaebelein; 12 vols.; Grand Rapids: Zondervan, 1976–92), 1:409–16, and D. J. A. Clines, "The Language of the New Testament," in *The International Bible Commentary* (ed. F. F. Bruce; Grand Rapids: Zondervan, 1986), 1012–18.

182. Other Useful Works

On verbal aspect: S. Porter, *Verbal Aspect in the Greek of the New Testament* (New York: Lang, 1989); B. M. Fanning, *Verbal Aspect in New Testament Greek* (Oxford: Oxford University Press, 1990).

On Greek word order: G. Hill (ed.), *The Discovery Bible* (Chicago: Moody, 1989), 549–54; I. Larsen, "Word Order and Relative Prominence in New Testament Greek," *Notes on Translation* 5 (1991): 29–34.

On the Semitic coloring of New Testament Greek: C. F. D. Moule, *An Idiom Book of New Testament Greek* (Cambridge: Cambridge University Press, 1963), 171–91; D. A. Black, "New Testament Semitisms," *The Bible Translator* 39 (1988): 215–23.

On Greek word study: J. P. Louw and E. A. Nida, *Greek-English Lexicon of the New Testament Based on Semantic Domains* (2 vols.; New York: United Bible Societies, 1988); G. Kittel and G. Friedrich (eds.), *Theological Dictionary of the New Testament* (trans. and ed. by G. W. Bromiley; 10 vols.; Grand Rapids: Eerdmans, 1964–76); C. Brown (ed.), *The New International Dictionary of New Testament Theology* (4 vols.; Grand Rapids: Zondervan, 1975–86).

On vocabulary study: B. M. Metzger, *Lexical Aids for Students of New Testament Greek* (Princeton: Theological Book Agency, 1974); T. A. Robinson, *Mastering Greek Vocabulary* (Peabody, Mass.: Hendrickson, 1991); W. C. Trenchard, *The Student's Complete Vocabulary Guide to the Greek New Testament* (Grand Rapids: Zondervan, 1992).

On reviewing paradigms: W. Mueller, *Grammatical Aids for Students of New Testament Greek* (Grand Rapids: Eerdmans, 1972).

183. Computer Software

Useful software programs for serious language study include *Accordance*, *BibleWorks*, and *Logos Bible Software*. Each of these programs allows searches for individual words or for various syntactical patterns.

Appendix 1

THE GREEK ACCENTS

184. Introduction

Greek, as we have seen (§10), has three accents: the acute (´), the grave (`), and the circumflex (ˆ): ἀκούω τὴν φωνὴν τοῦ θεοῦ. Notice that the accent stands over the *vowel* of the accented syllable, and over the *second vowel* of a diphthong. Although the accents originally indicated tone or pitch, today we make no such distinction between them.

Observe that:

(1) *A Greek word has as many syllables as it has vowels or diphthongs*: λόγος has two syllables (λό-γος), ἄνθρωπος has three (ἄν-θρω-πος), δοῦλος has two (δοῦ-λος), and ἀλήθεια has four (ἀ-λή-θει-α).

(2) *A syllable is long if it has a long vowel or a diphthong*: in βλέπω, βλέ- is short, while -πω is long; in δοῦλος, δοῦ- is long, while -λος is short. However, the diphthongs -αι and -οι are considered short when they are final. Hence the οι in λόγοι is short because it is final, but the οι in λόγοις is long because it is followed by another letter.

(3) *A word may be accented only on one of its last three syllables*. The last syllable is called the *ultima*; the syllable preceding the ultima is called the *penult*; and the syllable preceding the penult is called the *antepenult*.

185. General Rules of Accentuation

1. The *acute* accent.

   a. The acute may stand on either a long or a short syllable: λόγος, οἴκοις.

   b. The acute may stand on either of the last three syllables: ἄγγελος, λόγος, καρπός.

   c. The acute may not stand on the antepenult when the ultima is long: ἄγγελος, but ἀγγέλου.

   d. The acute may not stand on a long penult when the ultima is short: δούλου, but δοῦλος.

2. The *grave* accent.

a. The grave may stand only on the ultima.

b. The grave may stand on either a long or a short syllable.

c. If a word other than an enclitic follows immediately, the acute is changed to a grave:

υἱός, but υἱὸς θεοῦ.

3. The *circumflex* accent.

a. The circumflex may stand only on a long syllable: δοῦλος, but not λόγος.

b. The circumflex may stand only on the penult or ultima: δοῦλος, καρποῦ.

c. The circumflex may not stand on the penult if the ultima is long: δοῦλος, but δούλου.

186. Noun and Verb Accent

1. Noun accent is *persistent*, that is, the accent remains on the syllable that bears it in the nominative singular so far as the general rules of accent permit. The position of the accent in the nominative singular must be learned for each noun separately. When this is known, the above rules of accent apply. Note the following examples:

ἄνθρωπος	(short ultima)	δοῦλος
ἀνθρώπου	(long ultima)	δούλου
ἀνθρώπῳ	(long ultima)	δούλῳ
ἄνθρωπον	(short ultima)	δοῦλον
ἄνθρωποι	(short ultima)	δοῦλοι
ἀνθρώπων	(long ultima)	δούλων
ἀνθρώποις	(long ultima)	δούλοις
ἀνθρώπους	(long ultima)	δούλους

2. Verb accent is *recessive*, that is, the accent stands as far from the ultima as the general rules of accent permit:

λύω	ἐλυόμην
λύεις	ἐλύου
λύει	ἐλύετο
λύομεν	ἐλυόμεθα
λύετε	ἐλύεσθε
λύουσι(ν)	ἐλύοντο

187. Proclitics and Enclitics

A *proclitic* is a word that "leans forward" on the *following* word so closely as to form a single unit of accent with it. An *enclitic* is a word that "leans on" the *preceding* word so closely as to form a single unit of accent with it. Hence neither a proclitic nor an enclitic has an accent of its own.

The proclitics include:

1. The forms ὁ, ἡ, οἱ, and αἱ of the article.
2. The negative οὐ.
3. The prepositions εἰς, ἐν, and ἐκ (ἐξ).
4. The particles εἰ and ὡς.

The enclitics include:

1. The present indicative forms of εἰμί, except for the second singular form εἶ.
2. The forms of the indefinite pronoun τις/τι.
3. The unstressed forms of the personal pronouns: μου, μοι, με, σου, σοι, σε.

The proclitics have no special rules of accent; they simply have no accent. Enclitics, however, are a different matter. The following rules of accent apply to enclitics and words preceding an enclitic:

1. The word before an enclitic does not change an acute on the ultima to a grave:
   ἀδελφός μου, not ἀδελφὸς μου.

2. If the word before an enclitic has an *acute* on the *antepenult* or a *circumflex* on the *penult*, it receives a second accent (an acute) on the ultima:
ἄνθρωπός τις, ὁ δοῦλός σου, δῶρόν ἐστιν.

3. If the word before an enclitic is itself a proclitic or an enclitic, it receives an acute on the ultima:
εἴς με, ἄνθρωπός μού ἐστιν, ἀνήρ τίς ἐστιν.

4. An enclitic of two syllables retains its own accent when it follows a word that has an acute on the penult:
ὥρα ἐστίν.

5. An enclitic retains its accent when it begins a sentence or clause:

Matt 19:12: εἰσὶν γὰρ εὐνοῦχοι.
"For they are eunuchs."

THE GREEK ALPHABET SONG

Al - pha, Be - ta, Gam - ma, Del - ta, Ep - si - lon,____

Ze - ta, E - ta, The - ta, I - o - ta, Kap - pa, Lamb - da,____ Mu,

Nu, Xi, Om - i - cron, Pi, Rho, Sig - ma,____

Tau, Up - si - lon, Phi, Chi, Psi, O - me - ga.____

American Folk Tune

Appendix 3

KEY TO THE EXERCISES

The following is a key to the translation exercises found in Lessons 3–17. (The exercises in the remaining lessons are taken directly from the Greek New Testament, so that you may check your translations in these chapters with any English version.) When you have completed the exercises, check them with the key given here. If you have made mistakes, determine the point of grammar involved and be sure you understand exactly how and why you went wrong. Then read the Greek again, preferably aloud, until you are able to translate without reference to your version, the vocabulary, or the key. It should be noted that some sentences are capable of being translated in more than one way.

LESSON 3

1. You see. You write. You do not send.
2. He leads. He baptizes. He does not loose.
3. We hear. We prepare. We do not believe.
4. You write. You trust in. You do not save.
5. They see. They teach. They do not loose.
6. He baptizes. We teach. They do not hear.
7. Do I save? Does he heal? Do they send?
8. You are. We are. You are.
9. He will hear. He will baptize. He will have.
10. We will write. We will teach. We will preach.
11. You will not loose. You will not glorify. We will not trust in.

LESSON 4

1. A servant writes a law.
2. You know death.
3. Brothers loose servants.
4. Sons bring gifts.
5. You write words to apostles.
6. A son sees temples and houses.

7. A brother does not speak a word to a man.
8. A servant brings a gift to an apostle.
9. We know a way to a temple.
10. We do not hear words of death.
11. You speak to servants, but I speak to brothers.
12. Sons loose servants of apostles.
13. To both apostles and men we speak words of death.
14. You do not write words to sons.
15. Children hear words in a house, but crowds hear words in a wilderness.
16. He knows apostles and brings gifts to children.
17. You will see servants, but we will see men.
18. Apostles save brothers.
19. I am an apostle, but you are sons.
20. We are servants, but we will teach servants.
21. You are messengers and you bring gifts to men.
22. Apostles will save men from death.

LESSON 5

1. I loose the servant in the church.
2. We see the houses of the young men.
3. The messenger speaks words of death to the soldiers.
4. The brothers of the disciples will hear the words of God.
5. The apostle will write a parable for the crowds.
6. The sons of the apostles have love and wisdom and joy.
7. The disciples know the teaching of the apostle.
8. The prophet of God writes the words of Scripture.
9. The way of the Lord is the way of joy and boldness.
10. The hypocrites do not know the way of life and truth.
11. The apostle of the Messiah receives gifts from the synagogues.
12. God knows the heart of man.
13. I am the way and the truth and the life.
14. We will lead the disciples of the Lord and the prophets of God and the sons of the apostles out of the houses of sin.
15. The messengers know the gospel of truth, but tax collectors do not know the way into the kingdom of righteousness.
16. Soldiers take the gifts from the sons of the apostles.
17. I am a young man, but you are a man of God.

18. We do not know the day and the hour of salvation.

LESSON 6

1. The beloved apostle teaches the servant.
2. The church is good.
3. The disciples see the dead men.
4. The other man hears the word of God in the church.
5. The evil men speak bad words in the last days.
6. The good prophets speak new parables both to the faithful men and the faithful women.
7. We speak good words to the good apostles.
8. The Messiah of the kingdom saves the faithful men and the faithful women.
9. The good woman will see the good days of the kingdom of love.
10. The brothers are first, and the servants are last.
11. The wise women say good things.
12. The righteous men will lead the unclean men into the synagogue.
13. The apostle of the Lord speaks a good parable to the beloved disciples.
14. The ways are good, but the men are evil.
15. You will see the good days of the Lord of life.
16. The son of the unbelieving brother sees the worthy men.
17. The truth is good, and the hour is bad.
18. You speak the good words to the evil churches and the bad words to the brothers.
19. The unbelieving women will glorify God.

LESSON 7

1. The apostles loosed the servants.
2. We saw the blessed sons.
3. The disciples preached to sinners.
4. The Lord of life was saving the evil men.
5. The evil men left, but the good men believed the gospel.
6. You fled out of the evil houses and into the church of God.
7. In the beginning was the Word, and the Word was God.
8. Jesus suffered, but the disciples received life and salvation from God.

9. The apostle taught the disciples and kept leading the good men into the kingdom of love.
10. The Lord saw the evil men, but we see the good men.
11. You believed the truth and began to preach the gospel.
12. I heard and saw the disciples, but you heard and saw the Lord.
13. We were in the church, but you were in the houses of sin.
14. You were baptizing the faithful men, but we were teaching the disciples and glorifying God.
15. The Lord saved the evil women from sin.
16. You were not speaking words of truth, but evil men were believing the gospel.
17. The Lord was having joy and peace in the world.
18. He was in the world, but the world did not receive the truth.
19. The Messiah taught both in the temple and in the synagogue.

LESSON 8

1. The disciple reads a parable about the kingdom.
2. We throw the evil things out of the house.
3. The good women received good things from the faithful brother.
4. The sons of the prophets spoke words according to the truth.
5. Because of the glory of the Lord we were hearing a parable of love and peace.
6. Through the Scriptures we know the law of God.
7. God sent angels into the world.
8. We were in the church with the good apostles.
9. They bring the evil soldiers into the temple.
10. The young men led the good servants and the sons of the prophets to the houses of the disciples.
11. The sons of men are in the temple.
12. You speak against the law, but I speak words of truth.
13. Jesus suffered for the sins of the world.
14. The dead are under the earth.
15. The apostle was speaking about the sins of the children.
16. God sent the prophets before the apostles.
17. We were with the disciples in the wilderness.
18. The faithful apostle preached instead of the Messiah.
19. The Lord was leading the disciples around the sea and into the wilderness.

20. The apostles were teaching daily in the temple.
21. Christ died for the sins of men according to the Scriptures.

LESSON 9

1. Your disciples know the apostle and lead him into their house.
2. I teach my sons and speak to them the word of God.
3. I am a servant, but you are the Lord.
4. Our brothers saw us, and we saw them.
5. The Lord himself will lead me into his kingdom.
6. You will see death, but I will see life.
7. The apostle is faithful, but his servants are bad.
8. We saw you and spoke to you a parable of love.
9. You fled from us, but we kept teaching in the church.
10. In the last days Jesus will lead his disciples into the kingdom.
11. The men found their children and led them into their houses.
12. You received the Lord into your hearts, but we fled from the church.
13. I suffered, you sinned, but he himself saved us.
14. We saw the disciples of our Lord with our brothers.
15. Through you God will lead his children into the kingdom of love.
16. My brother received good gifts from you.
17. After the evil days we ourselves will see the good days.
18. We are with you in your houses.
19. We ourselves know the way, and through it we will lead you into the same church.
20. Because of me you will see the Lord.

LESSON 10

1. We have heard the truth.
2. We have known that God is love.
3. We have believed that you are the Holy One of God.
4. You have loosed the servant and have sent him into the church.
5. We have written words of truth because of our love for the apostle.
6. The Messiah has suffered and has known death.
7. You had loosed the servants of the faithful men because you were good.

8. You know that the Son of God has saved you.
9. We know that we have known him, because we have believed in him.
10. I have spoken the truth, but you did not believe me.
11. For us God has prepared a kingdom.
12. You have heard that I have sinned against the Lord.
13. I have had joy and peace, but you have suffered because you have not trusted in the Lord.

LESSON 11

1. This apostle knows that apostle.
2. These men hear those children.
3. This man sees that man in the temple.
4. This woman has peace in her heart.
5. We will hear this parable about the evil demons.
6. These men have joy, but those men have sin in their hearts.
7. This is the word of the Lord.
8. We know this man and lead him with his cloak into our houses.
9. We bring these gifts from the apostle into our church.
10. This man is a man of the world and an enemy of God, but that man is a friend of God.
11. Those apostles are disciples of this Lord.
12. After those days we will lead these disciples into the boat.
13. The apostles of the Lord ate bread and fruit in the wilderness.
14. He himself saw those signs in heaven.
15. With these faithful men the disciples heard good parables, but the people will hear words of death.
16. This woman has known the truth itself.
17. Into the same church Peter led these good blind men.
18. In those days we were in the field and were teaching those children.
19. This is the way of death and sin, and evil men lead their children into it.
20. This book is the word of God.
21. These men do not know the time of the day of the Lord.

LESSON 12

1. The servants are being loosed by the apostles.
2. The truth is being taught by the sons of the disciples.
3. The faithful disciple is being saved by the Lord.
4. The messenger is being sent by the apostle out of the house and into the church.
5. The crowds are being saved out of the world.
6. Evil men glorify themselves, but righteous men glorify God.
7. The evil disciples are being thrown out of the churches.
8. The men themselves receive life from the Lord.
9. The Scriptures are being read by the faithful disciples.
10. The good disciples are teaching one another the word of truth.
11. The faithful women are coming and are being baptized by the apostles.
12. The faithful children are being known by God.
13. You are becoming a good disciple.
14. The apostle is being led with his brothers into the church of God.
15. You are going out of the wilderness and into the house.
16. You are being saved from your sins by the Son of God.
17. The sinners are not coming out of the evil houses because they themselves do not believe in God.
18. The faithful woman is being saved by her Lord.
19. The sinners are receiving Christ into their hearts.
20. Apostles both pray for sinners and preach the gospel to them.

LESSON 13

1. Therefore the servants have been loosed by the Lord.
2. Today I have been baptized by the good apostle.
3. For the Messiah rightly comes just as it has been written about him in the Holy Scriptures.
4. This man has not been baptized into Jesus.
5. We ourselves will loose the good servants.
6. Now you are sinners, but then you will be sons of God.
7. The righteous men themselves will see the Lord.
8. I know God and am known by him.
9. The demon has been thrown out of the man.
10. I am a sinner, but I am saved.

11. Not even the apostles themselves will teach the truth when they come into the church.

LESSON 14

1. For the words of the prophet were being written in the book.
2. There the writings of the apostles were being heard by the sinners.
3. In those days we were being taught well by the disciples of the Lord.
4. Then the crowd was going out to the Lord, but now it no longer sees him.
5. The demons were always being thrown out by the word of the Lord.
6. The crowds were going out of the wilderness and were going into the church.
7. Immediately the disciples themselves loosed the servants of the righteous man.
8. The apostles themselves received bread and fruit from the disciples.
9. We ourselves saw the Lord and believed in him.
10. Here the servants had been loosed by the good man.
11. These men became disciples of the Lord, but those men were still sinners.
12. The Lord was near, but he was not being seen by his disciples.

LESSON 15

1. The disciples were taught by the apostles of the Lord.
2. The words of the prophets were written in the Scriptures.
3. The apostles were sent into the world.
4. By the love of God the sinner was saved and became a disciple of the Lord.
5. The gospel was preached in the world.
6. We went into the church and were baptized.
7. In that day the word of God will be heard.
8. We saw the Lord and were seen by him.
9. You taught the children, but you were taught by the apostle.
10. The sinners were received into heaven.
11. The demons were thrown out of the evil men by the Lord.

12. God was glorified by his Son, and he will be glorified by us.
13. Salvation, joy, and peace will be prepared for us in heaven.
14. A voice was heard in the wilderness and will be heard in the earth.
15. The angels were sent into the world.

LESSON 17

1. The Word became flesh.
2. You are the light of the world.
3. This is my body.
4. We do not have hope because we do not believe in the Lord.
5. We were saved by grace through faith.
6. We no longer know the Christ according to the flesh.
7. A ruler came to Jesus by night and was taught by him.
8. The children received good things from their mother.
9. The chief priests and the scribes sent their servants into the temple.
10. The king comes into the city, but the scribe goes out to the wilderness.
11. The Son of Man will have the power of judgment in that day.
12. The priests have the law, but they do not have the love of God in their hearts.
13. In the resurrection the saints will have life and peace.
14. The sinners heard the words of Christ and received his mercy.
15. The nations do not know the will and the grace of God.
16. The disciples were baptizing in the name of Jesus.
17. Evil men are in the darkness of sin, but faithful men hear the words of the Lord and become his disciples.
18. I baptized you with water, but he himself will baptize you with the Spirit.
19. These are the words of the Holy Spirit.
20. The apostle spoke these things about the rulers of this age.
21. In that night the words of the gospel were preached to the sinners.
22. After the resurrection of Christ the bodies of the saints were seen.

Appendix 4

NOUN PARADIGMS

The Definite Article ("The")

		Singular				Plural	
	M.	F.	N.		M.	F.	N.
N.	ὁ	ἡ	τό		οἱ	αἱ	τά
G.	τοῦ	τῆς	τοῦ		τῶν	τῶν	τῶν
D.	τῷ	τῇ	τῷ		τοῖς	ταῖς	τοῖς
A.	τόν	τήν	τό		τούς	τάς	τά

Nouns

(1) First declension

Singular

	Feminine Nouns				Masculine Nouns	
	"day"	"glory"	"voice"		"disciple"	"young man"
N.	ἡμέρα	δόξα	φωνή		μαθητής	νεανίας
G.	ἡμέρας	δόξης	φωνῆς		μαθητοῦ	νεανίου
D.	ἡμέρᾳ	δόξῃ	φωνῇ		μαθητῇ	νεανίᾳ
A.	ἡμέραν	δόξαν	φωνήν		μαθητήν	νεανίαν
V.	ἡμέρα	δόξα	φωνή		μαθητά	νεανία

Plural

	Feminine Nouns				Masculine Nouns	
N.V.	ἡμέραι	δόξαι	φωναί		μαθηταί	νεανίαι
G.	ἡμερῶν	δοξῶν	φωνῶν		μαθητῶν	νεανιῶν
D.	ἡμέραις	δόξαις	φωναῖς		μαθηταῖς	νεανίαις
A.	ἡμέρας	δόξας	φωνάς		μαθητάς	νεανίας

(2) Second declension

	"man"	"gift"
	Singular	Singular
N.	ἄνθρωπος	δῶρον
G.	ἀνθρώπου	δώρου
D.	ἀνθρώπῳ	δώρῳ
A.	ἄνθρωπον	δῶρον
V.	ἄνθρωπε	δῶρον
	Plural	Plural
N. V.	ἄνθρωποι	δῶρα
G.	ἀνθρώπων	δώρων
D.	ἀνθρώποις	δώροις
A.	ἀνθρώπους	δῶρα

(3) Third declension

	Singular	Plural
	"body"	
N.	σῶμα	σώματα
G.	σώματος	σωμάτων
D.	σώματι	σώμασι(ν)
A.	σῶμα	σώματα
	"flesh"	
N.	σάρξ	σάρκες
G.	σαρκός	σαρκῶν
D.	σαρκί	σαρξί(ν)
A.	σάρκα	σάρκας
	"ruler"	
N.	ἄρχων	ἄρχοντες
G.	ἄρχοντος	ἀρχόντων
D.	ἄρχοντι	ἄρχουσι(ν)
A.	ἄρχοντα	ἄρχοντας

"race"

N.	γένος	γένη
G.	γένους	γενῶν
D.	γένει	γένεσι(ν)
A.	γένος	γένη

"king"

N.	βασιλεύς	βασιλεῖς
G.	βασιλέως	βασιλέων
D.	βασιλεῖ	βασιλεῦσι(ν)
A.	βασιλέα	βασιλεῖς

"city"

N.	πόλις	πόλεις
G.	πόλεως	πόλεων
D.	πόλει	πόλεσι(ν)
A.	πόλιν	πόλεις

Adjectives

(1) Consonant stem ("good")

	Singular			Plural		
	M.	F.	N.	M.	F.	N.
N.	ἀγαθός	ἀγαθή	ἀγαθόν	ἀγαθοί	ἀγαθαί	ἀγαθά
G.	ἀγαθοῦ	ἀγαθῆς	ἀγαθοῦ	ἀγαθῶν	ἀγαθῶν	ἀγαθῶν
D.	ἀγαθῷ	ἀγαθῇ	ἀγαθῷ	ἀγαθοῖς	ἀγαθαῖς	ἀγαθοῖ
A.	ἀγαθόν	ἀγαθήν	ἀγαθόν	ἀγαθούς	ἀγαθάς	ἀγαθά
V.	ἀγαθέ	ἀγαθή	ἀγαθόν	ἀγαθοί	ἀγαθαί	ἀγαθά

(2) ε, ι, ρ stem ("small")

	Singular			Plural		
	M.	**F.**	**N.**	**M.**	**F.**	**N.**
N.	μικρός	μικρά	μικρόν	μικροί	μικραί	μικρά
G.	μικροῦ	μικρᾶς	μικροῦ	μικρῶν	μικρῶν	μικρῶν
D.	μικρῷ	μικρᾷ	μικρῷ	μικροῖς	μικραῖς	μικροῖς
A.	μικρόν	μικράν	μικρόν	μικρούς	μικράς	μικρά
V.	μικρέ	μικρά	μικρόν	μικροί	μικραί	μικρά

(3) Two-termination ("impossible")

	Singular		Plural	
	M./F.	**N.**	**M./F.**	**N.**
N.	ἀδύνατος	ἀδύνατον	ἀδύνατοι	ἀδύνατα
G.	ἀδυνάτου	ἀδυνάτου	ἀδυνάτων	ἀδυνάτων
D.	ἀδυνάτῳ	ἀδυνάτῳ	ἀδυνάτοις	ἀδυνάτοις
A.	ἀδύνατον	ἀδύνατον	ἀδυνάτους	ἀδύνατα
V.	ἀδύνατε	ἀδύνατον	ἀδύνατοι	ἀδύνατα

(4) πᾶς ("all")

	Singular			Plural		
	M.	**F.**	**N.**	**M.**	**F.**	**N.**
N. V.	πᾶς	πᾶσα	πᾶν	πάντες	πᾶσαι	πάντα
G.	παντός	πάσης	παντός	πάντων	πασῶν	πάντων
D.	παντί	πάσῃ	παντί	πᾶσι(ν)	πάσαις	πᾶσι(ν)
A.	πάντα	πᾶσαν	πᾶν	πάντας	πάσας	πάντα

(5) πολύς ("much," "many") and μέγας ("great")

Singular

	M.	F.	N.		M.	F.	N.
N.	πολύς	πολλή	πολύ		μέγας	μεγάλη	μέγα
G.	πολλοῦ	πολλῆς	πολλοῦ		μεγάλου	μεγάλης	μεγάλου
D.	πολλῷ	πολλῇ	πολλῷ		μεγάλῳ	μεγάλῃ	μεγάλῳ
A.	πολύν	πολλήν	πολύ		μέγαν	μεγάλην	μέγα

Plural

	M.	F.	N.		M.	F.	N.
N.	πολλοί	πολλαί	πολλά		μεγάλοι	μεγάλαι	μεγάλα
G.	πολλῶν	πολλῶν	πολλῶν		μεγάλων	μεγάλων	μεγάλων
D.	πολλοῖς	πολλαῖς	πολλοῖς		μεγάλοις	μεγάλαις	μεγάλοις
A.	πολλούς	πολλάς	πολλά		μεγάλους	μεγάλας	μεγάλα

(6) ἀληθής ("true")

	Singular		Plural	
	M./F.	N.	M./F.	N.
N.	ἀληθής	ἀληθές	ἀληθεῖς	ἀληθῆ
G.	ἀληθοῦς	ἀληθοῦς	ἀληθῶν	ἀληθῶν
D.	ἀληθεῖ	ἀληθεῖ	ἀληθέσι(ν)	ἀληθέσι(ν)
A.	ἀληθῆ	ἀληθές	ἀληθεῖς	ἀληθῆ

Personal Pronouns

(1) First person ("I," "me," "us," "our")

	Singular	Plural
N.	ἐγώ	ἡμεῖς
G.	ἐμοῦ or μου	ἡμῶν
D.	ἐμοί or μοι	ἡμῖν
A.	ἐμέ or με	ἡμᾶς

(2) Second person ("you," "your")

	Singular	Plural
N.V.	σύ	ὑμεῖς
G.	σοῦ or σου	ὑμῶν
D.	σοί or σοι	ὑμῖν
A.	σέ or σε	ὑμᾶς

(3) Third person ("he," "her," "its," "their")

	Singular			Plural		
	M.	F.	N.	M.	F.	N.
N.	αὐτός	αὐτή	αὐτό	αὐτοί	αὐταί	αὐτά
G.	αὐτοῦ	αὐτῆς	αὐτοῦ	αὐτῶν	αὐτῶν	αὐτῶν
D.	αὐτῷ	αὐτῇ	αὐτῷ	αὐτοῖς	αὐταῖς	αὐτοῖς
A.	αὐτόν	αὐτήν	αὐτό	αὐτούς	αὐτάς	αὐτά

Demonstrative Pronouns

(1) Near demonstrative ("this," "these")

	Singular			Plural		
	M.	F.	N.	M.	F.	N.
N.	οὗτος	αὕτη	τοῦτο	οὗτοι	αὗται	ταῦτα
G.	τούτου	ταύτης	τούτου	τούτων	τούτων	τούτων
D.	τούτῳ	ταύτῃ	τούτῳ	τούτοις	ταύταις	τούτοις
A.	τοῦτον	ταύτην	τοῦτο	τούτους	ταύτας	ταῦτα

(2) Remote demonstrative ("that," "those")

	Singular			Plural		
	M.	F.	N.	M.	F.	N.
N.	ἐκεῖνος	ἐκείνη	ἐκεῖνο	ἐκεῖνοι	ἐκεῖναι	ἐκεῖνα
G.	ἐκείνου	ἐκείνης	ἐκείνου	ἐκείνων	ἐκείνων	ἐκείνων
D.	ἐκείνῳ	ἐκείνῃ	ἐκείνῳ	ἐκείνοις	ἐκείναις	ἐκείνοις
A.	ἐκεῖνον	ἐκείνην	ἐκεῖνο	ἐκείνους	ἐκείνας	ἐκεῖνα

Interrogative Pronouns ("Who?", "Which?", What?", "Why?")

	Singular		Plural	
	M./F.	N.	M./F.	N.
N.	τίς	τί	τίνες	τίνα
G.	τίνος	τίνος	τίνων	τίνων
D.	τίνι	τίνι	τίσι(ν)	τίσι(ν)
A.	τίνα	τί	τίνας	τίνα

Indefinite Pronouns ("Someone," "Something")

The Greek indefinite pronoun is identical to the interrogative pronoun apart from accentuation: the indefinite pronoun is an enclitic, throwing its accent back onto the preceding word (see Appendix 1).

Relative Pronouns ("Who," "Which," "That")

	Singular			Plural		
	M.	F.	N.	M.	F.	N.
N.	ὅς	ἥ	ὅ	οἵ	αἵ	ἅ
G.	οὗ	ἧς	οὗ	ὧν	ὧν	ὧν
D.	ᾧ	ᾗ	ᾧ	οἷς	αἷς	οἷς
A.	ὅν	ἥν	ὅ	οὕς	ἅς	ἅ

Indefinite Relative Pronouns ("Who," "Whoever")

Singular: ὅστις, ἥτις, ὅτι
Plural: οἵτινες, αἵτινες, ἅτινα

Reciprocal Pronouns ("One Another")

G.   ἀλλήλων
D.   ἀλλήλοις
A.   ἀλλήλους

Reflexive Pronouns ("-self")

There is no nominative of the reflexive pronoun. The first and second persons are made up of a combination of ἐμέ and σέ with αὐτός: ἐμαυτοῦ, ἐμαυτῷ, ἐμαυτόν; σεαυτοῦ, σεαυτῷ, σεαυτόν. The third person reflexive pronoun is declined like αὐτός: ἑαυτοῦ, ἑαυτῷ, ἑαυτόν, etc. In the plural, ἑαυτῶν, -οῖς, -ούς does duty for all persons.

Possessive Pronouns (Adjectives)

The possessive pronouns ἐμός ("my"), σός ("your"), ἴδιος ("his"), ἡμέτερος ("our"), and ὑμέτερος ("your") are declined like regular adjectives of the first and second declensions.

The Numeral εἷς ("One")

	M.	F.	N.
N.	εἷς	μία	ἕν
G.	ἑνός	μιᾶς	ἑνός
D.	ἑνί	μιᾷ	ἑνί
A.	ἕνα	μίαν	ἕν

Appendix 5

CASE-NUMBER SUFFIXES

First Declension Nouns

	1	2	3	4	5	Plural
N.	-α	-α	-η	-ης	-ας	-αι
G.	-ας	-ης	-ης	-ου	-ου	-ων
D.	-ᾳ	-ῃ	-ῃ	-ῃ	-ᾳ	-αις
A.	-αν	-αν	-ην	-ην	-αν	-ας

Second Declension Nouns

	Singular		Plural	
	M.	N.	M.	N.
N.	-ος	-ον	-οι	-α
G.	-ου	-ου	-ων	-ων
D.	-ῳ	-ῳ	-οις	-οις
A.	-ον	-ον	-ους	-α
V.	-ε	-ον	-οι	-α

Third Declension Nouns

	Singular		Plural	
	M./F.	N.	M./F.	N.
N.	-ς, none	none	-ες	-α
G.	-ος	-ος	-ων	-ων
D.	-ι	-ι	-σι	-σι
A.	-α or -ν	none	-ας	-α

238

Appendix 6

PERSON-NUMBER SUFFIXES

Primary Suffixes

	Active	Middle/Passive	Active	Middle/Passive
	Singular		Plural	
1.	-ω	-μαι	-μεν	-μεθα
2.	-εις	-σαι (-η)	-τε	-σθε
3.	-ει	-ται	-ουσι(ν)	-νται

Secondary Suffixes

	Active	Middle/Passive	Active	Middle/Passive
	Singular		Plural	
1.	-ν	-μην	-μεν	-μεθα
2.	-ς	-σο (-ου, -ω)	-τε	-σθε
3.	none (or movable ν)	-το	-ν or -σαν	-ντο

Appendix 7

SUMMARY OF PREPOSITIONS

Prepositions with One Case

Preposition	Case	Meaning
ἀνά	accusative	*up*
ἀντί	genitive	*instead of, in place of, for*
ἀπό	genitive	*from, away from, of*
εἰς	accusative	*into, to, for, in*
ἐκ	genitive	*out of, from, by*
ἐν	dative	*in, within, by, with, among*
πρό	genitive	*before*
πρός	accusative	*to, toward, with*

Prepositions with Two Cases

Preposition	Case	Meaning
διά	genitive	*through, by*
	accusative	*because of, on account of*
κατά	genitive	*against, down*
	accusative	*according to*
μετά	genitive	*with*
	accusative	*after*
περί	genitive	*about, concerning, for*
	accusative	*around*
ὑπέρ	genitive	*for*
	accusative	*above, over*
ὑπό	genitive	*by*
	accusative	*under*

Prepositions with Three Cases

Preposition	Case	Meaning
ἐπί	genitive	*upon, on, at, about*
	dative	*upon, on, at, about*
	accusative	*upon, on, at, about*
παρά	genitive	*from*
	dative	*with*
	accusative	*beside, by*

Appendix 8

WORDS DIFFERING IN ACCENTUATION OR BREATHING

ἀλλά   *but*
ἄλλα   *other things*

αὐτή   nominative feminine singular of αὐτός
αὕτη   nominative feminine singular of οὗτος

αὐταί   nominative feminine plural of αὐτός
αὗται   nominative feminine plural of οὗτος

εἰ   *if*
εἶ   *you are*

εἰς   *into*
εἷς   *one*

ἔξω   *outside*
ἕξω   *I will have* (future indicative of ἔχω)

ἡ   nominative feminine singular of the definite article
ἥ   nominative feminine singular of the relative pronoun
ἤ   *or*

ἦν   *he was* (imperfect indicative of εἰμί)
ἥν   accusative feminine singular of the relative pronoun

ὁ   nominative masculine singular of the definite article

ὅ   nominative/accusative neuter singular of the relative pronoun

ὄν   nominative/accusative neuter singular of the present participle of εἰμί

ὅν   accusative masculine singular of the relative pronoun

οὐ   *not*

οὗ   genitive masculine/neuter singular of the relative pronoun

τίς, τί, etc.   *Who?, What?*

τις, τι, etc.   *a certain one, a certain thing*

ὤν   nominative masculine singular of the present participle of εἰμί

ὧν   genitive plural of the relative pronoun

Appendix 9

PRINCIPAL PARTS OF SELECTED VERBS

(Parentheses signify that this principle part does not appear in the New Testament.
Blanks signify that this principle part was not found in any ancient Greek literature.)

Present	Future	Aorist	Perfect Active	Perfect Middle	Aorist Passive
ἀγαπάω *love*	ἀγαπήσω	ἠγάπησα	ἠγάπηκα	ἠγάπημαι	ἠγαπήθην
ἄγω *lead*	ἄξω	ἤγαγον	(ἦχα)	ἦγμαι	ἤχθην
αἴρω *take up*	ἀρῶ	ἦρα	ἦρκα	ἦρμαι	ἤρθην
ἀκούω *hear*	ἀκούσω	ἤκουσα	ἀκήκοα	(ἤκουσμαι)	ἠκούσθην
ἁμαρτάνω *sin*	ἁμαρτήσω	(ἡμάρτησα) ἥμαρτον	ἡμάρτηκα	(ἡμάρτημαι)	(ἡμαρτήθην)
ἀφίημι *forgive*	ἀφήσω	ἀφῆκα	ἀφεῖκα	ἀφεῖμαι	ἀφέθην
βαίνω *go*	βήσομαι	ἔβην	βέβηκα	(βέβημαι)	ἐβήθην
βάλλω *throw*	βαλῶ	ἔβαλον	βέβληκα	βέβλημαι	ἐβλήθην
γίνομαι *become*	γενήσομαι	ἐγενόμην	γέγονα	γεγένημαι	ἐγενήθην
γινώσκω *know*	γνώσομαι	ἔγνων	ἔγνωκα	ἔγνωσμαι	ἐγνώσθην
γράφω *write*	γράψω	ἔγραψα	γέγραφα	γέγραμμαι	ἐγράφην

244

Present	Future	Aorist	Perfect Active	Perfect Middle	Aorist Passive
διδάσκω *teach*	διδάξω	ἐδίδαξα			ἐδιδάχθην
δίδωμι *give*	δώσω	ἔδωκα	δέδωκα	δέδομαι	ἐδόθην
δοξάζω *glorify*	δοξάσω	ἐδόξασα	(δεδόξακα)	δεδόξασμαι	ἐδοξάσθην
ἐγείρω *raise*	ἐγερῶ	ἤγειρα		ἐγήγερμαι	ἠγέρθην
ἐλπίζω *hope*	ἐλπιῶ	ἤλπισα	ἤλπικα		
ἔρχομαι *come*	ἐλεύσομαι	ἦλθον	ἐλήλυθα		
ἐσθίω *eat*	φάγομαι	ἔφαγον			
ἑτοιμάζω *prepare*	ἑτοιμάσω	ἡτοίμασα	ἡτοίμακα	ἡτοίμασμαι	ἡτοιμάσθην
εὑρίσκω *find*	εὑρήσω	εὗρον	εὕρηκα	(εὕρημαι)	εὑρέθην
ἔχω *have*	ἕξω	ἔσχον	ἔσχηκα		
θεραπεύω *heal*	θεραπεύσω	ἐθεράπευσα	(τεθεράπευκα)	τεθεράπευμαι	ἐθεραπεύθην
ἵστημι *stand*	στήσω	ἔστησα ἔστην	ἕστηκα	(ἕσταμαι)	ἐστάθην
καλέω *call*	καλέσω	ἐκάλεσα	κέκληκα	κέκλημαι	ἐκλήθην
κηρύσσω *preach*	κηρύξω	ἐκήρυξα	(κεκήρυχα)	(κεκήρυγμαι)	ἐκηρύχθην
κρίνω *judge*	κρινῶ	ἔκρινα	κέκρικα	κέκριμαι	ἐκρίθην
λαμβάνω *take*	λήμψομαι	ἔλαβον	εἴληφα	(εἴλημμαι)	ἐλήμφθην

Present	Future	Aorist	Perfect Active	Perfect Middle	Aorist Passive
λέγω say	ἐρῶ	εἶπον	εἴρηκα	εἴρημαι	ἐρρήθην
λείπω leave	λείψω	ἔλιπον	(λέλοιπα)	λέλειμμαι	ἐλείφθην
λύω loose	λύσω	ἔλυσα	(λέλυκα)	λέλυμαι	ἐλύθην
μένω abide	μενῶ	ἔμεινα	μεμένηκα		
ὁράω see	ὄψομαι	εἶδον	ἑόρακα ἑώρακα		ὤφθην
πάσχω suffer	(παθοῦμαι)	ἔπαθον	πέπονθα		
πείθω trust in	πείσω	ἔπεισα	πέποιθα	πέπεισμαι	ἐπείσθην
πέμπω send	πέμψω	ἔπεμψα	(πέπομφα)	(πέπεμμαι)	ἐπέμφθην
πιστεύω believe	(πιστεύσω)	ἐπίστευσα	πεπίστευκα	πεπίστευμαι	ἐπιστεύθην
ποιέω do	ποιήσω	ἐποίησα	πεποίηκα	πεποίημαι	(ἐποιήθην)
σώζω save	σώσω	ἔσωσα	σέσωκα	σέσωσμαι σέσωμαι	ἐσώθην
τηρέω keep	τηρήσω	ἐτήρησα	τετήρηκα	τετήρημαι	ἐτηρήθην
τίθημι place	θήσω	ἔθηκα	τέθεικα	τέθειμαι	ἐτέθην
φιλέω love	(φιλήσω)	ἐφίλησα	πεφίληκα	(πεφίλημαι)	(ἐφιλήθην)

Greek-English Vocabulary

(The following list includes all words introduced in the vocabularies. The section numbers indicate the first appearance of the word in a vocabulary.)

ἀγαθός, -ή, -όν, *good*, §46.
ἀγαπάω, *I love*, §127.
ἀγάπη, ἡ, *love*, §41.
ἀγαπητός, -ή, -όν, *beloved*, §46.
ἀγγέλλω, *I announce*, §127.
ἄγγελος, ὁ, *angel, messenger*, §36.
ἅγιος, -α, -ον, *holy, saint*, §46.
ἀγοράζω, *I buy*, §160.
ἀγρός, ὁ, *field*, §36.
ἄγω, *I lead*, §26.
ἀδελφός, ὁ, brother, fellow believer, §36
ἀδύνατος, -ον, *impossible*, §46.
αἷμα, αἵματος, τό, *blood*, §115.
αἴρω, *I take up, I take away*, §127.
αἰτέω, *I ask*, §127.
αἰών, αἰῶνος, ὁ, *age*, §115.
αἰώνιος, -ον, *eternal*, §46.
ἀκάθαρτος, -ον, *unclean*, §46.
ἀκήκοα, 2 perf. of ἀκούω, §75.
ἀκολουθέω, *I follow*, §127.
ἀκούω, *I hear*, §26.
ἀκούσω, fut. of ἀκούω, §26.
ἀλήθεια, ἡ, *truth*, §41.
ἀληθής, ἀληθές, *true*, §122.
ἀλλά, *but*, §36.
ἀλλήλων, *one another*, §148.
ἄλλος, -η, -ο, *other*, §46.
ἁμαρτάνω, *I sin*, §56.
ἁμαρτία, ἡ, *sin*, §41.
ἁμαρτωλός, ὁ, *sinner*, §36.
ἀμήν, *truly*, §97.
ἀμνός, ὁ, *lamb*, §79.

ἄν, a particle adding an element of indefiniteness to a clause, §154.
ἀνά, prep. with acc., *up*, §62.
ἀναβαίνω, *I go up, I ascend*, §127.
ἀναγινώσκω, *I read*, §62.
ἀνάστασις, ἀναστάσεως, ἡ, *resurrection*, §115.
ἀνέῳξα, 1 aor. of ἀνοίγω, §62.
ἀνήρ, ἀνδρός, ὁ, *man, husband*, §115.
ἄνθρωπος, ὁ, *man, person*, §36.
ἀνίστημι, *I raise, I rise*, §164.
ἀνοίγω, *I open*, §62.
ἀντί, prep. with gen., *instead of, in place of, for*, §62.
ἄξιος, -α, -ον, *worthy*, §46.
ἀξίως, *worthily*, §97.
ἄξω, fut. of ἄγω, §26.
ἅπας, ἅπασα, ἅπαν, *each, every, all, whole*, §122.
ἀπέθανον, 2 aor. of ἀποθνήσκω, §62.
ἀπέρχομαι, *I go away, I depart*, §83.
ἀπεστάλην, 2 aor. pass of ἀποστέλλω, §104.
ἄπιστος, -ον, *unbelieving, faithless*, §46.
ἀπό, prep. with gen., *from, away from, of*, §41.
ἀποδίδωμι, *I give back, I pay*, §164.
ἀποθνήσκω, *I die*, §62.
ἀποκρίνομαι, *I answer* (takes the dat.), §85.
ἀποκτείνω, *I kill*, §127.
ἀπόλλυμι, *I destroy*, §164.
ἀποστέλλω, *I send*, §127.

ἀπόστολος, ὁ, *apostle*, §36.
ἄρτος, ὁ, *bread*, §79.
ἀρχή, ἡ, *beginning*, §41.
ἀρχιερεύς, ἀρχιερέως, ὁ, *high priest, chief priest*, §115.
ἄρχομαι, *I begin*, §85.
ἄρχω, *I rule* (takes the gen.), §85.
ἄρχων, ἄρχοντος, ὁ, *ruler*, §115.
ἀσθενέω, *I am weak, I am sick*, §127.
ἀσπάζομαι, *I greet*, §85.
αὐτός, -ή, -ό, *he, self, same*, §68.
ἀφίημι, *I send away, I forgive*, §164.
ἄχρι, *until, up to* (takes the gen.), §92.

βαίνω, *I go* (always compounded in the NT), §127.
βάλλω, *I throw*, §56.
βαπτίζω, *I baptize*, §26.
βαπτίσω, fut. of βαπτίζω, §26.
βασιλεία, ἡ, *kingdom, reign*, §41.
βασιλεύς, βασιλέως, ὁ, *king*, §115.
βέβληκα, 1 perf. of βάλλω, §75.
βεβάπτισμαι, perf. mid./pass. of βαπτίζω, §92.
βέβλημαι, perf. mid./pass. of βάλλω, §92.
βήσομαι, dep. fut. of βαίνω, §127.
βιβλίον, τό, *book*, §79.
βλασφημέω, *I revile, I blaspheme*, §127.
βλέπω, *I see*, §26.
βλέψω, fut. of βλέπω, §26.
βούλομαι, *I wish, I am willing*, §85.

γάρ, *for* (postpositive), §92.
γε, *indeed, really, even* (postpositive).
γέγραμμαι, perf. mid./pass. of γράφω, §92.
γέγραφα, 2 perf. of γράφω, §75.
γεννάω, *I give birth to*, §127.
γένος, γένους, τό, *race*, §115.
γῆ, ἡ, *earth, land*, §41.
γίνομαι, *I become, I am* (takes a complement), §85.
γινώσκω, *I know*, §36.

γλῶσσα, *tongue, language*, §41.
γνῶσις, γνώσεως, ἡ, *knowledge*, §115.
γραμματεύς, γραμματέως, ὁ, *scribe, teacher of the law*, §115.
γραφή, ἡ, *Scripture, writing*, §41.
γράφω, *I write*, §26.
γράψω, fut. of γράφω, §26.
γυνή, γυναικός, ἡ, *woman, wife*, §115.

δαιμόνιον, τό, *demon*, §79.
δέ, *now, but* (postpositive), §36.
δεῖ, *it is necessary* (impersonal verb; takes the acc. and inf.), §139.
δείκνυμι, *I show*, §164.
δεύτερος, -α, -ον, *second*, §46.
δέχομαι, *I receive*, §85.
δέω, *I bind, I tie*, §127.
δηλόω, *I show*, §127.
διά, prep. with gen., *through, by*; with acc., *because of, on account of*, §62.
διάβολος, ὁ, *slanderer, devil*, §79.
διαθήκη, ἡ, *covenant*, §41.
διακονέω, *I serve, I minister to*, §127.
διακονία, ἡ, *service, ministry*, §41.
διάκονος, ὁ, *minister*, §36.
διδάξω, fut. of διδάσκω, §26.
διδάσκω, *I teach*, §26.
διδαχή, ἡ, *teaching*, §41.
δίδωμι, *I give*, §164.
διέρχομαι, *I go through*, see §83.
δίκαιος, -α, -ον, *righteous, just*, §46.
δικαιοσύνη, ἡ, *righteousness*, §41.
δικαιόω, *I justify*, §127.
διό, *therefore*, §92.
δοκέω, *I think* (δοκεῖ, *it seems*), §127.
δόξα, ἡ, *glory*, §41.
δοξάζω, *I glorify*, §26.
δοξάσω, fut. of δοξάζω, §26.
δοῦλος, ὁ, *servant, slave*, §36.
δύναμαι, *I am able, I can*, §164.
δύναμις, δυνάμεως, ἡ, *power*, §115.
δυνατός, -ή, -όν, *powerful, possible*, §46.
δύο, *two*, §122.

δώδεκα, *twelve*, §122.
δῶρον, *gift*, §36.

ἑαυτοῦ, *himself, herself*, §148.
ἐάν, *if* (used with non-ind. moods), §154.
ἐὰν μή, *except, unless* (used with subj.), §154.
ἔβαλον, 2 aor. of βάλλω, §56.
ἐβαπτίσθην, 1 aor. pass. of βαπτίζω, §104.
ἔβην, 2 aor. of βαίνω, §127.
ἐβλήθην, 1 aor. pass. of βάλλω, §104.
ἐγγίζω, *I come near*, §160.
ἐγγύς, *near*, §97.
ἐγείρω, *I raise*, §127.
ἐγενήθην, 2 aor. dep. of γίνομαι, §104.
ἔγνωκα, 1 perf. of γινώσκω, §75.
ἔγνων, 2 aor. of γινώσκω, §56.
ἐγνώσθην, 1 aor. pass. of γινώσκω, §104.
ἔγνωσμαι, perf. mid./pass. of γινώσκω, §92.
ἐγράφην, 2 aor. pass. of γράφω, §104.
ἐγώ, *I*, §68.
ἐδιδάχθην, 1 aor. pass. of διδάσκω, §104.
ἐδοξάσθην, 1 aor. pass. of δοξάζω, §104.
ἔθνος, ἔθνους, τό, *nation, Gentile*, §115.
εἰ, *if* (used with ind. mood.), §154.
εἶδον, 2 aor. of ὁράω, §56.
εἰμί, *I am*, §26.
εἶπον, 2 aor. of λέγω, §56.
εἴρηκα, 1 perf. of λέγω, §75.
εἰρήνη, ἡ, *peace*, §41.
εἰς, prep. with acc., *into, to, for, in*, §41.
εἷς, μία, ἕν, *one*, §122.
εἰσέρχομαι, *I go into, I enter*, §83.
εἶχον, impf. of ἔχω, §56.
ἐκ, prep. with gen., *out of, from, by*, §41.
ἐκάλεσα, 1 aor. of καλέω, §127.
ἕκαστος, -η, -ον, *each, every*, §46.

ἐκβάλλω, *I throw out, I cast out*, §62.
ἐκεῖ, *there, in that place*, §97.
ἐκεῖνος, -η, -ο, *that*, §79.
ἐκηρύχθην, 1 aor. pass. of κηρύσσω, §104.
ἐκκλησία, ἡ, *church*, §41.
ἐκπορεύομαι, *I go out*, §85.
ἔλαβον, 2 aor. of λαμβάνω, §56.
ἐλείφθην, 1 aor. pass. of λείπω, §104.
ἔλεος, ἐλέους, τό, *mercy*, §115.
ἐλήμφθην, 1 aor. pass. of λαμβάνω, §104.
ἔλιπον, 2 aor. of λείπω, §56.
ἐλπίζω, *I hope*, §160.
ἐλπίς, ἐλπίδος, ἡ, *hope*, §115.
ἔμαθον, 2 aor. of μανθάνω, §56.
ἐμαυτοῦ, -ῆς, *myself*, §148.
ἐμός, -ή, -όν, *my, mine*, §148.
ἐν, prep. with dat., *in, within, by, with, among*, §41.
ἐντολή, ἡ, *commandment*, §41.
ἐξέρχομαι, *I go out*, §83.
ἔξεστι(ν), *it is lawful* (impersonal verb; takes the dat. and inf.), §139.
ἐξουσία, ἡ, *authority, right*, §41.
ἔξω, *outside* (takes the gen.), §97.
ἔξω, fut. of ἔχω, §26.
ἔπαθον, 2 aor. of πάσχω, §56.
ἐπείσθην, 1 aor. pass. of πειθω, §104.
ἐπέμφθην, 1 aor. pass. of πέμπω, §104.
ἐπί, prep. with gen., dat., and acc., *upon, on, at, about*, §62.
ἐπιθυμία, ἡ, *desire, lust*, §41.
ἐπικαλέω, *I call upon*, §127.
ἐπιστολή, ἡ, *letter*, §41.
ἐπιτίθημι, *I put on*, §164.
ἐπιτιμάω, *I rebuke, I warn*, §127.
ἐπορεύθην, 1 aor. dep. of πορεύομαι, §104.
ἐργάζομαι, *I work*, §85.
ἔργον, τό, *work*, §36.
ἔρημος, ἡ, *wilderness, desert*, §36.
ἔρχομαι, *I come, I go*, §85.
ἐρωτάω, *I ask, I request*, §127.

249

ἐσθίω, *I eat*, §56.

ἔσχατος, -η, -ον, *last*, §46.

ἔσκηκα, 1 perf. of ἔχω, §75.

ἔσχον, 2 aor. of ἔχω, §56.

ἐσώθην, 1 aor. pass. of σώζω, §104.

ἔτερος, -α, -ον, *other, different*, §46.

ἔτι, *still, yet*, §92.

ἑτοιμάζω, *I prepare*, §26.

ἑτοιμάσω, fut. of ἑτοιμάζω, §26.

ἔτος, ἔτους, τό, *year*, §115.

εὐαγγελίζομαι, *I preach the gospel, I bring good news*, §85.

εὐαγγέλιον, τό, *gospel*, §36.

εὐθύς, *immediately, at once* (also appears as εὐθέως), §97.

εὐλογέω, *I bless*, §127.

εὕρηκα, 1 perf. of εὑρίσκω, §75.

εὗρον, 2 aor. of εὑρίσκω, §56.

εὑρίσκω, *I find*, §56.

εὐχαριστέω, *I give thanks, I thank*, §127.

ἔφαγον, 2 aor. of ἐσθίω, §56.

ἔφυγον, 2 aor. of φεύγω, §56.

ἐχθρός, ὁ, *enemy*, §79.

ἔχω, *I have*, §26.

ἑώρακα, 1 perf. of ὁράω, §75.

ἕως, *until, up to* (takes the gen.), §92.

ζάω, *I live*, §127.

ζήσομαι, dep. fut. of ζάω, §127.

ζητέω, *I seek*, §127.

ζωή, ἡ, *life*, §41.

ἤ, *or*, §92.

ἤγαγον, 2 aor. of ἄγω, §56.

ἠθέλησα, 1 aor. of θέλω, §56.

ἠκούσθην, 1 aor. pass. of ἀκούω, §104.

ἦλθον, 2 aor. of ἔρχομαι, §85.

ἥλιος, ὁ, *sun*, §79.

ἡμάρτηκα, 1 perf. of ἁμαρτάνω, §75.

ἥμαρτον, 2 aor. of ἁμαρτάνω, §56.

ἡμέρα, ἡ, *day*, §41.

ἡμέτερος, -α, -ον, *our*, §148.

ἤνεγκα, 1 aor. of φέρω, §56.

ἤνεγκον, 2 aor. of φέρω, §56.

ἡτοίμακα, 1 perf. of ἑτοιμάζω.

ἡτοιμάσθην, 1 aor. pass. of ἑτοιμάζω, §104.

ἤχθην, 1 aor. pass. of ἄγω, §104.

θάλασσα, ἡ, *sea*, §41.

θάνατος, ὁ, *death*, §36.

θαυμάζω, *I am amazed*, §160.

θέλημα, θελήματος, τό, *will*, §115.

θελήσω, fut. of θέλω, §127.

θέλω, *I want, I will*, §127.

θεός, ὁ, *God*, §36.

θεραπεύω, *I heal*, §26.

θεραπεύσω, fut. of θεραπεύω, §26.

θεωρέω, *I see, I perceive*, §127.

θλίψις, θλίψεως, ἡ, *affiction, tribulation*, §115.

θρόνος, ὁ, *throne*, §79.

θυγάτηρ, θυγατρός, ἡ, *daughter*, §115.

ἴδε, *See!, Look!, Behold!*, §160.

ἴδιος, -α, -ον, *his, one's own*, §148.

ἰδού, *See!, Look!, Behold!*, §160.

ἱερεύς, ἱερέως, ὁ, *priest*, §115.

ἱερόν, τό, *temple*, §36.

Ἰησοῦς, ὁ, *Jesus*, §36.

ἱμάτιον, τό, *cloak, garment*, §79.

ἵνα, *that, in order that* (used with subj.), §154.

ἵστημι, *I stand, I cause to stand*, §164.

ἰσχυρός, -ά, -όν, *strong*, §46.

καθαρίζω, *I cleanse*, §160.

κάθημαι, *I sit*, §164.

καθίζω, *I seat, I sit*, §160.

καθώς, *just as, as*, §92.

καί, *and, also, even*, §36.

καὶ . . . καί, *both . . . and*, §36.

καινός, -ή, -όν, *new*, §46.

καιρός, ὁ, *time, occasion*, §79.

κακός, -ή, -όν, *bad*, §46.

καλέσω, fut. of καλέω, §127.

καλέω, *I call*, §127.

καλός, -ή, -όν, *good, beautiful*, §46.
καλῶς, *rightly, well*, §92.
καρδία, ἡ, *heart*, §41.
καρπός, ὁ, *fruit*, §79.
κατά, prep. with gen., *against, down;* with acc., *according to*, §62.
καταβαίνω, *I go down, I descend*, §127.
κεφαλή, ἡ, *head*, §41.
κηρύξω, fut. of κηρύσσω, §26.
κηρύσσω, *I preach*, §26.
κλῆσις, κλήσεως, ἡ, *calling*, §115.
κόσμος, ὁ, *world*, §36.
κράζω, *I cry out.*
κρατέω, *I take hold of*, §127.
κρίνω, *I judge*, §127.
κρίσις, κρίσεως, ἡ, *judgment*, §115.
κύριος, ὁ, *Lord, master*, §36.

λαλέω, *I speak*, §127.
λαμβάνω, *I take, I receive*, §36.
λαός, ὁ, *people*, §79.
λέγω, *I say, I speak*, §36.
λείπω, *I leave*, §56.
λέλυκα, 1 perf. of λύω, §75.
λέλυμαι, perf. mid./pass. of λύω, §92.
λίθος, ὁ, *stone*, §36.
λογίζομαι, *I consider*, §85.
λόγος, ὁ, *word, message*, §36.
λύσω, fut. of λύω, §26.
λύω, *I loose*, §26.

μαθητής, ὁ, *disciple*, §41.
μακάριος, -α, -ον, *blessed*, §46.
μανθάνω, *I learn*, §56.
μαρτυρέω, *I testify, I bear witness*, §127.
μαρτυρία, ἡ, *testimony*, §41.
μάρτυς, μάρτυρος, ὁ, *witness*, §115.
μέγας, μεγάλη, μέγα, *great, large*, §122.
μείζων, μεῖζον, *greater, larger*, §122.
μέλλω, *I am about to, I will* (takes the inf.), §139.
μεμάθηκα, 1 perf. of μανθάνω, §75.

μὲν . . . δέ, *on the one hand . . . on the other hand* (postpositive), §92.
μένω, *I remain, I abide*, §127.
μεριμνάω, *I worry, I am anxious*, §127.
μέρος, μέρους, τό, *part*, §115.
Μεσσίας, ὁ, *Messiah*, §41
μετά, prep. with gen., *with*; with acc., *after*, §62.
μετανοέω, *I repent*, §127.
μή, *not*, §26.
μηδείς, μηδεμία, μηδέν, *no one, none, nothing, no*, §122.
μήτηρ, μητρός, ἡ, *mother*, §115.
μικρός, -ά, -όν, *small, little*, §46.
μισέω, *I hate*, §127.
μόνος, -η, -ον, *only*, §46.
μυστήριον, τό, *secret*, §79.

ναί, *Yes!, Indeed!*
ναός, ὁ, *temple, sanctuary*, §79.
νεανίας, ὁ, *young man*, §41.
νεκρός, -ά, -όν, *dead*, §46.
νεός, -ά, -όν, *new*, §46.
νικάω, *I overcome*, §127.
νόμος, ὁ, *law*, §36.
νῦν, *now*, §92.
νυνί, *now.*
νύξ, νυκτός, ἡ, *night*, §115.

ὁ, ἡ, τό, *the*, §41.
ὁδός, ἡ, *road, way*, §36.
οἶδα, *I know*, §75.
οἰκία, ἡ, *house*, §41.
οἰκοδομέω, *I build up, I edify*, §127.
οἶκος, ὁ, *house*, §36.
ὄνομα, ὀνόματος, τό, *name*, §115.
ὅπου, *where*, §92.
ὅπως, *that, in order that* (used with subj.), §154.
ὁράω, *I see*, §127.
ὀργή, ἡ, *anger, wrath*, §41.
ὅς, ἥ, ὅ, *who, which, that, what*, §148.
ὅστις, ἥτις, ὅτι, *who, whoever, what, whatever*, §148.

251

ὅταν, *whenever*, §154.
ὅτε, *when*, §92.
ὅτι, *that, because*, §75.
οὐ, *not*, §26.
οὐαί, *Woe!, How terrible!*, §160.
οὐδέ, *and not, nor, not even*, §92.
οὐδὲ . . . οὐδέ, *neither . . . nor*, §92.
οὐδείς, οὐδεμία, οὐδέν, *no one, none, nothing, no*, §122.
οὐκέτι, *no longer*, §92.
οὖν, *therefore, then* (postpositive), §92.
οὐρανός, ὁ, *heaven*, §79.
οὗτος, αὕτη, τοῦτο, *this*, §79.
οὕτως, *thus, in this manner*, §97.
οὐχί, *no* (emph. form of οὐ), §92.
ὀφθαλμός, ὁ, *eye*, §79.
ὄχλος, ὁ, *crowd*, §36.
ὄψομαι, fut. of ὁράω, §127.

παιδίον, τό, *child*, §79.
πάλιν, *again*, §154.
πάντοτε, *always*, §97.
παρά, prep. with gen., *from*; with dat., *with*; with acc. *beside, by*, §62.
παραβολή, ἡ, *parable*, §41.
παραδίδωμι, *I betray, I hand over, I pass on*, §164.
παρακαλέω, *I urge, I exhort, I comfort*, §127.
παράκλησις, παρακλήσεως, ἡ, *encouragement, comfort*, §115.
παρρησία, ἡ, *boldness, confidence*, §41.
πᾶς, πᾶσα, πᾶν, *each, every, all, whole*, §122.
πάσχω, *I suffer*, §56.
πατήρ, πατρός, ὁ, *father*, §115.
πείθω, *I trust in*, §26.
πειράζω, *I test, I tempt*, §160.
πείσω, fut. of πείθω, §26.
πέμπω, *I send*, §26.
πέμψω, fut. of πέμπω, §26.
πέντε, *five*, §122.
πεπίστευκα, 1 perf. of πιστεύω, §75.
πέποιθα, 2 perf. of πείθω, §75.

πέπομφα, 2 perf. of πέμπω, §75.
πέπονθα, 2 perf. of πάσχω, §75.
περί, prep. with gen., *about, concerning, for*; with acc. *around*, §62.
περιπατέω, *I walk*, §127.
περισσεύω, *I abound*.
περιτομή, ἡ, *circumcision*, §41.
Πέτρος, ὁ, *Peter*, §79.
πέφευγα, 2 perf. of φεύγω, §75.
πιστεύσω, fut. of πιστεύω, §26.
πιστεύω, *I believe*, §26
πίστις, πίστεως, ἡ, *faith*, §115.
πιστός, -ή, -όν, *faithful*, §46.
πλανάω, *I deceive, I lead astray*, §127.
πλῆθος, πλήθους, τό, *multitude, crowd*, §115.
πληρόω, *I fill, I fulfill*, §127.
πλοῖον, τό, *boat*, §79.
πνεῦμα, πνεύματος, τό, *Spirit, spirit*, §115.
ποιέω, *I do, I make*, §127.
πόλις, πόλεως, ἡ, *city*, §115.
πολύς, πολλή, πολύ, *much, many*, §122.
πονηρός, -ά, -όν, *evil*, §46.
πορεύομαι, *I come, I go*, §85.
πότε, *when?*, §97.
πρίν, *before*, §139.
πρό, prep. with gen., *before*, §62.
πρός, prep. with acc., *to, toward, with*, §62.
προσέρχομαι, *I come to, see* §83.
προσευχή, ἡ, *prayer*, §41.
προσεύχομαι, *I pray*, §85.
προσκυνέω, *I worship*, §127.
προφήτης, ὁ, *prophet*, §41.
πρῶτος, -η, -ον, *first*, §46.
πῦρ, πυρός, τό, *fire*, §115.
πῶς, *how?*, §154.

ῥῆμα, ῥήματος, τό, *word, saying*, §115.

σάββατον, τό, *Sabbath*, §79.

σάρξ, σαρκός, ἡ, *flesh*, §115.
σεαυτοῦ, -ῆς, *yourself*, §148.
σέσωκα, 1 perf. of σώζω, §75.
σέσωσμαι, perf. mid./pass. of σώζω, §92.
σημεῖον, τό, *sign*, §79.
σήμερον, *today*, §92.
σκανδαλίζω, *I cause to stumble, I cause
  to sin*, §160.
σκότος, σκότους, τό, *darkness*, §115.
σός, σή, σόν, *your* (singular), §148.
σοφία, ἡ, *wisdom*, §41.
σοφός, -ή, -όν *wise*, §46.
σπείρω, *I sow*, §127.
σπέρμα, σπέρματος, τό, *seed,
  descendant*, §115.
σταυρός, ὁ, *cross*, §79.
σταυρόω, *I crucify*, §127.
στόμα, στόματος, τό, *mouth*, §115.
στρατιώτης, ὁ, *soldier*, §41.
σύ, *you*, §68.
σύν, prep. with dat., *with*, §62.
συναγωγή, ἡ, *synagogue*, §41.
συνέρχομαι, *I come together*, see §83.
σώζω, *I save*, §26.
σῶμα, σώματος, τό, *body*, §115.
σώσω, fut. of σώζω, §26.
σωτηρία, ἡ, *salvation*, §41.

τε, *and* (postpositive).
τεθεράπευκα, 1 perf. of θεραπεύω,
  §75.
τέκνον, τό, *child*, §36.
τελειόω, *I perfect, I complete*, §127.
τέλος, τέλους, τό, *end*, §115.
τελώνης, ὁ, *tax collector*, §41.
τέσσαρες, τέσσαρα, *four*, §122.
τηρέω, *I keep*, §127.
τίθημι, *I place, I put*, §164.
τιμάω, *I honor*, §127.
τίς, τί, *who?, which?, what?, why?*,
  §148.
τις, τι, *one, a certain one, someone,
  anyone*, §148.
τόπος, ὁ, *place*, §79.

τότε, *then, at that time*, §92.
τρεῖς, τρία, *three*, §122.
τρίτος, -η, -ον, *third*, §46.
τυφλός, ὁ, *blind man*, §79.

ὕδωρ, ὕδατος, τό, *water*, §115.
υἱός, ὁ, *son*, §36.
ὑμέτερος, -α, -ον, *your*, §148.
ὑπάρχω, *I am, I exist*, §85.
ὑπέρ, prep. with gen., *for*; with acc.,
  above, over, §62.
ὑπό, prep. with gen., *by*; with acc.,
  under, §62.
ὑποκριτής, ὁ, *hypocrite*, §41.
ὑπομονή, ἡ, *endurance, steadfastness*,
  §41.

φανερόω, *I reveal*, §127.
φέρω, *I bring, I bear*, §36.
φεύγω, *I flee*, §56.
φημί, *I say*, §164.
φιλέω, *I love*, §127.
φίλος, ὁ, *friend*, §79.
φόβος, ὁ, *fear*, §79.
φωνέω, *I call*, §127.
φωνή, ἡ, *voice, sound*, §41.
φῶς, φωτός, τό, *light*, §115.

χαρά, ἡ, *joy*, §41.
χάρις, χάριτος, ἡ, *grace, favor*, §115.
χείρ, χειρός, ἡ, *hand*, §115.
Χριστός, ὁ, *Christ*, §36.
χρόνος, ὁ, *time*, §79.
χωρίς, *without, apart from* (takes the
  gen.).

ψεύδομαι, *I lie*, §85.
ψυχή, ἡ, *soul, life*, §41.

ὧδε, *here, in this place*, §97.
ὥρα, ἡ, *hour*, §41.
ὡς, *as, about*, §154.
ὥστε, *so that, therefore*, §139.
ὤφθην, 1 aor. pass. of ὁράω, §104.

Subject Index

(The numerals refer to the sections of the grammar, not to the pages.)